The Philosophy of the Novel

The Philosophy of the Novel

the Novel

Lukács, Marxism and the Dialectics of Form

J.M. Bernstein

Lecturer in Philosophy, University of Essex

University of Minnesota Press · Minneapolis

Published by the University of Minnesota Press,
2037 University Avenue Southeast, Minneapolis MN 55414

Printed in Great Britain

ISBN 0-8166-1304-4
    0-8166-1307-9 (pbk.)

PN
3331
.L83
B47
1984

The University of Minnesota
is an equal-opportunity
educator and employer.

Contents

For Maggie

Preface

This book, like so many others, is more a product of accident than design. Seven years ago the thought of writing a book about Lukács and the philosophy of the novel had not even occurred to me. When I found myself, through dint of some unimaginable concatenation of circumstances, assigned to teach a course in literary theory I picked on Lukács's *The Theory of the Novel (TN)* because it seemed to me then, and still does, the most philosophical account of the novel available. Teaching it was an exciting and infuriating experience. It was exciting, both for me and my students because its grand Hegelian movement really did seem to illuminate the nature of the novel; it was infuriating because the detail of its argument, indeed the very structure of its argument, remained elusive. In 1977 the casual offer to give a paper on Lukács at a conference on Marxist literary theory was the catalyst for bringing my thoughts on Lukács together. Several commentators on *TN* had noted the continuity between it and Lukács's seminal work *History and Class Consciousness*. I decided, then, that it would be a worthwhile exercise to try to read his pre-Marxist theory of the novel from the perspective of his Marxist social theory. Thus the present work was born.

In fact, a great deal has been written about *TN*. These writings fall into roughly three categories. First, there are those historical accounts which attempt to place it in the context of the development of the young Lukács from bourgeois to Marxist. Here the writings of Andrew Arato and Paul Breines, Michael Löwy and György Márkus are prominent. Their scholarship has put all students of Lukács in their debt. Secondly, there are several short essays. The best of these – those by Paul de Man, Maire Kurrick and Ferenc Feher are worthy of separate mention – are interesting and acute in their criticisms. Unavoidably, however, in virtue of their length, these essays are all schematic, more schematic in fact than the original. Finally, there are those writers who have simply used Lukács's ideas in *TN* in the construction of their own literary theories. It would not be inappropriate in this context to make mention of Theodor Adorno, Walter Benjamin, Lucien Goldman, Edward Said and Fredric Jameson. None of this would be worrying or out of order were it not for the existence of claims like Adorno's, for example, that *TN* set a standard for philosophical aesthetics that has remained to this day; or Harry Levin's statement that *TN* in 'possibly the most penetrating essay that ever addressed itself to the elusive subject of the novel'. In other words, there appears to be a consensus about the importance of Lukács's essay without there existing anything like a credible or rigorous evaluation of what the theory states.

There are, I suspect, a number of reasons for this state of affairs. The extraordinarily condensed character of his argument combined with his predilection for employing abstract nouns instead of concrete examples certainly help make Lukács's essay easier to praise or allude to than analyse. The overtly Hegelian structure of his argument equally makes his essay difficult to analyse in a culture where Hegelian habits of thought are alien in the extreme. Then there is the issue of the genre of the essay. It is not an essay on the sociology of literature, nor is it what we would call the philosophy of art or literary theory. Part of the difficulty here, I suspect, is that we are ourselves not quite sure of what separates literary theory from the philosophy of literature; and no matter how we construe that difference, or the difference between those modes of analysis and the sociology of literature, Lukács's conception of philosophical–historical analysis will not fit into any of our established modes of theoretical analysis. Finally, there is the simple fact that neither Marxists, nor liberals, nor theoretical (post-) modernists feel strategically obliged either to defend or refute him.

In what follows I have tried to make Lukács's argument sufficiently precise for detailed objections to it to be raised. In order to achieve this, I have adopted the method of philosophical reconstruction rather than historical or textual analysis. Such a methodology involves taking what appears to be the 'truth' of the text in question and constructing one's analysis of the remainder of the text around this initial insight. As will become evident, my method of hermeneutical analysis is equally the method I believe Lukács was employing. Further, since I begin with what I take to be the 'truth' of what Lukács was saying, this essay naturally turns into an argumentative defence of his theory. This involves me in occasionally employing a terminology that Lukács did not have at his disposal. These departures from Lukács's own usages will be justified if they help clarify the status of his argument. While I have tried to be clear and precise about questions of methodology and genre, I have been unable to avoid Lukács's abstractness. What I have tried to do is make that abstract vocabulary itself more precise and a great deal more accessible to the philosophically untutored reader. Finally, I claim that once the details of Lukács's theory become clear, it becomes evident that in *TN* we have the rudiments of a Marxist theory of the novel.

I am painfully aware that in defending Lukács's theory in this way I have accumulated as many philosophical debts as I pay off for Lukács. The ones to which I am most sensitive are my construal of his philosophy of praxis in the opening chapter, my arguments concerning the nature of narratives in general in Chapter IV, and my theory about the narrative character of personal identity in Chapters V and VII. And then there is all that I have not said about my reading of Kant and my construal of transcendental subjectivity. I hope to be able to settle at least some of these debts in a forthcoming study, provisionally entitled *Identity and Totality: Interpretation and Representation in Social Theory.*

It is my pleasure to record here my thanks to Peter Hulme for his indispensable comments on the penultimate draft of this essay. Terry Eagleton's extensive comments on what is now the final chapter of this study alerted me to some egregious errors in the argument there. I hope the argument in Chapter III will convince him that Lukács's conception of 'the novel' is not an ideal type. Gillian Rose's encouragement is of a different order: her intellectual and political sympathy for what I am trying to do here (and elsewhere) has made it seem worth doing. Mrs Margaret Smith typed the manuscript quickly and efficiently; her grammatical sense salvaged more than one sentence.

This book is dedicated to my wife: without her patience it would never have been begun; without her impatience it would never have been completed.

Introduction

1 A MARXIST THEORY

It is universally agreed that Georg Lukács's *The Theory of the Novel* is one of its author's pre-Marxist works. After all, the book was written in 1914–15 and Lukács did not join the Communist Party until late in 1918. If further justification were needed for refusing *TN* a Marxist pedigree, then one might cite the work's lack of mention in its analysis of the transition to the modern world of alienation of class conflict or class relations. Indeed, the Marxist theory of class does not appear in the work at all. There are, it would appear, substantial historical and theoretical reasons for regarding *TN* as belonging to Lukács's pre-Marxist *oeuvre*.

And yet although originally appeared as an essay in 1916, it was published in unrevised book form in 1920, by which time Lukács had become a Communist. In their *The Young Lukács*, Arato and Breines note this as 'one of a number of philological curiosities' they have been unable to resolve.[1] Here is another curiosity: in his critical study of the Marxist Lukács's *The Meaning of Contemporary Realism*, Theodor Adorno says of *TN* that it had 'a brilliance and profundity of conception which was quite extraordinary at the time, so much so that it set a standard for philosophical aesthetics which has been retained ever since.'[2] One might, of course, take Adorno's statement as a rhetorical gesture designed to deflate the value of Lukács's properly Marxist works of literary criticism. Since, however, Adorno's criticism of the later Lukács can stand on its own, and further, Adorno points to the value of Lukács's early writings as the *basis* for even considering his later writings, it seems legitimate to take his appraisal of *TN* as literal. Another curiosity is Walter Benjamin's near-transcription of the historical and theoretical schema of *TN* in his 1936 'The Story-

teller'.[3] It might even be argued that Lukács's early work
provides the essential historical and theoretical schema *within*
which Adorno and Benjamin employ their distinctive, and quite
unLukácsian brand of literary criticism.[4] A final curiosity is
Lucien Goldman's explicit attempt to erect his sociology of the
novel on the basis of the framework provided by *TN*.[5]

These curiosities require explanation. One might have expected Lukács to revise or preface *TN* when publishing it in book
form given his apparent change in perspective from when the
book was written. With respect to the other curiosities one might
say that there is no reason why a clearly non-Marxist work
should not influence Marxist theory; but what we have before us
is more than influence. Adorno speaks of *TN* as setting a
'standard' for philosophical aesthetics; and the appropriations
of *TN* by Benjamin and Goldmann go beyond mere influence.
That the three leading Marxist literary theorists of this century,
apart from Lukács himself, have both praised and used *TN* in
such an unqualified manner requires explanation.

Assuming that all these writers are not completely mistaken in
their evaluation of *TN*, then the simplest and most direct
explanation of the phenomena before us is that *TN* is, as a
matter of fact if not intention, a Marxist work; or rather, more
precisely, a properly Marxist theory of the novel can be
excavated from *TN*. The initial steps of an argument to support
this view are not difficult to make out. There can be little doubt
that the seminal work in the history of western Marxism, as it
came to be called, is Lukács's *History and Class Consciousness*
(1923); and that it was this book which conditioned and made
possible Adorno's, Benjamin's, and Goldmann's (and
Horkheimer's) Marxism.[6] The Marxism of *HCC* was a
Hegelianised Marxism, with emphasis being placed on Marx's
dialectical 'method' as opposed to any particular doctrines. For
good or ill, the appropriateness of reading Marx in terms of his
Hegelian roots has been a central issue of western Marxism as a
whole; and the defence of the Hegelian reading of Marx, which
includes a Marxist reading of Hegel, has been a major, if not the
dominant, strand in that tradition.[7] In his harshly critical 1962
Preface to *TN*, Lukács notes that the work aimed at a fusion of
'left' ethics with 'right' epistemology (21). The 'left' ethic refers
to the Hegelian, dialectical and historical, elements of the

theory, while the 'right' epistemology refers to the neo-Kantian methodology of constructing ideal types that is used in the book. Lukács's retrospective claim that he was attempting to 'fuse' these methods is too strong, for as he points out it is only the first part of *TN* which is Hegelian, with the 'right' epistemology dominating its second part (13, 15–16). *TN*, then, is not a unified work; its two parts are constructed in accordance with different principles and methods. Hence, if a Marxist theory is to be excavated from *TN*, then that excavation, that philosophical reconstruction of Lukács's argument, will have to be guided by the Hegelian materials of Part I. To argue that an authentically Hegelian theory of the novel is present in *TN* is, however, neither new[8] nor the same as arguing that the theory is Marxist.[9]

The historical and dialectical procedures of Part I suggest the possibility that the gap between *TN* and a properly Marxist analysis might not be a very large one. That gap begins to disappear altogether when we recognise that the *operative* premises for Lukács's analysis of the novel are Marxist. I say 'operative' because clearly his stated premises are not Marxist; but his stated premises, I shall argue, do not validly license the inferences he draws from them.[10] The validity of his arguments concerning the novel require premises that are explicitly Marxist, indeed, the very particular construal of Marxist theory he defends in *HCC*. If the premises of his argument are Marxist, and his argument is valid, then his analysis itself must be Marxist. The absence of a class component in his analysis of the novel is compensated for in the premises of that argument.

There is, however, a more direct way in which a reader acquainted with *HCC* might perceive the analysis of the novel in *TN* to be Marxist. Lukács conceives of the novel in funda- mentally Kantian terms, that is, he conceives of the practice of novel writing as working within the Kantian analysis of the relation between man and world. The novel, we might say, is written against a background of Kantian assumptions, and these assumptions are constitutive of the form of the novel. In *HCC* Lukács identifies Kant's critical philosophy as the philosophy of our age, as the theory which most completely articulates our experience of ourselves and the world now. Kant's philosophy, for Lukács, is the philosophy of the bourgeois world; it philosophically consecrates the world of capital. Thus, from a

Marxist point of view, the Kantian system harbours the essential antinomies (contradictions) of bourgeois thought. The antinomies of Kant's philosophy are the antinomies of bourgeois thought; the novel gives phenomenological expression to those same antinomies. The analysis of the novel in *TN* repeats and extends the Hegelian – Marxist critique of Kant; in coming to understand the novel in these philosophical and historical terms the nature of our historical world is revealed and the way beyond it glimpsed. If this is correct, then the procedures and analyses of *TN* are closer to the programme for Marxist theory and criticism sketched in *HCC* than any of Lukács's later works of literary criticism.

2   PHILOSOPHY AND THE NOVEL

One of the difficulties in reading *TN* lies in establishing what sort of text it is; what kind of analysis of the novel is it attempting to provide? The very level of generality at which Lukács works seems to defy our ordinary modes of classification. Paul de Man's succinct statement of Lukács's project nicely captures the difficulty: 'The emergence of the novel as the major modern genre is seen as the result of a change in the structure of human consciousness; the development of the novel reflects modifications in man's way of defining himself in relation to all categories of existence.'[11] If Lukács is dealing with the 'structures of consciousness' and 'all categories of existence', then his concerns extend far beyond those of the sociology of literature or literary history as ordinarily understood. His concerns are those of philosophy; but traditionally philosophy has concerned itself with the analysis of things like knowledge, action, consciousness, justice, meaning, and art or beauty in general, and not with so mundane a phenomenon as the novel. The novel appears too small a vessel, too empirical and specific an item to be the focus of such large concerns.

Now a commonly accepted reading of Marx has him wishing to replace philosophical speculation about the nature of reality with (empirical) historical and sociological analysis. But if such a replacement or completion means anything, it must mean that Marxist theory inherits the task of attempting to comprehend the phenomena which had previously been the prerogative of philosophy. More simply, if Marxist theory too is concerned with changes in the structures of human consciousness and all the categories of existence, then it cannot be restrictedly classified as a sociological theory, or as an economic theory, or as an example of political economy. The very generality of Marxist theory forces it out of the domain of the empirical sciences of society and towards philosophy. Part of Lukács's goal in *HCC* is to criticise Marxism's comprehension of itself as an empirical science of society, and to give to Marxist theory a philosophical dimension. The providing of Marxism with *this* kind of philosophical dimension is, I think, what defines the programme of Hegelian Marxism.

In Chapter I Lukács's conception of philosophy, his conception of historical–philosophical analysis, is delineated through the reconstruction of the argument of the central essay in *HCC*. My goal in this reconstruction is not to evaluate the numerous and complex theses Lukács puts forward there; that task would require a book of its own. Rather, I want to reconstruct the *structure* of Lukács's argument, for it is that which best reveals his understanding of the relationship between Marxist theory and philosophy, his philosophical comprehension of the meaning of Marxist theory. I shall argue that Lukács's critique of representational social theory, including Marxist social theory so construed, and his critique of epistemologically-based philosophy, grounded in subject/object dualism, are two sides of the same coin; the two critiques, mutually entail one another. What representational social theory and epistemologically-oriented philosophy share is a conception of the relationship between man and world in which the fundamental relationship between the two is taken to be one of knowing (seeing, representing, imaging, picturing). Lukács claims that the universality of this 'contemplative' conception of the relationship between man and world is best explained as a product of the capitalist mode production. He terms the social mechanisms whereby the social world comes to appear as an object externally related to the individuals living in that world 'reification'. Since the social mechanisms which make the world appear as an object to be known are real, then the overcoming of reification, and with it our contemplative stance towards the world, can be altered only by changing the social relations which define men's relationship with reality. This *movement* of overcoming is directed against the specific social relations of capital; the comprehension of those social relations in their historical specificity is what defines the empirical moment of Marxist theory. Since, however, those same social relations are *categories* of existence, defining the historical meaning of the present, then their comprehension and practical overcoming is equally a philosophical movement. Marxism, for Lukács, is the philosophy of the present; it is the comprehension of the meaning of history from the perspective of the present. Because that meaning is mediated through men's social engagements, their needs, desires and actions; and further, because the end or goal of their actions is in part defined by those very actions themselves, then Marxism is a practical philosophy, a philosophy of 'praxis'. Marxism is a historically situated and practical philosophy; Lukács's conceptions of reification, contemplation and praxis are the central moments in his construction of a Marxist hermeneutic.[12]

The philosophy of the novel will be a hermeneutics of the practice of novel writing, a description and explanation of that practice of writing in terms of its historical specificity on the one hand, and in terms of the contemporary categories of existence on the other. Now that the novel is directly concerned with the modern categories of existence is explained by the novel being essentially Kantian in form (a social 'fact' which is revealed to us through the interpretation of the novel), where Kant's theory is in its turn recognised as being the most accurate philosophical articulation of the world of capital from the point of view of bourgeois thought (a thesis I argue for in Chapter I).[13] At this juncture it will prove useful to give a preliminary sketch of these 'Kantian' elements in Lukács's theory.

In *The Critique of Pure Reason* Kant offers an account of human knowledge and the knowable world. According to Kant the whole of the objective, knowable world is constituted as a causal world where everything that occurs is to be explained through causal laws. The objective world is a causally determined world without 'value' or any place in it for the expression of human freedom. Yet for Kant this fact is not simply so; on the contrary, that the world 'appears' this way is to be explained by the *forms* of human knowing, by the categories and concepts which we bring to the world in order that we may have knowledge of it. These forms of knowledge are products of the spontaneity of the human intellect, they are expressions of human freedom and rationality. Oversimplifying, Kant's thesis is that the world's appearance of being a causally determined domain is to be explained by the *imposition* of the category of causality on it by human beings in their cognitive activities.[14] Thus, the objective world's being causally constituted is, in part at least, a result or product of human activity. Because the objective, spatially and temporally extended world confronting human beings is causally constituted, then human freedom and spontaneity can gain no purchase on it; human freedom remains exiled within human subjectivity, unable to determine or shape the objective world in terms appropriate to itself. For Kant our spontaneity, freedom and rationality are what define us as human beings; yet, in the simplest expression of those powers in the act of knowing we construct a world in which there is no room for freedom or reason. What 'is' is determined by relations of cause and effect; human rationality hence becomes an 'ought' forever transcending the objective world.

It is not difficult to see in this description of a causally determined world resulting from human activity, and a 'world' of freedom exiled into interiority a metaphysical statement of the Marxist theory that in the historically conditioned exercise of our freedom and rationality we have created the 'alienating' world of capital which leaves no objective, social space where our freedom and reason may express itself. For Marx, pre-capitalist social formations were themselves permeated and structured (in part) by the normative values, the social ethic of the time; thus in pre-capitalist societies people's normative beliefs, their freedom and reason, were directly expressed in their social practices and institutions. If, from our historical vantage point, it seems correct to say that, for the most part, those beliefs were not rational nor those institutions 'free', that is not to deny those beliefs a determining role in the structuring of the practices and institutions concerned. In pre-capitalist societies, we might say, economic domination had a normative substratum; in capitalist societies economic domination is 'purely' economic. One of the consequences of capital's development of a purely economic sector, of capital's 'disenchantment' of the economy, is that all those social domains necessary for the continued existence of the economy must be equally 'disenchanted'. The non-normative exigencies of economic life thus come to determine all the major institutions of modern life. Thus in the name of economic rationality the social world as a whole comes to appear as a Kantian 'natural' world determined by non-normative, causal factors alone. Freedom and value must hence retreat into subjectivity.

What distinguishes and privileges the novel for Lukács is the way in which its form leads it both to accept and reject this exile of value in subjectivity. According to Lukács, pre-capitalist epic narratives were structured by value-systems and beliefs whose validity was authenticated by the practices and institutions of society at large; or better, what gave the normative beliefs which structured older narratives their objective validity was their capacity to structure ordinary social practices meaningfully. Because our social world is no longer value-oriented and structured in this way, then the novel cannot rely on antecedently validated value assumptions. As an epic genre the novel must attempt to represent the social world; thus, to the degree to which the novel has mimetic ambitions it must represent the objective world as devoid of value; but in so far as it is a 'literary' work it must give 'form' to what it represents. Aesthetic form in the novel is the surrogate for the value assumptions and beliefs of past narratives. Form *as* 'aesthetic', we might say, is the exile of value systems in fiction; literary form is what value-systems become when they are exiled into an 'autonomous' domain.

For Lukács the novel is a dialectic of form-giving and mimesis, a dialectic of interpretation and representation. These two aspects or moments of the novel correspond to the Kantian worlds of freedom and causality, ought and is; the dialectic of the novel is the attempt to write the world as it is in terms of how it ought to be. The novel is *premised* by the gap between is and ought; the practice of novel writing both recognises the gap and through the instrumentality of form attempts to bridge it.

But the novel, according to Lukács, is Kantian in form in a more radical way. The dialectic whereby the world as it is is figured as it ought to be has the structure of a Kantian synthesis of the manifold, that is, a structure in which a discrete set of events is bound together into a unity through the application of abstract concepts or categories. Novel narration, then, attempts to 'constitute' a world in the same sense in which the application of the categories in judgement is constitutive of experience in the *Critique of Pure Reason*. The significant difference between the two, and what gives Lukács's employment of Kant's vocabulary its metaphorical tone, is that the categories and concepts at issue in the novel are ethical concepts or categories rather than epistemic ones. Thus, where Kant argues that his categories are necessary for experience for without them experience would be unintelligible, the novel argues that without its ethical figuration of experience life would be meaningless; where Kant argues that because it is we who give the world its intelligibility (because the categories constitutive of experience come from us) the world we know is transcendentally ideal, which is to say, the world we know is not the world as it is in itself, the novel recognises that the price of its ethically constituting experience is that it remain a 'fiction'. (The novel's 'fictionality', we shall see, is specific to it.) It has been argued that Kant's demonstration of the necessity of the categories for experience turns on their being necessary for the possibility of self-consciousness or personal identity; without the categories, the argument goes, we could not have experiences of ourselves as distinct individuals, we would not be able to say who we are.[15] The novel, I shall argue, contends that unless we are able normatively or ethically to narrate our experience we are unable to say who we are. Conversely, the world as the novel finds it, the world prior to the novel's ethical figuration or constitution of it, the world where freedom is exiled into subjectivity, is a world we cannot narrate (except fictionally), a world in which we are unable to say who we are. For Lukács, then, the Kantian contours of the novel explicate not merely the internal workings of the novel, but equally the place or space of (the institution of) the novel in our social world. That the novel has, or has had, such cultural significance is to be explained by the slack and absences in the social world which devolve upon the institution of the novel to take up and complete.

It is sometimes suggested that the novel is so 'formless' a genre that it cannot be defined.[16] Lukács claims that the novel is a dialectic of form-giving and representation. What sort of

definition is this? What Lukács offers us is an interpretation of
the practice of novel writing. He assumes that the writing of
novels is a rule-governed activity; the constitutive rules of that
practice are what give the novel its specificity as a genre. But
those rules are social rules, they define a social practice; in
interpreting those rules we give them a social context and an
historical location, a context and a location which those rules
themselves presuppose or assume, implicitly or explicitly. Thus,
it is the novel itself, its form, which tells us it is a dialectic of form-
giving and mimesis, that the world it represents is a world in
which value is *exiled* in subjectivity. The novel itself, we might
say, tells us of a past in which value beliefs were grounded
in a form of life, and that our value beliefs are like the
unintelligible remnants of a lost world. The practice of novel
writing itself constructs a past and a present; in interpreting that
practice Lukács attempts to make explicit the historical specificity of the novel, that is, he attempts to reconstruct and
explicate, give theoretical contours to the history the novel
constructs for itself. That it is this which Lukács is doing has
rarely been appreciated. Confusions about the nature of his
project are most evident in the diverse accounts of what he is
about in comparing the novel with Homer's epics. The dominant interpretation of this comparison claims that Lukács is
there offering some kind of speculative philosophy of history
with the Homeric world figuring as a past utopia, a narrative
Garden of Eden. That this reading of Lukács is mistaken, and
that the procedures of *TN* are as hermeneutic as those of *HCC*, is
argued for in Chapter II. Unavoidably, much of the argument
of this chapter is negative; false leads are tracked down, and
Lukács's own mistaken account of the premises of his argument
is clarified and corrected.

The argument proper concerning the nature of the novel
begins in Chapter III. The chapter opens with an account of
Lukács's central theoretical concepts: form and life. After
briefly demonstrating how his argument as a whole concerning
the form of the novel can be reconstructed in terms of a series of
practical deliberations of the form 'In order to achieve y in
circumstances c it is necessary for me to do x', thus showing how
what is at issue in giving an account of the form of the novel is
giving an account of a rule-governed activity, I go on to analyse

the dialectic of form-giving and mimesis itself. One of the difficulties which surfaces from this analysis is how an abstract category or concept can unite a diverse series of events. In Chapter IV I argue that in order for an abstract ethical system to be applied to experience it must be, to use the Kantian term of art, schematised', that is, it must be given some kind of temporal form. This leads me into a consideration of Lukács's analysis of time in the novel in his remarks on Flaubert's *Sentimental Education*. His analysis of time in the novel occurs in Part II of *TN*, and consequently suffers from a lack of the kind of historicisation to which he subjects his categories in Part I. In order to make good this deficit I propose a very general account of the connection between narrative and temporal forms which is capable of being historicised.

In claiming that the novel is a dialectic of form-giving and mimesis Lukács is saying that the novel is structured by the kind of subject/object dualism which dominates epistemologically-oriented philosophy. One of the ways in which this dualism is directly manifested in the novel is in the overt distinction in the novel between narrative and narration, between the story being told and its telling. In literary theory this problem is most often dealt with in terms of questions relating to, for example, point of view, first person narration versus omniscient narrators, and the like. What interests Lukács, however, is not the way in which writers handle this dualism, but its significance as a dualism constitutive of the form of novel writing. He claims that the story told in a novel always has the outer form of a biography of a problematic individual; the inner form is that individual's search for self-recognition. Lukács goes on to argue that this narrative is itself always but an image of the act of narration, of an author giving form to experience. At one level, these claims can be validated as results of a presumed authorial practical deliberation; hence their status of belonging to the form of the novel. At another level, however, I argue that this doubling of authorial subjectivity in the subjectivity of the problematic hero can only be explained in terms of the subject/object dualism which invades subjectivity itself in the modern era. What constitutes subjectivity in 'our' modern sense is that the subject is now split or divided within itself. Thus the doubling of subjectivity in the novel images the Kantian distinction between the transcendental subject and empirical subject, between, that is, the subject which gives form to experience and the subject so formed. Crudely, the empirical subject is the 'I' lost in a meaningless world; while the transcendental subject is the 'free' self who is unable to enter or determine the world. I argue in Chapter V that this division within the self as manifested in the novel tells the story of how the self has become unnarratable, unable to tell its story and say who it is.

While the concept of transcendental subjectivity is part of the repertoire of modern philosophy, it is not an easy concept to grasp. Because it is so remote from the concerns of most novel readers, I depart from Lukács's own argument in Chapter V and demonstrate how that concept arises and works itself out in the case of one problematic novel. The analysis of the divided self and transcendental subjectivity is continued in Chapter VI where I analyse Lukács's contention that irony is the guiding structural principle of the novel. In strategic terms, in terms of authorial deliberation, irony emerges as the form by which an author can register the subjectivity, in the privative sense of the term, of ethical form in the novel generally. That, however, simply raises the question: why irony and not, say, metaphor or allegory? From one perspective, I argue, irony of the kind at issue just is the direct tropic expression of a split subjectivity. In making this correlation between irony and the divided subject I should not want to be taken as intending to explain novelistic irony in terms of the divided subject. On the contrary, from another perspective the very idea of a transcendental subject is but a 'reifying' of one of the moments of an ironic discourse. Hence, in the novel the exile of value in (transcendental) subjectivity becomes the exile of authentic selfhood in language. Here, as elsewhere in this text, instead of using Kantian concepts to illuminate the novel, the forms of the novel come to serve as a commentary on Kant's philosophy.

In my final chapter I take up Lukács's theory of the novel and attempt to show how it can be extended to deal with the changes in the novel which go under the name of 'modernism'. In strategic terms, modernist novel writing involves simply a systematic 'de-formation' of the concepts constituting the classical, realist text. In more general terms, modernism exemplifies a deepening and making explicit the autonomy of literature from other social domains. This autonomy has sometimes been misunderstood by defenders of novelistic modernism as the novel, somehow, realising in this kind of writing its true 'fictive' and scriptual vocation. Much of this chapter, then, is spent showing how the *social* autonomy of literature should not be taken as revealing anything about the 'true' nature of literary artefacts. Nor, I argue, should the fact that in our social world certain phenomena have been exiled into language and literature lead one to conclude that these things really are just linguistic, literary or fictional items. In particular, I urge that the modernist critique of narrative is misplaced; what the antinomies in the novel form of narration presage is not the death of narrative but the necessity or need for a new, non-literary form of narration. What such a new form of narration will look like is not, however, a question for idle speculation, for the rudiments of it are already available in the Lukácsian theory of class praxis.

A Note on References

Unless otherwise noted all page references in the text of Chapter I are to: Georg Lukács, *History and Class Consciousness*, translated by Rodney Livingstone (London: Merlin Press, 1971). Unless otherwise noted all page references in the remainder of the text are to: Georg Lukács, *The Theory of the Novel*, translated by Anna Bostock (London: Merlin Press, 1971). The former work is referred to throughout as *HCC*, the latter work as *TN*. I have sometimes, especially for *TN*, substituted my own translation. Finally, all references in the text to Kant's *Critique of Pure Reason* are to the Norman Kemp Smith translation (London: Macmillan, 1929); following standard practice, these page references are marked 'A' or 'B', referring to the first and second editions of the *Critique*, respectively.

Acknowledgements

I should like to thank the Merlin Press for permission to quote from Rodney Livingstone's translation of *History and Class Consciousness*, and from Anna Bostock's translation of *The Theory of the Novel*.

I

From Contemplation to Praxis: Notes for a Marxist Hermeneutic

'Reification and the Consciousness of the Proletariat', which forms the theoretical centre of Lukács's *History and Class Consciousness*, provides a critique of the mechanistic and economistic Marxism of the Second International together with a critique of bourgeois philosophy. These two critiques are mutually entailed so that the autonomy of social theory and philosophy from one another is dissolved: social theory becomes philosophical, and must do so, and philosophy becomes a fundamental form of social and historical reflection. The discussion of German Idealism in Part II of the 'Reification' essay is not a mere stepping-stone to the reformulation of Marxist social theory, as if philosophy could be replaced by the sociology of knowledge, say, or relegated to the task of providing methodological guidance for analytic insight into social theory. If social theory (and finally social praxis itself) *completes* the movement of the philosophical tradition, this must be because social theory and praxis can 'complete' themselves only by becoming philosophical.

The critique of classical Marxism, with its hierarchical base/superstructure model whereby the structures of the economic base determine the form and content of those social domains necessary for its (the economy's) reproduction, is carried through by means of a threefold elaboration of traditional Marxist theory. First, Lukács attempts to generalise the critique of political economy (the programme of *Capital*) into a critique of bourgeois society as a whole. This is accomplished by means of a generalisation of Marx's concept of commodity

1

fetishism, the process whereby relations between persons take on the characteristics of a relation between things, and conversely, where relations between things (commodities) come to appear as 'social' (only goods – commodities – 'exchange' in the market-place). If the same processes which produce commodity fetishism in the economic domain are necessarily operative throughout society, producing what Lukács terms 'reification', then social reproduction must function in accordance with at least some uniform principles throughout society. If it could be shown that these principles were neither simply derived from, nor mere effects of, the 'economy', then any rigid base/superstructure hierarchy would be vitiated. This would equally vitiate Marxist theory's own traditional self-understanding since social production will include 'theoretical production' as one of its elements. Reflectionist and re-presentational conceptions of knowledge lead us to forget that theoretical practices occur 'in' society, and are therefore subject to the very mechanisms they represent. Secondly, then, social critique must involve an auto-critique of Marxist theory which can both situate theoretical practices generally, and simul-taneously account for the 'real' possibility of its own procedures, products and (with a specification of what this terms means) 'truth'. Finally, since the possibility of overcoming the ideologi-cal mystification of understanding produced by reification occurs within society, then a more generous conception of consciousness and action than that provided by classical Marxism is required. If it is the case that consciousness is never either fully mystified, as the determination of the superstructure by the base demands, nor fully in possession of the truth, as a representational reading of Marxist theory suggests, then 'in so far as the "false" is an aspect of the "true" it is both "false" and "non-false"' (xlvii); and its non-falsity must condition and make possible its access to the true. In so far as 'true' and 'false' are not mere properties or predicates of whole statements or propositions which refer to an independently existing domain of objects, but rather immanently signify, in a sense to be explained, society's own dynamically conditioned self-understanding and movement, then some states of individual and/or class consciousness must be capable of making an objective difference to the social structure as a whole.

Now the critique of mechanistic Marxism presupposes a critique of bourgeois philosophy because the representational nature of classical Marxist theory itself presupposes the validity of the traditional epistemological formulation of the relation between subject and object: objects, even 'social' objects, exist independently of knowing subjects; the fundamental relation between subject and object is epistemic in character, i.e. the primary link between subject and object is a representation (be it mental or linguistic) of the object had by the subject; and knowing proper occurs when there is a correspondence between the subject's representations of what is the case and what those representations are 'of'. Epistemology is the search for trans-historical foundations, methods or criteria which will ground the search for truth, making the correspondence between representation and object possible in principle. The critique of representational social theory proceeds on the basis of and is consubstantial with the critique of epistemology. Even if not a direct effect of reification, the problem of subject/object dualism as epistemically conceived is formally homologous with the general effect of reification on theoretical understanding; hence the critical dissolution of the theory–object schema (e.g. where *Capital* is thought to provide a theoretical representation of an externally existing 'object', viz. the capitalist mode of production), which is the primary task of the auto-critique of Marxist theory, implies and turns upon for its validity the critical dissolution of subject/object dualism which is the primary task of the critique of epistemology, or what I shall term 'metacritique'.[1] In fine, Lukács contends that there is an inner identity between the auto-critique of Marxist theory and the critique of epistemology. Representational theory discovers that it is one of the objects it thought it was talking about, and that its representational understanding of itself is due to the mechanisms of reification which it had heretofore hypothesised as belonging only to its object. As a consequence, Marxist theory's own self-understanding (as a representation of capital) must be false; its link or connection with its object cannot be one of representing or mirroring; it is, or can be somehow, a non-mechanically determined moment *in* the movement or activity of that object. Similarly, as the aporias of epistemological subject/object dualism illustrate—aporias which are instanced, for example, by Descartes' attempt to validate his ideas through a proof of the existence of God, by Hume's scepticism, or by Kant's idealist claim that we know appearances only and not the things themselves – there is no Archimedian point immanent in knowing consciousness which will allow it access to, or a foothold in, an absolutely transcendent object domain. It is, the critique of epistemology urges, the project of traditional epistemology itself which generates scepticism rather than the failure of that project. Knowledge neither has nor requires an a priori, trans-historical foundation to ground its endeavours. Further, the fundamental relation between subject and object is not primarily one of knowing (or what we think of as knowing); we are tethered to the world by means which are other than knowing or representing, and that it is these means which allow epistemic activities to occur in the first instance, and which give them their point.[2]

Not only is there an identity between the auto-critique of Marxist theory and metacritique, there is as well a unity in the positive resolution of these two critiques. This unity can be detected in the overall structure of the 'Reification' essay. Part I attempts the auto-critique of Marxist theory, while Part II contains Lukács's critique of epistemology. The two critiques merge in the discovery of history as the process and product (subject and object) of human activity. Part III interrogates the historicity of the present by asking after 'the "we" which is the subject of history, that "we" whose action is in fact history' (145). For Lukács that 'we' is the proletariat. But the comprehension of the proletariat as the standpoint of the present, as the historical place where the 'meaning' of the present reveals itself to us, is neither an act of pure social theory nor a pure philosophical discovery; rather, such a comprehension marks the union of these disciplines, and hence the historical overcoming of their false, if none the less historically-grounded and produced, separation. From the perspective of social theory the comprehension of the standpoint of the proletariat fulfils the demand for an account of the possibility of a social theory, for theory's self-comprehension of its unique conditions of existence. Lukács contends that 'the self-understanding of the proletariat is ... simultaneously the *objective* understanding of the nature of society. When the proletariat furthers its own class-aims it simultaneously   achieves   the   conscious   realisation   of the – *objective* – aims of society' (149). From a philosophical perspective the comprehension of the standpoint of the proletariat functions as a hermeneutical key which focuses and makes sense of what is at issue in current cultural self-interpretations, that is, it reveals the historical significance of current self-interpretations.[3] Hence as social theory becomes reflective as a result of its auto-critique and philosophy becomes historical as a result of metacritique their formerly isolated ventures conjoin.[4] Indeed, for Lukács the objective validity of Marxist theory, the superiority of Marxist social theory to other social theories, and the privileged character of the Marxist hermeneutic as compared to other post-epistemological hermeneutical enterprises (Heidegger's or Foucault's, for example) resides, at least in part, in the inner identity of auto-critique and metacritique, and the way in which these two critiques are resolved in the hermeneutical comprehension of the proletariat and proletarian class consciousness.

A lacuna in this sketch of Lukács's joining of social theory and philosophy is its silence on the question of practice, on the relation between historically-situated theory and radical social action. In fact, Lukács's claim for there being an inner identity between auto-critique and metacritique rests on his contention that both traditional social theory (including traditional Marxist theory) and modern, epistemologically-oriented philosophy are subject to unresolvable antinomies because of their joint maintenance of a *contemplative stance* towards reality. The proper *historical* comprehension of the Siren's call of contemplation requires Lukács's theory of reification; the overcoming of the contemplative stance towards reality, and with it the correspondence theory of truth, demands a new (or renewed) conception of human praxis. Only with this reconstructed understanding of historical praxis and truth can Lukács's image of philosophy (and philosophical activity) be made visible; and only then can we portray what a philosophy of the novel would be for him.

2   REIFICATION AND CONTEMPLATION

Contrary to his own later self-criticism that in *HCC* he falsely identified alienation (by which he presumably means reification) with objectification, Lukács carefully premises his account of reification on Marx's analysis of commodity fetishism, which, he notes, 'is a *specific* problem of our age' (84). There is a qualitative difference between pre-capitalist societies which include commodity exchange in an episodic manner and capitalism where it is universal, 'permeating every expression of life' (84, 85–6). The aim of production in pre-capitalist societies is the creation of use-values; so even when supply exceeds demand, allowing use-values to become a means of exchange (and hence commodities), exchange value is still bound up with and determined by use-value. Under the capitalist mode of production 'exchange value is *the only form* in which the value of a commodity can manifest itself or be expressed.;[5] which is to say, exchange value assumes a form of its own when it becomes universal, for were there other forms in which the value of a commodity could be expressed then use-value would remain a/the determinant of exchange value. It is in the domination of use-value by exchange value that the origin of reification is to be found, for when this occurs the intrinsic properties or qualities of things no longer determine their value; rather qualitatively heterogeneous things are equated in relation to monetary value or price. Strictly speaking, then, 'to say that something is reified is not to emphasise that a relation between men appears as a relation between things. It is to emphasise that a relation between men (use-value) appears in the form of a property of a thing (exchange value). To be non-reified, then, is really to be a property of a thing, or, by analogy, to be a use-value.'[6]

None the less, if we depict the social processes necessary for exchange value to dominate use-value we can discover the basis of the specifically Lukácsian sense of reification. If commodities are to possess both use-value and value in exchange, then the process which produces these commodities must be equally two-sided. Only concrete human activity can create use-values; but value creating labour, labour which creates exchange value is *abstract* human labour, that is, 'equal, comparable labour, measurable with increasing precision according to the time socially necessary for its accomplishment' (87). It is no mental act (of comparison) which produces the commensurability of heterogeneous labours; abstract labour is the product of a specific social process whereby labouring is rationalised through its fragmentation into repeatable specialised operations whose time for accomplishment is converted through their intensification from an empirical average figure into an objectively calculated and conditioned fixed work-stint which is imposed on the worker.

Now it is in the *effects* of this rationalisation of the division of labour, which is both premise and product of commodity production (87), that Lukács locates the form of reification, compatible but not identical with the properly Marxian form noted above, which he regards as most significant for social analysis. Reification must be located at this juncture and not elsewhere because it is a necessary condition for the establishment of a rationalised work process that the rest of society – law, politics, and everyday life – be subject to these same processes of rationalisation: 'As the commodity becomes universally dominant ... the fate of the worker must become universal as otherwise, industrialisation could not develop in this direction' (91). Reification requires the separation of the worker from his means of production; this occurrence produces the 'free' worker whose labour power itself takes on the character of a commodity. With the commodification of labour power, and the rationalisation of those social domains necessary to sustain it, reification comes to inhabit and dominate all the major institutions of bourgeois society.

The Lukácsian analysis of reification derives from a generalisation of one aspect of Marx's theory of labour and value; since that theory is specific to the capitalist mode of production, then so must be reification. The historical specificity of reification will be significant for our later analysis of Lukács's identification of the proletariat as the identical subject–object of historical genesis. Having ascertained the grounds for reification in the labour process we need to say something more precise about its nature.

As a multivalent term of social analysis Lukács employs reification to specify a social process, the conditions for that process, and the paradigmatic societal effects of that process. Hence, it is not surprising that reification should be a synonym for alienation, rationalisation, atomisation and the deactivation of the subject; nor that these terms should signify different levels of analysis, which levels denote different aspects and/or levels of social structure and experience.[7] The core of the process of reification itself is the separation (alienation) of labour from the labourer (87) in virtue of the separation of the labourer from (direct control over) the means of production. As we have seen, the abstraction of labour this separation requires is brought about through the fragmentation of the work process itself, and hence, by extension, through the fragmentation of the product of labour. Lukács captures this idea in his contention that in a developed capitalist society the 'unity of a product as a commodity no longer coincides with its unity as a use-value' (89). This fragmentation of the object of production pre-supposes and effects a fragmentation and a deactivation of the producing subject. Because the subject must be made a component of the mechanically regimented and structured system of production then those psychological attributes re-quisite for the labour process must be 'separated from his total personality and placed in opposition to it so as to facilitate their integration into specialised rational systems and their reduction to statistically viable concepts' (88). The mechanised system of production, like the market itself, comes to confront the worker as a 'pre-existing and self-sufficient' (89) system, functioning in accordance with nature-like laws (103). The radical autonomy of market and work process from individual control on the one hand, and the necessity for the individual worker to submit him- or herself to the discipline of the market and work process on the other engender a deactivation of the subject.

This moment in Lukács's theory provides the sociological basis both for his critique of representational theory and for his critique of epistemology.

As labour is progressively rationalised and mechanised his lack of will is reinforced by the way in which his activity becomes less and less active and more and more *contemplative*. The contemplative stance adopted towards a process mechanically conforming to fixed laws and enacted independently of man's consciousness and impervious to human intervention, i.e. a perfectly closed system, must likewise transform the basic categories of man's immediate attitude to the world. (89)

To take a contemplative stance toward reality is not something individuals can do or not do as they please; nor, therefore, is 'contemplative' meant to signify in Lukács's theory a psychological property of individuals. The contemplative stance is a categorial appearance form of (individual) social existence in capitalist social formations. It is an appearance form because, on one level, it is false to assert that individuals stand in a merely contemplative relation to the world: individuals do work, transform the natural world, and produce new instruments of production. Further, and more importantly, the mechanised social systems toward which men take a contemplative stance are in fact produced and reproduced as the unintended consequences of intentional social practices (working, buying, selling, etc.). Finally, then, as human products these systems are *ultimately* subject to human (class, not individual) control. The contemplative stance is none the less categorial: social systems do confront individuals *as* mechanical processes conforming to natural laws; individuals can investigate such systems attempting to ascertain their operative laws, hoping thereby to be able to manipulate them to their social advantage (in a manner analogous to the way in which by learning the laws of nature we attempt to manipulate it, through technology, to our 'natural' advantage). Individuals must adjust themselves to what appears to be outside, external and impervious to them. Contemplation, then, denotes a form of external relatedness; under its sway social domains manifest themselves as 'objects' outside and independent of the individual. In pre-capitalist (slave and feudal) societies the contemplative stance was a social privilege of the non-labouring classes. Only under capital does contemplation become categorial and hence constitutive of our relation to the social world.[8] With the social production of the contemplative stance our primordial practical engagement with the world is (apparently) severed; the world becomes a picture, an object to be pictured. For Lukács, categorial contemplation is a historically produced and derived mode of relatedness to the world.[9]

Rationalisation produces a reified world; or conversely, looking at the situation from the perspective of the subject, rationalisation produces for the subject an object for contemplation, that is, something which presents itself *as* an object which is to be understood in the manner of the objectifying sciences of the natural world (physics, chemistry, astronomy, etc.). The social world, however, does not present itself as just one, complexly structured object; on the contrary, within what we might recognise as the social world different sub-sections within it present themselves as structurally autonomous and closed systems of relations. Fragmentation as a product of rationalisation infects the social system as a whole by producing an apparently heterogeneous range of discrete and structurally isolated 'objects'. Paramount among these objects is 'the economy', the object of economics. Pre-capitalist social formations can be distinguished from capitalism on the basis of the way in which the latter transformed political domination into economic domination in a specialised economic sphere, and hence discovered a uniquely economic mode for the extraction of surplus labour (90–2). But it is more than a question of transformation which is at issue here for, in part at least, the making and sustaining of the autonomy of the economy is a cause and effect of reification, that is, we are here witnessing the actual production of a social domain operating in accordance with *naturlich* laws of determination. The autonomy of the economy is thus a double autonomy: the economy is autonomous from individual social control (and is thus an 'object' for contemplation), and it is (immediately) autonomous from other social domains. Clearly the same process of rationalisation is responsible for both forms of economic autonomy.

Autonomisation is a species of fragmentation evidenced on the macroscopic features of the social structure. The double autonomy of the economy infects other domains of social activity both by requiring their rationalisation as a condition for its existence, thus giving them an equally reified character; and by forcing them thereby to fold back upon themselves and leave their essential (hidden but real) connection with the economy and one another socially invisible. The immediate autonomy of the different domains of society (economy, state, judicial system, family, etc.) requires an equal fragmentation of the individual. Thus the sciences of society (economics, political science, sociology) and human behaviour (psychology, psychoanalysis, linguistics) come into being in *response* to the historical production of these now discrete objects. Where others have sought to blame the objectifying methods of the social and human sciences on the ideological dominance of positivism, Lukács grounds the *culture of positivism* in the auto-objectification of society itself: reified sub-systems of the social world present themselves as 'objects'; the overall complement of which is the institution of categorial contemplation induced through the deactivation of the now individualised and isolated subject.

Lukács's critique of social theory, his auto-critique of the representational construal of Marxist theory, thus turns on his claim that representational theories of man and society generally are grounded in the auto-objectification of society, in the autonomisation and fragmentation of social domains and their components. Categorial contemplation, because constitutive of man's immediate relation to society, grounds the epistemic appropriation of social relations through the production of representational theories. The epistemological consequences of categorial contemplation, which together form what might be termed the 'positivism effect', have three essential aspects. First, because of their apparent entrapment in deterministic systems, the data investigated and used in social theory are taken to be *natural*, ready-made and value-neutral. What goes along with this, of course, is that the goal of social inquiry is taken to be the production, through induction, of testable law-like generalisations. Secondly, given the capacity of the new sciences to generate such law-like generalisations, there occurs an increasing displacement of critical self-consciousness by *methodology*; that is, critical reflection is replaced by canons of methodological rules which are taken to be sufficient analyses of the nature of inquiry itself (104, 106). Methodology, for Lukács, is synonymous with a loss of self-consciousness. Thus, finally, and for Lukács most importantly, the success of these sciences in producing laws and methodologies begets a dissolution of their understanding of the social totality, and as a consequence there occurs a 'bracketing' of the historical and ontological conditions grounding both theory and phenomena:

the more intricate a modern science becomes and the better it understands itself methodologically, the more resolutely it will turn its back on the ontological problems of its own sphere of influence and eliminate them from the realm where it has achieved some insight. The more highly developed it becomes and the more scientific, the more it will become a formally closed system of partial laws. It will then find that the world lying beyond its confines, and in particular the material

base which it is its task to understand, *its own concrete underlying reality*
lies, methodologically and in principle *beyond its grasp.* (104)

For Lukács the inability of classical and modern economic
theory to discover the material substratum of exchange value is
the prime example of the positivism effect. Representational
theory thus deepens categorial contemplation by making social
appearance into theoretical truth. By freezing social data in
deterministic systems, representational theories, be they bourgeois or Marxist, empty radical social action of any possible
meaning. The deactivation of the subject becomes complete
when the autonomy of a social system, whether stagnant or
evolving, is theoretically canonised.

Anomalous within this pattern of fragmentation is (are) the
domain(s) of culture, for its (their) autonomisation does not
generate an auto-presentation of a domain of discrete objects
awaiting scientific analysis. On the contrary, *it is the value-
orientation of cultural artefacts within an autonomous sphere* which
produces their specifically problematic character. It is this
problematic character which forms the centre of the analysis in
The Theory of the Novel. None the less, by way of anticipation, we
can detect the confluence of the cultural problematic with the
positivism effect by taking a quick look at the division (or strife)
between intrinsic and extrinsic approaches to literary criticism.
Intrinsic approaches – textual analysis, practical criticism, and
the like – are premised upon the autonomy/anomaly of their
object: the constitutive autonomy of the literary *as* literary and
nothing else engenders its own form of deactivation and
contemplation, namely, repeating the essential movements of
the text itself. To desire less would be to fail to respond to the
value demands, the 'insights' which the texts proclaim for
themselves; to attempt more would be to fail to respect the
'integrity' of the text, that is, would be to go beyond the domain
of its validity. In time, the fragility of the value claims made by
literary texts, their validity residing only in the restricted sphere
of literature itself, yielded the defensive postures of 'criticism as
literature' or 'criticism as performance' (presumably a 'literary'
performance); criticism thus attempts to secure for itself what it
takes to be the autonomous value of its object. The ultimate
muteness of this form of criticism naturally summoned up its
spectre; extrinsic criticism, which *explains* the text in accordance

with principles and laws drawn from some other domain (sociology, linguistics, psychoanalysis, etc.). Each such reductive programme is subject to a double failure: on the one hand, each project stands exposed before the claims of competing projects. This is inevitable since, seen aright, the *diversity* of critical projects *is* problematic or, what is the same, is a product of reification. On the other hand, all reductive procedures stand exposed before the claims of Literature itself, its tacit assertion of possessing an autonomous basis for its value claims. And the *enforced* (i.e. socially produced) autonomy of literature makes this counter-charge in part true.

The legitimacy of intrinsic criticism derives from its success in appropriating for itself the value basis of its object, while the legitimacy of extrinsic criticism derives from the representational truth of its laws which, as causal generalisations, must naturally deny the existence of any transcendent value claims. Thus the legitimacy of each approach cancels out the legitimacy of the other. Categorial contemplation lies behind both approaches, but here, as nowhere else, the result of contemplation is overtly antinomic since there exist good reasons from either perspective for rejecting the claims of the other perspective. From the point of view of Lukácsian theory the antinomy between extrinsic and intrinsic criticism is an expression of the more general antinomies between fact and value, and between determinism and freedom (where these two antinomies are regarded as overlapping). Under capital value claims come to be inscribed in a domain whose immediate autonomy is an expression of the inability of those values to permeate everyday life. Values thus must be regarded as subjective, as saying what 'ought' to be, as fictions. Extrinsic criticism fowards the recognised exigencies of existing psychosocial mechanisms to *explain* the fiction of literary value. Intrinsic criticism grasps the indubitable freedom of the individual subject as the support required and sufficient for its programme of holding up the claims of literary insight against society. Neither side can made decisive inroads against the claims of the other side.

Categorial contemplation and its antinomies form the terminus of Lukács's generalisation of Marx's concept of commodity fetishism. Beginning with the autonomy of the economic moment of social reproduction achieved by capital, Lukács goes on to demonstrate the 'reified' consequences of this autonomy for the rest of society. As its autonomy makes the economy a law-governed world of social objects, so the social domains necessary for its reproduction equally become (on the appearance level) law-governed worlds of social objects. Categorial contemplation is the subjective corollary and effect of this process of reification, of making social practices appear as things. Cultural positivism is the expression of categorial contemplation within the social and human sciences; while the antinomy of intrinsic and extrinsic criticism is an expression of categorial contemplation within the domain of literature. More significantly, the pheno-menon of categorial contemplation reverberates back on the starting-point of the analysis, namely, Marx's theory itself. Lukács does not want to argue that Marx's theory is an example of what he (Lukács) has just criticised; only that, given his critique of the paradigms of formal rationality, Marx's theory cannot be construed as a representation of an independently existing social object; the relation of Marx's theory to its competitors cannot be that his corresponds to reality (and is therefore true), while theirs do not so correspond (and are therefore false). Nor can it be the case, although both Lukács's and Marx's language sometimes appears to suggest this, that Marxist theory is true because it penetrates to the essence or reality of social phenomena, while bourgeois theories are false because they remain trapped within the appearances thrown up by the underlying reality. That conception of appearance and reality, be it metaphysically idealist as in Plato or metaphysi-cally realist as in Locke and contemporary scientific realists, presupposes the same contemplative conception of knowledge and its objects as is at work in the paradigm of formal rationality.[10] How, then, is the 'truth' of Marx's theory to be conceived? Lukács's auto-critique of the representational com-prehension of Marxist theory requires that the truth of that theory be reinterpreted, and in a manner which allows it to comprehend its 'own concrete, underlying reality', a reality which, we know, will be social and historical in character.

   Lukács's auto-critique of Marxist theory poses the question of the nature of the truth and meaning of that theory; and it is thus an attempt to rethink the truth of social theories which guides

Lukács's analysis of 'The Antinomies of Bourgeois Thought' (Part II of the 'Reification' essay) in philosophy. The philosophical critique of reification and categorial contemplation involves an analysis of the metaphysical and epistemological presuppositions of categorial contemplation. Lukács accomplishes his rediscovery and dissolution of categorial contemplation, and with it the positivism effect, at the level of philosophical theory by tracing its manifestations in the history of German Idealism from Kant to Hegel. These manifestations are the antinomies or dualisms of the philosophical tradition. Thus Lukács seeks to complement his sociological critique of reification and contemplation with a philosophical critique. Only the confluence of the two critiques will validate the overall critique while simultaneously opening up the question and possibility of discovering an historical substratum for critique itself.

3 METACRITIQUE: ON THE ANTINOMIES OF BOURGEOIS THOUGHT

The 'antinomies of bourgeois thought' are in reality the antinomies of Kant's critical philosophy. Kant's system is 'critical' in that it renounces the possibility of knowledge of the 'whole' as exemplified in the systems of classical rationalism, while simultaneously providing a critique of the dogmatic scepticism found in traditional empiricism. Empiricism accepts the rationalist account of what philosophical knowing is but denies its possibility. Kant denies the rationalist account of philosophical knowledge, limiting philosophical reflection 'to the study of the "possible conditions" for the validity of the forms in which its underlying existence is manifested' (10); in fine, Kant limits philosophy to providing an account of the conditions for the possibility of experience. The critique of critical reflection is metacritique.

What however, justifies Lukács in regarding Kant's system as exemplifying the antinomies of bourgeois thought? Lukács's answer is that

philosophy stands in the same relation to the special sciences as they do with respect to empirical reality. The formalistic conceptualisation of the special sciences becomes for philosophy an immutable given substratum and this signals the final and despairing renunciation of every attempt to cast light on the reification that lies at the root of this formalism. (110)

Hence if it can be shown that the positivism effect which marks the contemplative relation of social theory to reality equally infects Kant's philosophy, and further, that his philosophy makes that reified world appear 'as the only possible world, the only conceptually accessible, comprehensible world vouchsafed to us humans' (ibid.), then the categories and antinomies of his system can be regarded as existence-forms of bourgeois society, that is, as the philosophical equivalents of categorial contemplation. The very demonstration of this confluence, however, will be Lukács's metacritique itself, since it will relocate philosophical reflection in its historical substratum, while simultaneously revealing that the question of the historical substratum of thought marks the terminus of the philosophical attempt to untie the antinomies which haunt Kant's system.[11]

Since we shall be continually returning to the antinomies in Kant's system in later chapters, for present purposes it will suffice to examine his concept of the thing in itself as the theoretical focus where the different rays of the positivism effect intersect. Lukács identifies two apparently heterogeneous problematics which assemble themselves around the thing in itself: on the one hand, there is the problem of matter, that is, the problem of the content of concepts and categories, and hence of the source or causal origin of perceptual data; on the other hand, there is the problem of the whole or the ultimate object(s) (substance) of knowledge. Both problematics have their origin in Kant's 'Copernican turn' whereby the grounds for the possibility of knowledge are displaced from the external world (or God) to the knowing self. Roughly, in the First Critique in place of traditional metaphysical talk about things or substances represented we receive talk about our representations of things or substances; and in place of discourse about God's creating, ordering and connecting of things, we receive discourse about the self's ordering and connecting perceptual manifolds. This point can be made perspicuous by taking the following sentence: 'The transcendental unity of apperception forms out of all possible appearances, which can stand alongside one another in one experience, a connection of all these according to laws' (A 108); and substituting into it 'God' for 'transcendental unity of apperception', 'substances' for 'appearances' and 'representations', and 'world' for 'experience', we would thus get: 'God forms out of all possible substances, which can stand alongside one another in one world, a connection of all these substances according to laws' – a sentence which could have been written by Leibniz or appeared in Kant's own (pre-critical) 'Inaugural Dissertation'.[12] The philosophical replacement of God by man is the 'turn' by which questions of knowledge, questions relating to how it is we come to know about the world, replace questions of metaphysics, questions relating to the ultimate nature of reality. This is not to say that Kant believes that the world lacks an ultimate reality; only that, being finite creatures, we possess no way of knowing about such things. Our finite perspective on things is absolute 'for us'. Kant is committed to the thesis that knowledge of the ultimate nature of the world is forever prohibited to finite creatures like ourselves.

Thus the removing of the totality (the world) and the material substratum of thought (the self) as objects of knowledge comes to be the immediate goal of Kant's transcendental procedure, and jointly represents the primitive meaning of the thing in itself. Human beings do not know things in themselves, they do not know how the world really is (as God created it and perceives it, say), because all human acts of cognition involve the imposition (or use) of thought-forms, what Kant calls 'categories', in accordance with which the manifold of perceptual data is organised ('synthesised'). Categories are a human contribution to the knowing situation in virtue of which there comes into being 'a knowing situation', a relation between a knowing subject and an object known. Thus for anything to be an object is for it to be an object of a judgement; thus how things are apart from our activities of judging and synthesising we can not say. Totality, then, is what is suppressed in restricting knowledge to appearances only, to what appears within the horizon of human cognitive activity; while the material (or immaterial!) substratum of thought is bracketed out of experience in virtue of making the categories, which are brute products of an *un*intelligible spontaneity (B 158), the minimum necessary conditions for the possibility of knowledge.[13] This double bracketing of totality and self corresponds to the third moment of the positivism effect. Since what is knowable is so only in virtue of being brought under the categories of thought, then apart from the categories what appears is meaningless, and can only be taken as merely and unintelligibly 'given'. This corresponds to the first moment of the positivism effect. Finally, relating to the second moment of the positivism effect, since the basis of thought, the data of knowledge, and the whole of what can be known have been eliminated from both philosophical (transcendental) and empirical investigation, science can perfect itself through methodological refinement alone, and it is debarred from radical self-reflection. (Perhaps another way of putting this last point would be to say that Kant displaces teleology from the metaphysical level into the methodology of the natural sciences. In this way the world is made 'safe' for deterministic physics while the rationality of science becomes formal, a methodological prescription.)

The antinomic character of the thing in itself is neatly captured in Jacobi's famous dictum that he was unable to find his way into Kant's system without presupposing the thing in itself, but with the presupposition of the thing in itself he was unable to stay in the system. Kant deflects the question of the totality into transcendental reflection, letting self-activity provide the necessary conditions for (the possibility of) objectivity; but because man is not God and does not materially produce the world the problem of totality must resurface elsewhere in the system as the question of the source of perceptual data and as the question of the ultimate object(s) of knowledge. Because Kant's criticism of metaphysics employs the fundamental structures of metaphysical thought, the problems of the tradition naturally recur within his system. While the positivism effect falls out as a direct consequence of making the Copernican turn, the duality of the thing in itself, as limiting concept and as cause, reveals the positivism effect to have an essentially antinomic structure.[14]

To have detected the roots of positivism in Kant is not original to Lukács; to have specified the thing in itself as the meeting ground for those thoughts is what gives his analysis its fineness and interest. But Lukács presses his analysis further when he seeks to ground the positivism effect in Kant on the antinomies of freedom and necessity, is and ought; antinomies which function throughout Lukács's writings as the philosophical figures *par excellence* of reification. With the installation of the primacy of the antinomy of freedom and necessity, the problems of the thing in itself come to appear as an iridescent after-image of the more fundamental experience of freedom finding its limits pre-inscribed within the self; an experience which gives phenome-nological expression to the thus far only conceptually analysed contemplative relation.

Kant's Copernican turn gave an unprecedented role to human activity in the grounding of objectivity in knowledge and morals. Only the spontaneously produced forms of the intellect make knowledge and right action possible. In the case of knowledge the spontaneously produced and synthesising activities of the categories ground its possibility; while in ethics the Categorical Imperative is the law which the will gives to itself as the condition for its own continued free employment. As one commentator has put it: 'Reason, in Kant's philosophy, is essentially free; freedom is essentially rational; and both consist ultimately in spontaneity.... [S]pontaneity is the *ontological* foundation of both freedom and rationality in Kant's philo-sophy.'[15] One might naturally deduce from this that any restriction on the exercise of our spontaneous powers would be a restriction upon our essential nature, a manifestation of a lack of freedom, of necessity and irrationality, and hence contrary to it. Since necessity and irrationality contradict the essential nature of the self, one would suppose that by its nature the self would desire to overcome all limitations and restrictions on its spontaneous powers. This, at any rate, was the line of argument adopted by Fichte in order to overcome the antinomies in Kant's system, and it is the meaning of Fichte's speculative declaration that 'the self strives to fill out the infinite.'[16]

Kant's own conception of activity, however, places stronger, more permanent restrictions on it, taking more cognisance than Fichte of the situation and the content of reason as opposed to its principle and inner nature. Indeed, the pivotal category of Kant's epistemological system is that of cause and effect; it stipulates that *all* happenings in the world must be presupposed to conform to the causal principle that every event happens in accordance with some causal rule if they are to be knowable. What makes an event part of an objective system, which is to say, a part of a world, is its conformity to this principle; and *nothing in the world* can be regarded as an exception to this rule. The world, our world, is thus constituted as a world by its subsumption under the law of cause and effect.

Whence then freedom? In the domain of knowledge all that can be said is that freedom in the form of spontaneity is itself the producer of the category of causality.[17] Perhaps it would not be too unjust to say (as Marx might have) that we impose causal necessity upon ourselves in the very act of constructing an objective world; our freedom, operating behind our back, negates itself by the very form of its expression. What then of ethical, practical activity? The law of practical action is the law of freedom; but how can this law (*Wille*) and the capacity for action it determines (*Willkür*) gain purchase on the world if everything in the world occurs in accordance with the law of cause and effect? That the will, which is essentially free in its constitution, cannot penetrate experience is precisely what makes Kant's conception of the relation between freedom and necessity antinomic, and further makes the perspective of action itself contemplative: 'freedom and the autonomy that is supposed to result from the discovery of the ethical world are reduced to a mere *point of view from which to judge* internal events [i.e. the maxims governing particular intentions]. These events, however, are seen as being subject in all their motives and effects and even in their psychological elements to a fatalistically regarded objective necessity' (124). As a consequence of the diremptive antagonism between freedom and necessity the self becomes split into an empirical self governed by the law of cause and effect (thus belonging to what Kant terms the world of 'phenomena'), and a transcendental self governed by the law of freedom (and thus belonging to a 'noumenal' domain). The ethic which results is purely formal in the same manner in which positivistic science is formal; subjective form articulates and/or rationalises material contents which it is unable to truly penetrate and determine. The data remain inviolate in their givenness.

Kant's two worlds theory (a causally determined phenomenal domain and a self-determining noumenal domain) gives philosophical expression to the experience of an essentially free self confronting a predetermined, mechanistically ordered, reified world; where only the transcendental ideality of that world, the sense of its categorial structure being the product of self activity, serves as a critical reminder of the worldliness of the world.[18] For there to be anything we would recognise as a 'world' it must be a world for us, acceding to our place and participation in it; but Kant's worlds, which are our own, are, as phenomena, a domain of sheer indifference and as thing in itself (noumenon) a sheer beyond (not even a world). The sign of the uninhabitability of the world, of its dislocation from mind and self, is given by the gap between 'is' and 'ought'; '"ought" presupposes an existing reality to which the category of "ought" [the Categorical Imperative, the law of freedom] remains *inapplicable* in principle' (160). In the permanent transcendence of what ought to be beyond empirical reality that reality is philosophically legitimated and frozen in its indifference to rational human desire, which in its turn becomes 'a wish, a utopia' (ibid.).

Kant's theory provides a vision of a rational and active human subjectivity, while depriving that subjectivity of a world in which to act. 'Nothing in the world of phenomena', Kant says, 'can be explained by the concept of freedom, the guiding thread in that sphere must always be the mechanics of nature.'[19] The terms for a resolution of the antinomies are thus set: freedom must be able to determine the objective world, and the material substratum of that world must be determinable through practice. Indeed, Lukács goes so far as to say that 'the essence of praxis consists in annulling that *indifference of form* (subjectivity) *towards content*' (126). Three steps are necessary for this to be the case, and the antinomies thus untied.[20] First, the dualism between judgement (knowledge) and action must be overcome through the recognition that the unity and intelligibility of the world is the unity of action and deed as opposed to judgement. Hence both subject and object become products of action, their underlying affinity for one another residing in the ultimate subject of action. But this Fichtean primacy of practical reason founders on the nature of the subject, for the absolute self or subject, the primordial agent, is in Fichte a theoretical construct, and hence, like Kant's transcendental ego, deprived of concrete, empirical existence. Further, while Fichte was the first philosopher clearly to enunciate the principle that every image of mind and world reciprocally imply one another, and in this way to grasp the worldliness of the world, it remains mysterious on his account how individual minds, empirical or transcendental, can produce a world. Hence the second step in overcoming the Kantian antinomies becomes the denying of any privilege to the individual subject; action remains contemplative if the subject of action is conceived to be the isolated individual (135, 193). Social action can become praxial only if the isolated and egoistic individual of bourgeois society is transcended. And this entails denying that the subject of action is 'given' (186–7). Finally, then, if the object is the result of action, and the acting subject must itself be regarded as produced, then subject and object must be regarded as in process, or, what is the same, as reciprocally determined products of history. History becomes the locus of the genesis of both subject and object (142–4).

Kant's thought philosophically articulates and consecrates the antinomies of reified consciousness; the reified world of capital is the historical substratum of Kant's thought, and the antinomies of his system are theoretically (philosophically) untied with the discovery of history as the only possible locus and basis for human thought and action. Such is Lukács's metacritique; philosophy leaves the terrain of pure reflection and becomes historical.

4   HISTORY AS PHILOSOPHY (OF PRAXIS AND TRUTH)

Marxism ... had to be a revolutionary philosophy precisely because it refused to be a dogmatic philosophy of history. Two moments which succeed each other perpetually in it, each time at a higher level, composed its spiral movement – a reading of history which allows its philosophical meaning to appear, and a return to the present which lets philosophy appear as history.

(Maurice Merleau-Ponty)

whatever the fate of 'class consciousness' in a theory of revolution, its significance stands as a permanent goal of social epistemology .... For its claims are that history alone has excavated what we recognize as social position, that our place in society has become unknown to us, that knowledge of the self is acquired only together with knowledge of the self's society, of its stand in society – as though what is 'unconscious' in an adult is not merely his psychic past but his social present, equally painful and difficult to recognize – and that just as having a self requires taking a stand upon the self, so having a place means assuming that place.

(Stanley Cavell)

Philosophy becomes historical when it recognises that the thought-forms and structures which it seeks to analyse are themselves products of history, whose meaning can only be recovered through the recovery of their social basis (placement) and historical genesis. These two, social basis and historical genesis, represent the *mediating* forces of history which give meaning to theoretical concepts, and are hence the *totality* to which those concepts as elements belong as parts to a whole.[21] 'The essence of history', Lukács claims, 'lies precisely in the change undergone by those *structural forms* which are the focal points of man's interaction with the environment at any given moment and which determine the objective nature of both his inner and his outer life' (153). Structural forms are linked meaning and causal relations between man and man, and man and environment; they are social practices and positions conceived as both signifying and power relations which structure everyday life. Again, structural forms are the constitutive (i.e. the categorial) concepts governing particular institutional practices. Since the internal structure of institutions changes over time and further, changes in its relations to other institutional complexes, then the existence-forms of human life must themselves be subject to historical alteration. Structural forms, unlike Kantian categories and concepts, or empiricist ideas and impressions, are not the possession of individuals as such; it is those forms, rather, which inhabit and determine us. For Lukács 'man himself is dialectical' (187), which is to say, man can only think himself in terms of the ever-mutating structural forms of history. Hence Lukács rejects all reductive forms of humanism and 'anthropology' which would attempt to measure history against an abiding standard of human nature.

Such a thorough-going rejection of trans-historical touchstones for 'truth' raises two interlocking difficulties; on the one hand, it appears to open all theory to the charge of relativism;

on the other hand, since it discounts the possibility of a priori and trans-historical reflection on human thought and action, it appears to eliminate the possibility of philosophical thought as traditionally conceived, and tacitly urges a replacement of philosophy by sociology, above all by the sociology of knowledge. It is beyond question that 'The Standpoint of the Proletariat' (Part III of the 'Reification' essay) is meant to answer these problems; the issue is whether in providing an answer Lukács relapses into the kind of theorising he had earlier refuted.

Lukács poses the problem of the standpoint of the proletariat in quasi Fichtean terms: reality must be conceived as act as much as object, that is, if both the material substratum and, objects of human thought and action are not to be impenetrable 'givens', then they must be regarded as products of human action. In Fichte the absolute self is the ultimate subject–object of thought and action from which all else flows. Such an absolute self, we noted, was a theoretical hypostatisation which in reality was incapable of either thought or action. Further, the Fichtean self was both trans-historical in character and, arguably, an 'individual' subject. History cannot be the product of individuals *per se*, however, for to suppose that would be to return to some form of humanism. Hegel's historical and trans-individual notion of the 'World Spirit' fares no better as the ultimate subject–object of history since its perspective always transcends the peoples who function as instruments of its realisation. Hegel's concept of Spirit must be regarded as mythological since it always lacks concrete historical actuality (146–7).[22] Yet the question remains: who is 'the "we" which is the subject of history, that "we" whose action is in fact history' (145)?

Traditional readings of Lukács state that it is the proletariat which is the subject–object of history, and that it is the standpoint of the proletariat which allows us to see history aright, in its 'true' order of unfolding and meaning. This standpoint, however, is not the possession of existing individual proletarians; they, like us all, are subject to ideological mystification and illusion, and hence only the 'ascribed' class consciousness of the proletariat, that ideal type of class consciousness individual proletarians would have if they penetrated the illusory forms of reified thought thrown up by capital, is fully objective. So stated, it certainly sounds as if the ascribed class consciousness of the proletariat is an ideal type construction on the model of a Fichtean absolute subject, and that when ascribed class consciousness becomes actual, then the proletariat becomes in reality the subject–object of all historical genesis – as if all history had been awaiting the arrival of the proletariat in order to redeem it. And this argument certainly parallels a traditional Marxist thesis which claims that the proletariat is a historically unique class in that it is the first and only class in history which can realise its class interest only through the dissolution of *all* class antagonism (80). If all history is the history of class conflict, then the proletariat, in fulfilling its particular class interest, unties the riddle of history and does so knowingly. On this reading the standpoint of the proletariat represents a historically produced 'transcendental ego' whose act of self-realisation through becoming self-conscious allows history itself to be completed and dissolved. History becomes philosophy by producing within itself a standpoint in accordance with which its meaning can be deciphered and that meaning realised.

History does become philosophy for Lukács by producing the proletariat as the bearer of its meaning; but the proletariat does not on his account have the status of an absolute subject. To transcribe the standpoint of the proletariat into a Fichtean absolute subject through the addition of history and class to Fichte's subject concept would return Lukács's philosophy to the standpoint of contemplation. Contemplative consciousness can stand outside history only if history can be reduced to a 'natural' sequence, that is, only if there is a speculative philosophy of history which has a natural terminus. But as the Hegelian transformation of Fichtean theory makes evident 'history has no end' (147), or rather, to think of history as having an end necessitates adopting a speculative/spectatorial relation to history, which in its turn involves a relapse 'into the contemplative duality of subject and object' (148). Since Lukács denies that the standpoint of the proletariat is contemplative, it follows that the interpretation of it as a standpoint transcending historical determination must be incorrect.

Marxism is a historical philosophy of the *present*, 'it is the self-knowledge of capitalist society' (229, 16); hence the ideology and theory of dialectical and historical materialism are historically produced and conditioned. The application of a method and a 'logic' to any phenomena are dependent upon the nature of that phenomena; thus for Lukács the method of truth for any particular epoch is specific to that epoch.

The substantive truths of historical materialism are of the same type as were the truths of classical economics in Marx's view: they are truths within a particular social order and system of production. As such, but only as such, their claim to validity is absolute. But this does not preclude the emergence of societies in which by virtue of their different social structures other categories and other systems of truth prevail. (228)

Nor, Lukács continues, can Marxist theory be unproblematically applied to pre-capitalist social formations (237–38), for in those formations the purely economic forces of society had not yet achieved the kind of autonomy from other social institutions and domains (e.g. the political and religious domains) which would have permitted them to produce specifically reified social relations. Since the system of truth applicable to capital is derived from and allows the decipherment of reified social relations, and since those relations are specific to capital, then that system of truth is not historically generalisable. The double dialectic of subject–object and immediacy–mediation, which represents the dialectical logic of capital, is an immanent aspect of capital's social ontology, hence the logic of capital must be historically specific (ibid.).

It is in the experience of the proletariat that the double dialectic of subject–object and immediacy–mediation conjoin and intertwine. Beginning with the logic of immediacy–mediation, the experience of the proletariat is distinct from that of the bourgeoisie in that while they share the same immediate experience of reified social relations, 'the motor of class interests keep the bourgeoisie imprisoned within this immediacy while forcing the proletariat to go beyond it' (164). Both in work and daily life the proletarian discovers that what he initially takes to be a feature of life within his subjective control is in reality part of an impersonal and objective social process (165–7, 225–8). More precisely, work experience reveals the proletarian as both producer and commodity, as a fabricator of use-values and as a component in the production of exchange values, as subject and as object. So in the *experience* of the proletariat the logic of mediation reveals the dialectic of subject and object. This supplies a hint as to the historical specificity of the double dialectic, and of the place of the proletariat in the decipherment of reified social relations. What is not said here is anything about either the philosophical meaning of that experience or its connection with a presumed class praxis.

What is it the proletarian discovers in experiencing the theft of his subjectivity in the processes of capital production? It is this: in becoming aware of himself as a commodity, commodity relations themselves becomes self-conscious, that is, they come to know themselves for what they are: social relations between men submerged in the guise of quantitative relations between things (168–9). This discovery is of the utmost significance for, Lukács argues, 'the uniqueness of capitalism is to be seen precisely in its abolition of all "natural barriers" and its transformation of all relations between human beings into purely social relations' (176). It is precisely the socialising function of capital, *which is the philosophical significance of capitalist development*, which the proletarian experience unearths, and which 'intention' now passes to the proletariat as the horizon of its class action, and hence as the constitutive meaning of that action. The proletariat is the failure and remnant of the capitalist revolution; it remains, in the reduction of its labour power to the labour time sold to the capitalist, a subjectivity locked in the objective forms of capital productive relations. The secret of commodity relations, and what makes them fetishistic, is that in them 'all given factors are determined (a) as mediating terms in relations of recognition among free persons [i.e. as social relations] and (b) as objectifications (or embodiments) of abstract human labour time [i.e. as quanta of embodied labour time, and hence as quasi-natural determinants].'[23] The commodity form, then, is a type of natural determination capable of characterising the structure of social relations as a totality. Equally, however, these relations are themselves a product of human labour, and it is that which the spontaneous de-reifying experience of the proletariat reveals. Now because what proletarian experience reveals is the *social* relations of production, proletarian action can only be class action; to say that proletarian action is necessarily class action is to claim that its intention can only be realised through the transformation of the structural forms, the social relations of production themselves. Merleau-Ponty has captured this moment in Lukács's thought better than anyone:

The philosophical reading of history is not a simple application of concepts of consciousness, of truth and totality, badly disguised under historical rags, for this focusing, this placing in perspective, is accomplished in history itself by the proletariat. In creating an expropriated class – men who are commodities – capitalism forces them to judge commodities according to human relations. . . . It is not the philosopher who looks for the criteria of a judgment of capitalism in a conception of the 'reign of freedom'. It is capitalism which gives rise to a class of men who cannot stay alive without repudiating the status of commodity imposed upon them. The proletariat is commodity seeing itself as commodity. . . . The realisation of society that capitalism has sketched, left in suspense, and finally thwarted is taken up by the proletariat because, being the very failure of the capitalistic intention, it is, by position, 'at the focal point of the socialising process' (176). . . . The 'socialising' function of capital passes to the proletariat. At the same time, the proletariat *is* this philosophical meaning of history that one might have thought was the work of the philosopher, because it is the 'self-consciousness of the object' (178).'[24]

It is not philosophical reflection – be it transcendental, a priori, or some form of intellectual intuition – which discovers the meaning of history; rather, historical experience itself reveals that meaning in the social experience of a class attempting to make sense of its social placement, its participation and non-participation in social processes and the possibilities and impossibilities (social miseries) such involvements incur. And, of course, that meaning is historical; it is *the* meaning of history, the best sense which can be made of present social processes, but only for now.

It is at this juncture that a difficulty in Lukács's analysis arises in the form of an unresolved tension between objective and subjective accounts of proletarian class consciousness. The dualism Lukács was attempting to overcome can be easily stated: Is the proletariat to be defined in terms of its being or in terms of its praxis? To define the proletariat by its being is to reduce it to what the congealing social processes of capital have made it, namely, abstract individuals filling places within the predetermined objective structures of capital production. This is inadequate since it would reduce proletarian class consciousness to what it is determined to be by capital; the horizons of proletarian self-consciousness would be dictated by capital production itself. Alternatively, to define the proletariat strictly in terms of its self-making, what it has achieved through class struggle, would leave the structural determinants of that action out of account. Moreover, such a radically subjectivist position would eliminate all truth and meaning in the philosophical sense we have been attempting to locate. In resolving this either/or Lukács hesitates between a properly constructivist conception of class consciousness, and a more reductive account which ties proletarian class consciousness to horizons determined by capital itself. The account of class consciousness in the 'Reification' essay is usually read in terms of the latter alternative. In that case class consciousness 'is nothing but the expression of historical necessity' (177), an 'objectively impelled' irruption in the 'dialectics of history' (197). Only by the awakening of proletarian class consciousness, Lukács appears to be arguing, can the potentialities ossified in the natural tendencies of historical development become actual. Hence historical necessity becomes a historical freedom when the proletariat consciously grasps its position as the subject – object of history, and thus realises the ends which, like a destiny, history holds out for it.

In the essay 'Class Consciousness' Lukács did interpret proletarian class consciousness in terms of an objectively ascribed class consciousness, that is, in terms of an 'objective possibility', namely, the 'thoughts and feelings which men would have in a particular situation if they were *able* to assess both it and the interests arising from it in their impact on immediate action and on the whole structure of society' (51). And it is certainly tempting to identify this 'objective possibility' with the 'objectively impelled' consciousness of the 'Reification' essay. None the less, the reductive dogmatism (who is in a sufficiently privileged position to be able to validate such a counterfactual act of reflection?) of the former (and earlier) essay is not equivalent with the praxial conception of truth found in the 'Reification' essay. In the case of the earlier account appropriate class consciousness (i.e. that consciousness in virtue of which individual proletarians can come to preceive themselves *as* a class), the content of their class interests, and hence the appropriate goals for class action, are all determined by the structure of the totality and its determination of the place of consciousness within itself. Such is not the significance of the later account of praxis. There what is objectively impelled by the historical totality is *only* the emergence of class consciousness itself; this necessity, however, while causally conditioned is philosophical and intensional in character. Only the proletariat as a class can realise the socialising process set in train by the bourgeois revolution, and their objective place in the relations of production – as subject and object – provides the experiential conditions under which they can awaken to that task. What the social placement of the proletariat does not do is causally guarantee that class consciousness will be achieved (there are always countervailing ideological forces operative), or causally determine what the precise contents of that class consciousness are to be (the goals of proletarian action cannot be 'read off' of the structures of capital production – and making the reading counterfactual does not make the reading any easier or more legitimate). 'Dialectical trends,' Lukács reminds us, 'do not constitute an infinite progression that gradually nears its goal in a series of quantitative stages' (82). The achievement of proletarian class consciousness requires a 'qualitative revolution in the structure of society' (ibid.).

Lukács does sometimes appear to be suggesting that the awakening of proletarian class consciousness itself constitutes the sought-after revolution in the structure of society. Hence, holding on to his conception of ascribed class consciousness, it would then follow that in the overcoming of ideological mystification proletarian class consciousness is achieved and the old order is thereby overturned. It is difficult to conceive of what kind of conception of society and history would allow the mere overcoming of false belief to constitute a radical change in the form of social relations. Only by deleting the counterfactual account of ascribed class consciousness can sense be made of the idea of proletarian class consciousness itself constituting a structural alteration of social relations. If the existence of proletarian class consciousness involves (and requires) new forms of social relations, then it must function as a *goal* of revolutionary activity; but since revolutionary activity would not occur unless the proletariat possessed some class consciousness, then equally we must construe proletarian class consciousness as a means to revolutionary action. Proletarian class consciousness is both the means and the end of revolutionary activity; it is 'an aspiration towards society in its totality' (174), an intention towards totality and the totality which is intended.

Prior to the achievement of proletarian class consciousness the 'dialectical mechanics of history' work unimpeded, and the contradictions within the historical process will continue to reproduce themselves at higher levels of intensity until proletarian class consciousness is achieved (197–8). It is in the non-existence or failure of proletarian class consciousness 'that the objective necessity [causally construed] of history consists' (ibid.). The arrival of proletarian class consciousness means the arrival of the task and intention of practically abolishing the 'actual forms of social life' (177); but since proletarian class consciousness is itself an intention toward totality it cannot be fully realised within the existing social order. On the contrary, the rightness or wrongness of class action is gauged 'by the evolution of proletarian class consciousness' (199), by, that is, the degree to which in the practical overcoming of the objective/objectified forms of social life a truly social consciousness is achieved. 'Socialisation is the process in which the proletariat, as identical subject – object of history, transforms itself from a class within capitalism into the human base of a new economic order, from the object of social development into its subject.'[25]

One set of tendencies within the dialectic of capital forces and relations of production reproduces the structural contradictions of the system, while a countervailing cluster of tendencies presses toward further socialisation, and hence toward proletarian class consciousness. Proletarian class consciousness depends for its existence on both existing tendencies in the objective world and on the dissolution of existing structural laws and tendencies (178), and hence on the replacement of reified social relations by an authentic class praxis. Praxis is the form of knowing and acting appropriate to a class subject which has transcended (is transcending) a contemplative relation to the social world; it is the form of social action whereby proletarian class consciousness is constituted, and in being constituted reciprocally institutes itself as a new form of social action and reflection. Praxis participates in the duality of proletarian class consciousness as means and end by being that form of social action which is itself instrument and *telos*. Indeed, the link between proletarian class consciousness and praxis is so intimate that in defining Lukács's concept of praxis Merleau-Ponty includes class consciousness as one of its components.[26]

Proletarian class consciousness is the form of understanding appropriate to the class situation of the proletariat; as such it is as much an intention as a representation. Since the character of that intention is under-defined by the given conditions for action an essential component of proletarian deliberation is constituent-ends reasoning, a reasoning of what the end itself is to be. This reasoning is continually subject to refinement as class action alters the conditions for action, and simultaneously reveals the degree to which various ends (forms of social and political organisation, for example) do or do not accord with the global class project. Theory is less a representation of the world to be tested through experimentation than mutable possibilities for self-understanding producing sub-projects and actions within the global project which bring into being qualitatively new states of affairs possessing possibilities and tendencies of their own.

What is at issue in the practical activity prescribed by the Lukácsian subject is not simply a particular truth, but the very being of the object world. For the existence of this object world is validated in revolutionary practice. Revolution is therefore an ontological 'experiment'. What is tested in it is the very rationality of the *stance assumed* by the subject, the truth of its thinking in general.[27]

Proletarian class consciousness is the practical overcoming of contemplative reason, and thereby of the antinomies defining spectatorial consciousness. For example, Lukács conceives of the overcoming of the antinomy of freedom and necessity as involving a twofold dissolution. First, as the necessity governing the object world is recognised as not timelessly categorial but historically instituted through reification and rationalisation, then necessity becomes subject to praxis, that is, to the praxial interrogation of objective structures and the production of different forms of social relations which express or correspond to human interiority rather than standing as 'objects' outside of and anterior to subjectivity. Secondly, freedom itself must be relocated from individual to class subjects, for truly free action is praxial in character, it produces a 'world' (so recovering the worldliness of the world) rather than simple events 'in' a world. Analogously, since what 'is' is no longer categorially encapsulated within a deterministic system of causal laws but now includes progressive and regressive historical tendencies (some of which are causal, some intensional), then what ought to be 'must' be relocated from a noumenal realm of normative subjectivity into the potentialities of the existing social world, where this 'must' has the double sense of a potentiality and a decision, an acquiring or having of a social place by assuming that place.

Most importantly, truth itself can no longer be theorised as a relation between a representation and a world since neither pole of the representation – world dualism can maintain its isolation from the other under the weight of praxial interrogation. Truth cannot be a correspondence between thought and reality because the world thought is to mirror is changing and being changed through, in part, the efficacy of thought. 'Thus thought and existence are not identical in the sense that they "correspond" to each other, or "reflect" each other, that they "run parallel" to each other or "coincide" with each other (all expressions that conceal a rigid duality). Their identity is that they are aspects of one and the same real historical and dialectical process' (204). Earlier Lukács had said: 'But reality is not, it becomes – and to become the participation of thought is needed' (ibid.). History becomes philosophical when the meaning of history, the truth of history, is displaced into historical becoming, and hence into revolutionary praxis itself. Historical relativism, whereby all truth is made relative to the perspective of individual classes, and its theoretical counterpart 'absolutism', where truth transcends every and all class and historical standpoints, are both products of a contemplative conception of the relation between mind and world which regards change and becoming as necessarily antithetical to the very idea of truth.

Truth acquires a wholly novel aspect when becoming is recognised as constitutive of human being, when theory is divorced from its presumptive attachment to eternal (and forever external) objects, thereby overturning optical images of truth and allowing action itself to acquire an interrogative and an assertive character (189).[28]

It is history as the genesis of truth which praxis institutes and interrogates; and it is history which is the dual process of asserting and interrogating.

There is only one knowledge, which is the knowledge of our world in a state of becoming, and this becoming embraces knowledge itself. But it is knowledge that teaches us this. Thus, there is that moment in which knowledge looks back on its origins, recaptures its own genesis, equals as knowledge what it was as event, gathers itself together in order to totalise itself, and tends toward consciousness. The same whole is, in the first relationship, history; in the second, philosophy. History is philosophy realised, as philosophy is history formalised, reduced to its internal articulations, to its intelligible structure.[29]

Whatever the political sense of revolution amounts to, pro-letarian revolutionary praxis contains on Lukács's account a potential philosophical meaning, which is the giving to and acknowledgement of history as the making, asserting and questioning of what it is to be human.

5   LITERATURE AS A CULTURAL PRACTICE

History's course is a becoming of meanings transformed into forces or institutions.

(M.Merleau-Ponty)

The goal of *History and Class Consciousness* was to develop a cultural interpretation of Marxism for only in-so-far as Marx's analysis of capital could become an interpretation of capitalism – the forms or modes of life of persons in and under capital – could Marxist theory develop into a Marxist culture, a revolutionary culture capable of overthrowing capital.[30] If Marxist theory were to remain a representation of capital, then revolution could amount to no more than either an automatic collapse of capital and the equally automatic coming into being of socialism attended by the appropriate forms of consciousness (which would make consciousness under socialism as determined as it is under capital[31]) or, at best, a brief, and conceptually impossible,[32] moment when superstructural activity was allowed to determine the economic base. Representational or contemplative Marxist theory makes it impossible for us to live what is supposed to be the truth of our social life.

Cultural Marxism regards history as a cultural process 'in which practical activity generates not just events, but these events in a definite structural and functional order through which they take on meaning and coherence.'[33] Practical activity, which always occurs in accordance with given structural forms (153), is equally the production and reproduction of those forms. While Lukács gives ontological priority to process and agency over system and structure, since systems are products of agency, he denies that agents can stand outside systems and structures for, culturally understood, practical agency is always a form of social practice.[34] Because practices are social, because they produce, reproduce and participate in social systems and structures, they are capable of possessing goals or meanings which are not the goals or meanings of the agents who perform them. Practices may have meanings which outrun their intended meaning because as social the field of intentionality and meaning itself must be taken as wider than the field of consciousness. Only on this assumption, that there are ends or meanings latent in social practices which are not intentional properties under the direct control of the agents of those practices, does it make sense to speak of finding a meaning in history, of structures being made, re-made or decomposed through practical agency, and of historical tendencies which are not mere mechanical tendencies but rational (or irrational) tendencies, tendencies which are meanings: assertions, questions or denials. It is because practices can have a meaning at all only as elements of a wider set of practices that we can speak of the meaning or sense of a practice as outside the conscious awareness of those participating in the practice; but once this recognition is made, then the possibility is always there that practices will precipitate meanings which belie or contradict the presumed purposes of those practices.

A conception of literature determined by the theoretical principles espoused in *History and Class Consciousness* would be a theory of literature as a certain kind of social practice, a type of rule-governed activity. A conception of literature as a type of practice stands opposed to accounts of literature which define it in terms of some one or set of essential properties which are thought to be constitutive of the literariness of all literary artefacts, and which are thus required to be necessarily present in every recognised member of the class of literary objects. Such theories collapse when it is shown that not everything we would recognise as literature was always taken as such, that is, when it is demonstrated that what counts as literature is not univocal either through history or across cultures. That this is so should not be surprising since there is no reason to believe that literature is a natural kind (in the way that gold or uranium are natural kinds) as essentialist accounts presuppose. Thus even if it could be demonstrated that language as such possesses a unique 'poetic function' it would still not follow that literature could be defined in naturalistic terms.

Consider, for example, Roman Jakobson's account of poetics as a species of linguistics.[35] His theory specifies six factors which are present in every speech event, and then correlates each of these factors with a specific function. Beginning with the four most evident factors, we can say that every speech event involves someone ('the addresser') saying something ('the message') to someone ('the addressee') about something ('the context'). Each factor allows for the accomplishment of a particular task; but in any given speech event only one of these functions will be dominant. Corresponding to the context is the referential or cognitive function of language where what is being talked about is central. With the addresser is correlated the emotive or expressive function of language; here it is the attitude or feeling of the speaker which is most prominent. When the emphasis falls on getting the addressee to think, feel or do something in particular it is the conative function of language which is dominant. Finally, corresponding to a set towards the message for its own sake is the poetic function of language.

Now if Jakobson is correct in claiming that every speech event involves all the functions of speech, and speech events differ with respect to which of the functions is dominant, then his theory resolves some of the difficulties in earlier theories. The mimetic and expressive aspects of literary discourse are present in the referential and emotive functions which are elements of all speech events. In literary discourse however these functions are subordinated to and controlled by the poetic function. Further, the emphasis on the message for its own sake does *explain* fictionality since the overall effect of the dominance of the poetic function is to deepen 'the fundamental dichotomy of signs and objects';[36] that is, it focuses our attention on the saying itself apart from what is said or expressed. To say the same thing in another fashion: the poetic function involves the partial suspending or bracketing of the other functions of languages so the message itself can become an object of contemplation.

A simple question arises here: what linguistic features promote the set towards the message and the attendant bracketing or subordinating of the other linguistic functions? In a famous dictum Jakobson states: 'The poetic function projects the principle of equivalence from the axis of selection into the axis of combination.'[37] Consider the sentence 'The cat sat on the mat.' Moving horizontally, each unit of the sentence is *combined* with the one next to it in accordance with phonetic and syntactic rules. Each unit, however, was *selected*, along an imaginary vertical axis, from a range of possibilities. Instead of the 'c' in 'cat' an 'r' could have been selected; both combine with '-at' to form a noun designating a natural kind of four-legged animal, and to that degree they are equivalent. Further, in place of the whole word 'cat' we could have selected 'tabby', 'pussy' or even 'lion'. Normally equivalence is vertical, running along the axis of selection. Poetic language, however, generates equivalence along the axis of combination. Things that are usually simply *next* to one another are rendered through various devices *similar* to one another.

There can be little doubt that the different devices of metre, rhyme and rhythm do make a text appear to fold back upon itself so as to bracket the non-poetic functions of language. But can *all* the specifically literary meanings of a text be garnered through the application of linguistic tools? Are there not literary conventions or codes, genre assumptions for example, which are not reducible to purely linguistic devices? Conversely, could we not, with a little ingenuity, discover the same kinds of patterning in non-literary texts which Jakobson claims to be dominant in literary texts? One complex error appears to vitiate Jakobson's proposal: *he conflates the purely linguistic contribution to poetic meaning with poetic meaning itself*.[39] His theory is *reductionist* in that he makes the literary (poetic) an element of the linguistic and thereby denies that there exists anything which is specifically literary and non-linguistic in character. Analogously, one might say that although all sciences subordinate other linguistic functions to the referential no purely linguistic analysis of the referential function would allow us to comprehend the specific character of these sciences. Literature has forms which belong to it alone, and these forms change through time; they are historically and socially heterogeneous in character.

Literature is one (complex set of) social practice(s) among others. The specificity of literature relates to the specifically literary ways of 'going on', of writing, reading and talking about (writing about, criticising) certain texts. The institution of literature will involve a structuring or system of these practices: there will be practices of producing, exchanging (distributing) and consuming literature in a definite structural and functional order. Recently, there has been a general recognition of the need for an institutional or procedural account of literature.[39] Yet the accounts given by the new institutionalists do not fare much better than their predecessors. The reasons for their failure are instructive. Consider two such accounts:

(i) Literary texts are defined at those that are used by the society in such a way that the text is not taken as specifically relevant to the immediate context of its origin.[40]

(ii) Our construction of texts as performances depends on three deep-level constituents, or what Wittgenstein might call literary ways of going on, which govern the process of naturalisation – expectations of contemplative pleasures from attending to both mimetic and stylistic features of a work, a readiness to become affectively engaged in concrete situations without the usual commitments and consequences that accompany emotions in ordinary experience, and an assumption that the text will establish in internal terms (although not exclusively so) relationships that focus one's reflections on the quality and significance of the specific actions presented. None of these procedures is unique to literary discourse. What is distinctive is how recurrently all three are present when we take a discourse to be a literary one.[41]

The most striking feature of both accounts is that they define literature in terms of our practices of *consuming* literature, of what we are about in treating certain *given* texts as literature. Ironically, the practices of consuming literature, and by extension the practices governing the packaging of literature for the consumer (e.g. education and criticism) are given priority over the practices of literary production. Such accounts, then, are contemplative in the first instance because they take literary texts as given, and fail to question the nature of literary production. But these accounts are contemplative at a deeper level; they assume, like Jakobson, that since the goal of literature is not to refer, communicate or express, then the nature of literary consumption will be a special kind of contemplation, a special way of regarding the message for its own sake, a way, that is, of detaching the texts from its immediate context of origin and of attending to its 'internal' way of ordering. As with the classical Kantian conception of art, literature is regarded as internally purposeful (ordered and meaningful) while lacking any external, practical (epistemic or ethical) purpose. The very nature of literature, then, participates in the Kantian closure and fragmentation of experience: the external world, the world of reference, is constituted as a valueless (qualitatively empty) domain governed by the law of cause and effect; value is inner and private. To value experience, the external world, is to fictionalise, to figure the world in the image of desire and wish.

According to Lukács modern literature, those practices of literary production which take as their point of departure the autonomy of literature from other domains, is precisely the attempt to 'write' the objective world in the image of a presumed human freedom, a presumed sense of the value of a finitely constituted life. Thus, the *principle* of art in modernity achieves in its abstraction from experience what everyday practices cannot: the cancellation of the indifference of content *vis à vis* form (137–9). By attending to the consumption of literature, procedural theories capture the (truly) contemplative character of literature without comprehending either the reason why literature has become contemplative – what contemplation *means* for us – or the nature of the productive capacities of modern literature. In claiming that the principle of modern art and literature is the cancellation of the indifference of content *vis à vis* form, the principle that a concrete totality may spring from 'a conception of form oriented towards the concrete content of its material substratum' (137), the principle that art 'transforms the transcendental point of view into the common one' (138, following Fichte), we mean nothing more elaborate than the common recognition that modern literature, in tune with the denaturalising, socialising functions of capital production, does not function in subservience to traditional (natural) models, myths, plots and values. In terms of the novel this freedom is equivalent to the autogenetic, self-creating or making capacities of the novelistic hero (Robinson Crusoe, say) and the world-making, world-constituting powers of the novel author (para-digmatically: Joyce). The modern novel then takes up the principle of freedom inscribed by the bourgeois revolution, the view 'that all social problems, cease to transcend man and appear as products of human activity' (135), and provides it with a fictional (unreal) realisation. The source of the fictionality of the novel is its assumption that it is individuals, heroes or authors, that are world-makers (135). For Marx 'individualism' is the appearance form of social productivity, of the denaturalisation of society, of the sociality of the first truly social formation. None the less, the significance of modern literature is its figuring of transcendental constitution (become intellectual intuition) in everyday experience. Because isolated individuals cannot as such be world-makers, novelistic praxis is a pseudo-praxis; the condition for the novel being praxial, worldly and world-making, is its fictionality (or, looking at the novel from the bourgeois point of view: praxis is necessarily a fiction). The nature of novelistic fictionality, then, is inscribed by its pseudo-praxial nature.

For Lukács the nature of fictionality, like the nature of literature itself is not generalisable, that is, it is not a trans-historical natural kind. Fictionality cannot be reduced to, say, the systematic use of expressions and terms lacking reference or the use of speech acts without their usual practical and existential commitments (literature represents not things but our linguistic representations of things). What makes a Greek tragedy, a medieval mystery play or a modern lyric poem all fictions, all literature, is not the same for each (although that *we* count each of them as works of fiction or imagination is governed by a uniform set of practices).

Lukács's theory of the novel will examine the practices of novel production. That those purely literary practices have the characteristics they do, that we go on writing in 'this' way and not otherwise, is dictated on the one hand by the traditions (history) of narrative prose fiction – those earlier practices permit of us going on in this way – and, on the other, by the connection of those practices with other contemporaneous, non-literary, social practices. Anachronistically, in accordance with the argument of the 'Reification' essay, *The Theory of the Novel* will take up the problem of novel production as instantiating the modern principle of art (literary production as pseudo-praxis, as a fictional intellectual intuition), and consider the consequences and antinomies that arise from the instantiation of that principle. Of course, to claim that such a principle is instantiated is not to claim that it is consciously adopted; rather, the principle appears to underlie, be presupposed by or be implicit in, the practices of novel writing. As we have said, those practices are literary practices because they are recognisable extensions of previous literary practices; but that those practices and the principle underlying them are as they are cannot be explained merely through reference to previous practices. Equally we must refer to the context and conditions which precipitated a *need* for an alteration of given practices. How to go on writing is in part determined by the existing repertoire of writing practices, and in part determined by the need (and social necessity) of making those practices commensurable with other social practices. Determination here is not a matter of causal efficacy (necessary or sufficient), but a matter of invitation and constraint, of rules being open to new possibilities (the invitation) but rules none the less (with all the exclusiveness and constraint that implies). Commensurability is neither simply causal or logical in character, although the need to make certain practices commensurable now may be causally occasioned and have logical limits. Rather, commensurability is conceptual, it involves making sense of one set of practices in connection with other social practices; but such making sense is not only a conceptual activity, for what is made sense of is one's life and the lives of others.[42] What is important is that we be able to live the manifold of our practices; their presumed unity and difference answering to our need to make sense of our life, ourselves, to see a point in our different activities in relation to one another. Much, if not all, of what goes under the name of ideology is really but a form and effort of commensuration under the spell of categorial appearance forms. The study of ideology is but a study of one species of commensuration.

Lukács is not offering in *The Theory of the Novel* either a philosophy of the novel, if we mean by that the project of understanding experience in its unchanging forms, or a sociology of the novel. If the novel is a historically specific mode of human activity, then it is an impossible object for philosophical analysis as traditionally conceived. A necessary condition for there being a philosophy of the novel is that philosophy become historical. Not all understanding of the historical present, however, is sociological, an explaining of what is in terms of its causal conditions, functional placement or constituting rules. If traditional philosophical analysis tends to elide the historical specificity of its objects, traditional sociological analysis tends to err in the opposite direction, seeing only the historical specificity of its objects. If practices can have meanings and goals which transcend agents' awareness and ends, then some practices can be appropriated, their meaning grasped only by seeing them as unknowingly pointing beyond themselves; those practices must be regarded not as trans-historical limits on consciousness, but as a historical stage in the development of consciousness.[43] Because the historical meaning of such practices is unknown (in the first instance) to its agents, because it is an 'unconscious' element of the practices, the consciousness of the practice will be fraught, its 'unconscious' significance manifesting itself in terms of unresolvable tensions and ambiguities.

Lukács's theory of the novel is the appropriation of the historical meaning of the novelistic practices of writing. It is a Marxist interpretation of the novel because it locates the antinomies of novel writing within a grammar of contemplation; the meaning of those antinomies, as Lukács's account of the antinomies of bourgeois thought makes plain, is their gesture towards praxis. In the revelation of the novel's *pseudo*-praxis the nature of human praxis proper is adumbrated. Because Lukács failed in 1915 to recognise the theoretical framework underlying his analysis, and as a consequence drew false or unsubstantiated conclusions from that analysis, does not make the analysis false or non-Marxist (although the conclusions drawn are both unsubstantiated and non-Marxist). The meaning or truth of a practice or text does not always lie in its conscious intention. Such is a governing principle of hermeneutics; a principle consciously upheld by the Lukács of *History and Class Consciousness*. As a consequence, the Marxist Lukács could allow his younger self to accompany him into the world of praxis, knowing the truth of what he had earlier said but not then understood.

II

Lukács's Aesthetic:
The Epic and the Novel

It has become a common strategy in analysing the novel to place it against the background of earlier narrative forms, above all the Homeric epic. Auerbach's *Mimesis*[1] and Scholes and Kellogg's *The Nature of Narrative*[2] represent two perspicuous examples of this strategy. Auerbach's study of the 'representation of reality in western literature' (the sub-title of *Mimesis*) attempts to elucidate the nature of modern mimetic literature by showing how it developed from earlier descriptive practices which were prevented from employing the concrete representational practices of the novel by a variety of socio-historical assumptions and beliefs. Thus, for example, while the Christian view of man, each one unique and valuable in God's eye, provided the ideological materials necessary to defeat the rigid separation of high style (suitable for tragic subject-matter and lofty personages) and low style (suitable for comic subject-matter and ordinary personages), the Christian view of the relation between God and world displaced the centre of gravity from the world to God, and thereby required a form of 'realism' quite distinct from what preceded or followed: figural realism.[3] The power and suggestiveness of Auerbach's analyses are beyond question. None the less, his work has been less influential than its reputation would lead one to except. Rather simply, it has proved impossible to locate the theoretical, structural core of Auerbach's history, and it has therefore proved difficult to build on what he began.

By contrast, Scholes and Kellogg open their essay with the presentation of a structural *combinatoire* of narrative forms. Narrative breaks down into the empirical and the fictional. Empirical narrative forms may concern themselves with either questions of fact (history) or questions of experience (mimesis).

Fictional narrative forms may be directed towards beauty (romance), or goodness or truth (allegory). Diagrammatically, their theory may be presented like this:

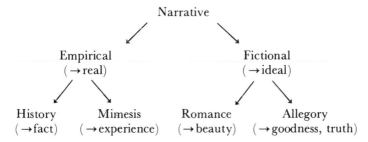

In itself this breakdown of the forms of narrative appears to possess at least a prima facie plausibility.[4] Difficulties arise when they attempt to process these structural possibilities through a historical, developmental sequence. Oral epics are a development of the mythic impulse.

> The epic story-teller is telling a traditional story. The primary impulse which moves him is not a historical one, nor a creative one; it is *re*-creative. He is retelling a traditional story, and therefore his primary allegiance is not to fact, not to truth, not to entertainment, but to the *mythos* itself – the story as preserved in the tradition which the epic story-teller is re-creating.[5]

Epics, like the Homeric epics, are part of this oral tradition. If this is correct, and we are to identify the 'Narrative' of our diagram with the epic tradition, then it follows that modern narrative forms will be crystallisations of possibilities latent in the narratively homogeneous unity of the epic. In other words, epic narratives are undifferentiated narratives where the *differences* which constitute the heterogeneity (truth or beauty or goodness) of modern narrative practices are significantly absent.

As soon as this theoretical paradigm is proffered, we are forced to notice how susceptible it is to the familiar paradox of continuity versus discontinuity. Either the later heterogeneous developments of narrative are latent but present in the epic, in which case history itself becomes irrelevant; that is, like bad Hegelian history, history can only implement (and so repeat) what is anterior to it (so contingency and novelty disappear). Or history is productive; but then the epic becomes superfluous since it possesses none of the *differentia* of later narrative forms; we have no way of connecting epic narrative with later narrative forms. Part of what is wrong with Scholes and Kellogg's story, and thus part of the reason for the existence of the paradox, is that history is here viewed endogenously: change and permutation are conceived as *internal* potentialities; thus what is later is either embryonically present in the past or not there at all. In order to generate the requisite complexity that would allow us the possibility of avoiding this late flowering of the organicist view of history, and permit us the employment of an exogenuous conception of historical change, we require more elements in our story.

Scholes and Kellogg's account of narrative is admittedly formalist (proto-structuralist) in nature. Thus it is not surprising that the place or function of history in their account tends to be anomalous. The purely literary materials they deploy are too thin to capture the historical specificity of either the epic or novel forms; assuming, that is, that these forms have some historical specificity, and are not simply members of a Platonic (Fryean) universe of literary forms. Anachronistically, Part 1 of Lukács's *The Theory of the Novel*, 'The forms of great epic literature examined in relation to whether the civilisation of the time is an integrated or problematic one', attempts to provide a solution to the paradox concealed in the formalist approach to literature and literary history. Lukács claims not only that there are different literary forms, but that they change in response to changing socio-historical circumstances. According to him the novel is the epic of modernity (post-feudal society); the novel is to modern society what the epic was to the integrated world of the Greeks. The difference between epic and novel is analogous and internally related to the differences between the societies of which they are a part. The central difference between ancient and modern society is that the former is integrated while the latter is problematic. Lukács's distinction between integrated and problematic societies naturally evokes the central terms of modern social analysis: community versus society; *Gemeinschaft* versus *Gesellschaft*; organic versus mechanical; unalienated versus alienated; and so forth. What might strike us as odd, having this evocation of modern sociological analysis before us, is that these terms of art are, on the whole, restricted in their application to distinguishing capitalism from all that went before it. This suggests, in its turn, that perhaps Lukács's use of the term 'epic' is intended not as a referring expression for some well-known Greek narratives, but rather as the marker for an historical experience, an historical tradition from which the novel is to be excluded. From here it would be but a short step to identifying the conceptual structure of *TN* with that of *HCC*, and further, to see in *TN* a hermeneutics of the novel rather than a theory of the novel embedded in a putative universal philosophy of history.

As a working hypothesis, I want to suggest that the *function* of Lukács's historiographical schema is not to forward a universal philosophy of history of any sort, but rather to aid in the establishing of the historical specificity, the historical uniqueness of the novel and its world, the world of capitalism. To be sure, Lukács is not always clear that it is specifically about capitalism he is writing, although his arguments in fact depend on Marx's and Simmel's accounts of the specificity of the capitalist era for their validity. Whenever Lukács strays from that position, as he occasionally does in his opening chapter, his arguments becomes obscure and inadequate. As I shall argue in section 4 below, Lukács's treatment of the concept of 'totality' suffers from precisely this defect.

Further, I want to argue that, in a fashion compatible with his hermeneutic interpretation of Marxist theory, Lukács's concept of the epic is a hermeneutical *construct*, an act of historical awareness from the perspective of the present by which that present can begin to come to self-consciousness of its historical situation. I say 'begin' because, as is insufficiently appreciated, Lukács's initial hermeneutical construction of the epic as the ancestor of the novel is not itself his theory of the novel, but the means by which the conceptual vocabulary of that theory is provided with an historical dimension. The theory itself is an account of the actual practices of novel writings. Thus what is presented here is a parenthesis, albeit an essential parenthesis, but nevertheless a pause in the argument which allows us to clarify the nature of the claims being made about the epic.

Now if what is at issue in the discussion of the epic is the construction of an ancestor for the novel, then two points follow.

First, both the necessity and the validity of that construction are to be evaluated in hermeneutical terms, that is, in terms that clarify, again, the historical significance of current self-interpretations. The point at issue, then, is not an empirical one of point-by-point noting what might be taken as formal features peculiar to the novel and asking after their historical ancestry;[6] rather, what is at issue is 'our' awareness, in the novel and elsewhere, of being poised in a historical space of distance and dissonance, and how we are going to understand that space. It is no accident, then, and this is the second point, that accounts of the historical specificity of the novel have so often begun and focused on *Don Quixote*, which performs, in an exemplary manner, an act of historical distancing and locating through the construction of 'a past of romance'; and that Lukács, in Part II of *TN*, where he provides a historical typology of the novel, locates the 'origin' of the novel in that quixotic performance. Because I think Cervantes' gesture is historically quixotic, I shall argue for a different founding moment for the novel in Chapter V. None the less, as the example of *Don Quixote* illustrates, and as our hermeneutic procedure requires, in locating the historical specificity of the novel the only relevant history is the one the novel itself gives, or chooses not to give. It is the novel's giving or withholding of the past which is the focus, the beginning and the end, of Lukács's theory of the novel. Yet, if this is so, then the meaning or sense of 'epic' in Lukács, and its conceptual corollary 'totality', cannot be revealed in full until the meaning of the novel itself is revealed.

Lukács is not offering us in *TN* a universal philosophy of history, be it a priori or empirical. Nor is the Homeric world an analogue of Rousseau's state of nature, a hypothetical zero-point from which the moral development or degeneration of the species can be chartered. The epic does not represent either the real or fictive 'origin' of the novel, and thus a narrative paradise to be regained. The terms 'epic' and 'novel' do not signify for Lukács two unproblematical empirical items which may be illuminated through a contrastive analysis; rather, those terms mark the poles of an act of historical reflection by which the novel can be brought into consciousness in its historical specificity and antinomic complexity.

It would be an understatement to say that this is not the usual understanding of Lukács's procedure or argument. In support of this view this chapter will take the following path: In section 1 I attempt to clarify Lukács's characterisation of the Homeric epic, and refute the claim, however briefly, that his reading of the epic is critically illegitimate. In the following section Lukács's juxtaposition of the 'subjectless' epic and modern subjectivity is examined: his praise of the former does not entail the possibility or the desirability of recovering such a subjectless state. Section 3 refutes the thesis that Lukács is constructing a universal philosophy of history in the traditional sense. Lukács's own confusions about totality are critically examined in section 4. The central contention of Chapter I of *TN*, a point almost universally ignored by Lukács's critics, is that the modern *autonomy* of art and literature is a product of reification or fragmentation, and that it is that autonomy which makes the novel problematic. In the final section I say a little about the meaning of this claim, and show how it follows from Lukács's hermeneutical procedure.

One of the crucial issues that runs through the chapter is his puzzling thesis, also generally ignored, that the epic cannot be interpreted. I defend this claim here by showing how it follows from the fact of the Homeric epic coming from an *oral* culture – a feature of the epic world not mentioned by Lukács. By stressing orality as a condition of epic literature its specificity begins to come into view; but it is this very specificity that prohibits the Homeric epics from being a model to be imitated, and requires us to regard them as boundaries to a tradition of writing, a tradition from which, for reasons having nothing to do with the distinction between oral and writing cultures, the novel, in the very act of appropriating that tradition to itself, is excluded.

1 A World Without Subjects

The theoretical pair which function throughout *TN* as the bearers of conceptual coherence are 'form' and 'life'. Form is what in-forms, gives order and structure to any material substratum. Platonic Ideas, Aristotelian essences and Kantian categories appear to be examples of form.[7] In face, Aristotelian essences and Kantian categories lack one of the necessary features of form for Lukács, namely, that it yield 'significance' and 'meaningfulness'. Thus in the first chapter of *Soul and Form* Lukács states: 'Science affects us by its forms; science offers us facts and the relationship between facts, but art offers us souls and destinies.'[8] Forms then order and evaluate; they are principles of intelligibility in the dual sense of the cognisable and the meaningful; where it is assumed that not everything which is comprehensible is thereby meaningful. Life is what is in-formed by form; it is experience in its immediacy and vitality, with all its attendant corporeality and complexity. For Lukács life is not a bare substratum for the play of forms; it includes pains and pleasures, fears and desires, even social practices. But these of themselves do not make a life meaningful; they are rather a potential for meaningfulness. Finally, it goes without saying, this dualism is primarily conceptual and not ontological, for it is just the understanding of the locus of form, its ground and origin, which fluctuates throughout the course of history. If the ontological status of life and form could be known a priori then history would be more like the elimination of errors than a course of production or discovery. Plato's Form/Life distinction is paradigmatic – it gives us a sense of what is at stake – but not exhaustive; it is just one historical realisation of the possible relations which may hold between these items.

Crudely, the epic world is one in which *no* distinction, analytic or otherwise, can be drawn between these two components of experience. It is this thought – echoing Schiller's category of the naive – which structures his account of the epic as a product of an integrated civilisation. The first and dominant feature of the epic which marks it out as product of a social structure where the dualism of life versus form is absent is its objectivity, its appearance of not being authored from any one individual perspective as opposed to any other individual perspective. Hegel's statement of this thesis was doubtless the origin of his contention.

On account of the objectivity of the whole epic, the poet as subject must retire in the face of his *object* and lose himself in it. Only the product, not the poet, appears.... Because the epic presents not the poet's own inner world but the objective events, the subjective side of the production must be put into the background precisely as the poet completely immerses himself in the world which he unfolds before our eyes. This is why the great epic style consists in the work's seeming to be its own minstrel and appearing independently without having any author to conduct it or be as its head.[9]

In a theoretical sense, the Homeric texts are anonymous; in reading them there is no question as to whether the narrator is reliable or unreliable for that distinction has no point in the epic context. Hence it is appropriate to say of them that they have no intention for us to recover (other than, of course, to repeat the traditional story); they are devoid of a beginning or origin (they make sense only in a world where repetition is of the essence). And this is so whether intention is construed narrowly as an antecedent conception in the mind of the author upon which the work somehow depends, or more broadly as the interplay between blindness and insight, as the link between 'idiosyncratic view and the communal concern'.[10] For the Greek world of the Homeric age the connection between authorship and authority had not yet been made because it was not necessary; it was not necessary because there was no place or need for the idiosyncratic view to stand outside the communal concern.

Analogous to his conception of the epic as subjectless with respect to its author is Lukács's contention that the epic is subjectless at the level of the hero. 'The epic hero', he says, 'is, strictly speaking, never an individual. It is traditionally thought that one of the essential characteristics of the epic is the fact that its theme is not a personal destiny but the destiny of the community' (66). In the same way in which in integrated societies there is no space for the idiosyncratic, individual perspective to stand outside of the communal concern in the production of literary works, so thematically no individual life can be regarded as more important than, or as uniquely different from, the fate of the community as a whole. Achilles is not a representative Greek warrior; rather the fate of the Greek army as a whole ebbs and flows with Achilles' fortunes. The claim, then, is not that in the Greek world there were no individuals; it is rather that epic individuals are constructions of their societies (integral components of them) and not simply individuals *in* a society which constrains them in their possible actions. They cannot conceive of their lives independently from

that of the community, and thus their fate cannot be disconnected from the communal fate.

Together these two claims can be summarised by the thesis
that the Homeric age (and subsequent ages down to the time of
Socrates) lacked a conception of subjectivity, where subjectivity
can be interpreted as a condition in which there is a 'space' or
gap between what is given in experience and that given's truth
or beauty or goodness. Subjectivity entails the existence of a gap
between self and other, self and world, and the self and its deeds.
In each case this space manifests itself as the need to establish an
order or relation with respect to the given. Interpretation,
explanation and the establishing of contractual relations are
examples of the ways in which we attempt to bridge this gap.
Lukács begins his account of the epic age with a clear denial that
any such gap existed in that time. 'Each action of the soul', he
says, 'becomes meaningful and perfect in this duality; complete
in meaning – in sense – and complete for the senses; complete
because actions detach themselves from the soul and become
autonomous, they find a meaningfulness of their own and draw
a circle around themselves' (29). Deeds do not have both a
public and a private life, an intention, motivation, reason or
inner worth and effects or consequences, but only a public
meaning (for both agent and spectator) in the Greek world.

This is Lukács starting-point: the Greeks of the epic age
lacked a conception of subjectivity, and as a consequence
produced narratives which were doubly subjectless – they
possessed neither authors not heroes in our sense of these terms.
Because there did not exist the possibility of providing alternative interpretations of the same phenomena neither history
(the production of different explanations of the same phenomena) nor fiction (the creating, authoring, of counterfactual
worlds which serve as alternative interprerations of a shared
domain of experience) existed as independent narrative impulses. Before attempting to assess the theoretical significance of
this thesis it is worth while eliminating an obvious objection to
what has been said thus far. Lukács is often accused of
mythologising, like his (German) eighteenth- and nineteenth-
century forerunners, the world of the ancient Greeks. Fredric
Jameson, echoing a commonplace objection, states that
Lukács's analyses of the novel depend on a kind of

literary nostalgia, on the notion of a golden age or lost Utopia of narration in the Greek epic ... [while] such a conception of literary history may simply be taken as an organizational fiction, as a mythological framework, for the concrete analyses of the book; in the long run, the historical inadmissibility of the framework returns to vitiate the individual analyses.[11]

Interestingly, the leading historicist literary critic of Lukács's generation provides a remarkably similar analysis of the epic age. Auerbach, in the well-known opening chapter of *Mimesis*, 'Odysseus's Scar', begins with an affirmation of Schiller's contention, which can be heard echoing throughout the pages of *The Theory of the Novel*, that what Homer depicts is '"simply the quiet existence and operations of things in accordance with their natures"': Homer's goal is "already present in every point of his progress".'[12] And in the same way in which it is important to Lukács's thesis concerning the subjectlessness of the epic that its heroes suffer no transformations or development as persons, so we find Auerbach stating that Greeks heroes 'have no development. and their life-histories are clearly set forth once and for all.... Homeric heroes ... wake each morning as if it were the first day of their lives: their emotions, though strong, are simple and find expression instantly.' Again, Lukács's statement that meaning is wholly present to the senses in Homer is repeated in Auerbach's claim that the basic impulse of the Homeric style is 'to represent the phenomena in a fully externalized form, visible and palpable in all their parts, and completely fixed in their spatial and temporal relations.' The central thesis of Lukács's analysis is the claim that the Greeks did not possess a conception of human subjectivity, an understanding which would require of any self that it interpret the phenomena presented to it. Now Auerbach's contrast between the Old Testament and Greek representations of reality is precisely that between a 'subjectivistic –perspectivistic procedure, creating a foreground and background, resulting in the present lying open to the depths of the past', and a style which 'knows only a foreground, only a uniformly illuminated, uniformly objective present.' According to Auerbach's analysis each Biblical personage possesses a background, each changes and progresses through the course of his life, and each is a multilayered personality. None of these things can be predicated of Homeric characters; and it is that which is revealed by the uniform objective presentation of the Homeric style.

This peculiarity of the Homeric style generates a final important contention which Lukács and Auerbach share. The lack of perspective and depth in the Homeric texts (especially the *Iliad*) or, what is the same, their indifference towards the 'truth' (in any sense we would recognise), entails the remarkable corollary that those texts are not themselves susceptible to interpretation. They may be philologically analysed, or a transcendental topography of the Greek mind may be given in accordance with them (32); but they offer us no foothold for interpretation just because they represent (are the product of) a self-enclosed universe where nothing is concealed. They possess no teaching ('truth') nor any secret second meaning, although later generations attempted to make them productive of truth by reading them allegorically. This is part of what Lukács means when he says that the metaphysical compass of the life of the Greeks was narrower than our own, and that we could not, as part of our life, place ourselves inside it (32). We cannot, even as a *part* of our life, give objective *self-evidence* to the primeval images of Greek life because their self-evidence is a function of (is made possible by) the closed nature of the Greek world. We can enter into an hermeneutical dialogue with a text only when, roughly, the elements of form and life, motif and theme, can be separated; for only then is there discourse in our sense, that is, a saying or speaking *about* some subject-matter. The Trojan War is not the subject-matter for a history or poem (although we sometimes treat the *Iliad* as a poem because it is not history; but then we sometimes treat it as a historical document as well), or for a philosophical examination of war and its evils. In fine, the Homeric texts are ontologically anomalous; they are not of the same status as later texts, and they do not relate to their social milieu in any of the obvious ways that other texts do. As we shall see later, there is a comprehensible reason for all this.

Of course, it does not follow from Auerbach and Lukács agreeing that either of them is correct. Nor would the position be radically altered by mentioning works on Homer (Redfield's *Nature and Culture in the Iliad*; Frankel's *Early Greek Poetry and Philosophy*) and Greek tragedy (Jones' *On Aristotle and Greek Tragedy*; Vernant's 'Greek Tragedy') which are more recent but whose line of argument parallels the one suggested here. None the less, recent research, with fifty-odd years of anthropology behind it, has tended to reinstate the view that the Greeks did not possess a conception of subjectivity in its modern sense. If Lukács is mythologising the past, it is not because he has mischaracterised it. This does not rule out the possibility that he rightly characterises the epic world while misconstruing its significance; but this turns out not to be the case.

2   SUBJECTIVITY AS ALIENATION

From the time of the collapse of the Homeric world the relation between form and life has been fraught. In the period of early and middle Greek tragedy this division first impresses itself upon men as the religious thought of the earlier epoch and the juridical and political thought which is that of the city (replacing the family as the central social unit) find themselves in uneasy conflict.[13] With Plato the divorce of form and life is complete (35); forms 'became the sole and absolute, the transcendent reality' (ibid.). From this time through the whole Christian era the problem will be one of mediating form (God, the Ideas) with life. Only with modernity is a new element added: history. This is Lukács's first full statement of the problematic character of modernity.

(i) We have invented the productivity of the spirit: that is why the primaeval images have irrevocably lost their objective self-evidence for us, and our thinking follows the endless path of an approximation that is never fully accomplished. We have discovered the creation of forms: and that is why everything that falls from our weary and despairing hands must always be incomplete.

(ii) We have found the only true substance in ourselves: that is why we have to place an unbridgeable chasm between cognition and action, between the soul and its structures, between self and world, why all substantiality has to be dispersed in reflexivity on the far side of that chasm; that is why our essence had to become a postulate for oursleves and thus create a still deeper, still more menacing abyss between us and our own selves. (33–4)

The logic of this passage is, with a twist, undeniably Kantian. Lukács takes it as given that the Kantian critical system provides the most lucid metaphysical portrayal of modernity. Lukács's twist is his denial of the a priori status of the categories, and the replacement of them by produced frameworks. Since this has been a constant strategy with respect to Kant in this century this claim should cause us no difficulty. From that premise, that the self makes the world, the rest of the passage follows without difficulty. Statement (i) claims that if we produce the forms of cognition, then knowledge can never be complete. For cognition to be complete essentialism would have to be true; for essentialism to be true the structure of the world and not transcendental subjectivity would have to be the ground of all possible knowledge. Since the productivity of forms denies that the object of knowledge grounds the possibility of knowledge, knowledge is in principle incomplete. In fine, nature is not itself a language in need of interpretation or another mind which can be understood; what nature is in itself we do not know. All that can be known is how things appear under the articulations of our creative subjectivity. This is the irony of our situation, and the source of the despairing tone of Lukács' account. The only world we can know is the world as it appears under the forms of creative subjectivity; but that world is not worth knowing because it is not *the* (thing in itself) world at all. The capacity to know and understand is what distinguishes man from the rest of nature; but this very power also permanently makes nature something forever beyond his grasp.

The metaphysical caesura which ironically stresses the relation of man to nature is repeated in the Kantian analysis of the self as stated in (ii). We create forms. From this it follows that there must be a self or subject which does the creating. It is to this self Lukács is referring when he says 'we have found the only true substance within ourselves.' Paradoxically, this self is as unknowable as the world which stands outside creative understanding, and for an analytically parallel reason. What can be known is articulated through the forms of creative understanding by the knowing subject; this knowing subject, the creative self, however, cannot itself be grasped by these forms. In every act of knowing there is an object known and a knowing self; so even if the object known is the self, it cannot be the knowing/creative self since this self will in all cases be doing the knowing. Thus a chasm opens up between the self as knower/creator and the self as known, between the transcendental and empirical ego. In Kant's system, since the forms of creative understanding give us knowledge of what may be the case, creative understanding, our 'essence', itself comes to represent what ought to be the case. The dualism within the self, the alienation of man from himself, hence takes the form of a dualism between fact and value, between what is and what ought to be.

Now if the hallmark of the epic is its subjectlessness, then it might plausibly be argued that subjectivity as such is what makes modernity problematic. In his Kierkegaard essay, 'The Foundering of Form Against Life', in *Soul and Form*, Lukács appears to be stating just such a thesis. Central to his argument in that essay is the contrast between a conventionalised psychology and an explanatory psychology, a contrast which exactly parallels that between a world in which interpretation in our sense plays no part and a world in which all action requires interpretation. Lukács states his thesis in the following way:

Where psychology begins, there are no more deeds but only motives for deeds; and whatever requires explanation, whatever can bear explanation, has already ceased to be solid and clear.... When psychology rules, then there are no gestures any more that can comprise life and all its situations within them. The gesture is unambiguous only for as long as the psychology remains conventional.[14]

In *Soul and Form* only art could provide the rounded deed; life was considered to be open and ambiguous. The historicism of *The Theory of the Novel* allowed Lukács to transpose the clarity of fiction to a past: the epic world. Thus in comparing a conventionalised psychology with an explanatory psychology we can perhaps elucidate the distance separating ancient and modern.

A deed requires explanation or interpretation just in case we can conceive the motive (reason, impulse, desire, want) behind an act as being different from its social description. Charitable acts may be done for egoistic, self-aggrandising motives, and courageous deeds are committed out of a fear of ridicule. Once a dualism of this sort can enter into our understanding of actions,

then we are immediately placed in an environment where while
the individual can identify his goals with those of the community
(if communal goals – interests – exist: Rousseau and Marx
have forced us to doubt that this is generally so for us), this must
be understood as an act *of identification*, no more. Individual goals
and communal concerns are here essentially dirempt from one
another because individual deeds *always* can be explained
independently from their social description. The 'always' of this
thesis derives from the introduction of an autonomous sphere of
action determination: the individual and his particular life
history. Individuals are congeries not only of dispositions to
actions of certain sorts, but also, and primarily, of individual
projects for self-realisation. Dispositions and projects stand in
a complex, multilayered, hierarchic relation to one another.
Each non-habitual action requires a resynthesis of the existing
complex, since each action must be given an ordered place in
a life history. Thus new acts do and must modify the interpretation of past deeds. And always the possibility of explanations not derived from the conscious ordering of wants and
desires can be introduced. The self's openness, its problematic
status is thus severely overdetermined. The self is open because:

  (i) it has a past whose sense can be altered by future actions and
      choices;
 (ii) it can choose courses of action for reasons which do not coincide
      with the social description of those actions;
(iii) its reasons for action may not be the same as the causes for its
      action, and the causes for an action may lie in unseen social
      determinations or in the remote depths of the individuals's
      psyche.

To the question 'Who is acting?', there exists no obvious
answer; but for us this is a tragedy, a loss. It marks the point
where the attempt to construct a self fails, where the self loses
what it inevitably takes to be its own. Our tragedy is that we
must ask the question 'Who is acting?' without ever being able
to answer it.

   None of this is the case in a conventionalised psychology.
First, there is no dualism within actions; the explanation of a
deed and its social description are necessarily identical; courageous deeds result from courage and nothing else. Secondly,

if explanation and social description are to be necessarily identical, then the self must be understood in terms of where it is (status) and what it does (action and its effects). Character is nothing but this interplay of social status and social action. Hence, we typically understand Achilles as someone who *is* a warrior and *is* his courage and pride; and similarly Odysseus is a household head and is his versatility and foresightedness.[15] Character, as expressed in epithets, is all the unity Homeric men possess. They are not a synthesis of their past history, continually remaking who they are with each act, but simply that history itself. Redfield nicely states the position thus:

> Homeric man, being objective, has no innerness. He expresses himself completely in words and acts, and is thus completely known to his fellows. He has no hidden depths or secret motives; he says and does what he is. Such a man is not an enclosed identity; he is rather a kind of open field of forces. He is open to others – to the words of other men and to the intervention of the gods. There is no clear line for him between *ego* and *alter*.[16]

Psychology remains conventional, then, when all actions of a certain type are to be understood in terms of reasons necessarily coterminus with their typification by social description, that is, where the distinction between description, cause, motive and reason is inapplicable (there exist no phenomena to which these terms may be applied); and character can be subsumed under epithets which make no reference to or assumptions about the inner nature of the person concerned. Because in a world inscribed by a conventionalised psychology the space where ambiguity and the need for interpretation and/or explanation does not exist, action may have just the palpability and outwardness Lukács ascribes to the deeds of the Greek heroes.

The claim that it is subjectivity which makes modernity problematic has a basis in Lukács's views about self and action. None the less, such a view must be mistaken (a) because the above analysis of the self under the conditions where an explanatory psychology is in force is *not* synonymous with the Kantian problematic of the self sketched earlier; and (b) because the opposite of conventional psychology man, the epic man, is not modern man, the Cartesian self and its progeny. Let us examine (b) first. To sustain (b) we need only cite

Auerbach's analysis of Genesis 22:1.[17] The episode of Abraham's near-sacrifice of Issac is fraught with qualities of self, action, interpretation, choice and understanding that have no comparison with anything found in Homer. Auerbach's results may be summarised in the following terms:

(i)   The relationship between God and Abraham signified by Abraham's 'Behold me!' is moral or ethical; Abraham indicates in these words his obedience, inferiority and dependence (all these terms are to be taken as possessing an ethical connotation).

(ii) Abraham's journey through the desert is as much psychological and theological as it is geographical.

(iii) From (i) and (ii) it follows that Abraham must be conceived as an autonomous agent with a complex psychological life. He must order his priorities, to son and to God, and so order the different dimensions of his relations, emotional, ethical and religious. It is essential to the Abraham story that these dimensions of the self be distinguishable. The self is shaped by *how* he orders them with respect to one another.

(iv) In general, Old Testament personages are continually engaged in struggles of development in which the dissolution of the self remains an abiding possibility.

(v)   Thus our sense of the self as an individual, at least, is applicable to Abraham: 'for it is only during the course of an eventful life that men are differentiated into full individuality; and it is this history of personality which the Old Testament presents to us as the formation undergone by those whom God has chosen to be examples.'

Old Testament discourse differs from the horizontal, metonymic, present structure of Homeric discourse by possessing a vertical, metaphoric, absent dimension which creates a foreground/background perspective which *is* the space of a synthetic self.

Returning now to (a), it should be evident that this synthetic self, although familiar, is not our self, not the modern self which Lukács finds problematic. The difference between the two appears to be this. While the Old Testament self is synthetic, thus possessing the capacity for self-reflection, what the self synthesises are events in accordance with *given* forms. But we have discovered the productivity of spirit, the creation of forms, and it is for this reason that we find 'the only true substance in ourselves'. For the authors of the Old Testament as well as later

Christian writers up to Dante this thesis is false. For them God is the author and source of form, and therefore only He, properly speaking, is true substance. It is this thesis about the status of forms Lukács has in mind when he states that 'The novel is the epic of a world that has been abandoned by God' (88). In Christian writings God provides closure for the world of forms; He Himself may serve as the close of the system or, through His creative acts, as the totaliser of a world of forms which stand outside Him. For Lukács Dante is the most exemplary of Christian writers, and the last great writer to have access to a historically uncompromised totality, albeit one possessing architectural as opposed to organic form. Dante's greatness resides in his ability to create representations of fully human individuals, possessing the inwardness and subjectivity of novelistic characters, while still being able to place those individuals in a harmonious universal order (68). Dante's achievement was accomplished by making the placing of individuals in the afterworld an 'absolute realization of [their] particular earthly personality'.[18] Without God and without an after world the totality of life as a possible experience of life is lost.

It is not, then, subjectivity *per se* which makes modernity problematic for Lukács: or, to put the same point in negative terms, Lukács's valorisation of the epic world is not reducible to a simple praise of its subjectlessness. Nor is there any indication anywhere in *The Theory of the Novel* that Lukács conceives of a return to such a state of affairs as either possible or desirable. The reflexive capacities of synthetic man and the freedom of modern man are not historically reversible aspects of the human condition. We can only conceive a lack of reflexion as a denial of the need and privilege to order and evaluate; we can only conceive of a denial of creative subjectivity as a denial of the relative autonomy of culture vis-à-vis nature. Lukács's thesis concerning the productivity of spirit is, I am suggesting, a metaphysical restatement of Marx's thesis that post-feudal society is the first society based on 'purely social' as opposed to 'natural' life forms. If statements like Feher's that in comparing epic and modern 'Lukács unambiguously decides in favor of the former'[19] are to be comprehended, then it is to Lukács's philosophy of history, where different forms of social relations are compared and evaluated, that we must turn.

3 PROGRESS OR REGRESS?

It is sometimes suggested that Lukács's explicit shift to Marxism
entailed a shift in his image of Utopia (if Utopia it is to
which he is gesturing). Thus Jameson claims that the embrace of
Marxism thematised in *History and Class Consciousness* requires
that 'the ultimate realization of a reconciled universe will now
be projected into the future, and with such a shift in perspective
we are already well within the Marxist theory of history.'[20] Yet
nothing in *The Theory of the Novel* denies the productivity of spirit
hypothesis; therefore Jameson's claim that the break between
an idealist philosophy of history and a materialist philosophy of
history lies in the former finding Utopia in the past and the latter
finding Utopia in an hypothesised (wished-for) future in no way
tells against Lukács's earlier work. Of course, if Lukács had
denied the possibility of some kind of future reconciliation, then
Jameson's charge would have some point. But while the
possibility of future reconciliation is doubtless an ambiguous
matter in *The Theory of the Novel*, for reasons which will become
evident in due course, it is hardly denied, as the whole of Part II,
and especially the chapters on Goethe, Tolstoy and Dostoievsky
bear witness to.

Yet Lukács does appear to be providing a Rousseauesque
account of degeneration from a totality of meaning where
philosophy – 'homesickness' (29) as Novalis has it – with its
needs and questions does not even exist ('happy ages have no
philosophy' (29)), to the fragmented, paradoxical world of
modernity. And this degeneration coincides, is identical, with
the shifting place of form with respect to life. For the epic world
no distinction between form and life could be drawn. In the
Tragic age although the 'pure immanence of life' (34) has been
destroyed, life as it is and life as it should be for the first time
being clearly distinguishable, none the less the tragic moment is
a holding together of those two things, life and essence, and thus
the question 'How can essence become alive?' receives a creative
answer in the lives of tragic heroes. All this passes away with the
birth of philosophy, when 'the essence, having completely
divorced itself from life, became the sole and absolute, the
transcendent reality' (35). Thus we have the three 'great and
timeless paradigmatic forms of world literature: epic, tragedy,
philosophy' (35). With the separation of life and form into the

separate domains of time and eternity the possibility of history, of time requiring the mediation of form, becomes possible; and it is thus here that the Greek world merges, meets and unites with the Biblical world in Christianity. Jewish and Christian universal histories allow history to be real without being absolute; the horizontal movement of history is, at every moment, linked vertically to the God who provides history with its form: paradise, fall and history, paradise regained.

But Lukács's story does not end with the universal history of the Jews and Christians; there is a final break to come. And that is the disappearance of form as transcendent and a priori. Our degradation is synonymous with the discovery of the productivity of forms by us; and the novel is the art form which is wholly of this world for it is the only art form which explicitly thematises the disappearance of a priori forms and struggles with its own necessary productivity and openness.

What makes us so suspicious of such a scheme is that we can imagine the very same materials employed to provide a story not of degradation but of progression. Thus Habermas uses materials very like Lukács's to forward a theory of social evolution – developmental, non-reversible stages of social progression – which is recapitulated in the moral growth of the individual.[21] Not only individuals learn, but societies learn as well; societies can learn because individuals are capable of development and maturation; but individuals can only realise different developmental possibilities in the context of social relations which possess 'room' wherein these acquired abilities can be manifested. What Lukács describes as the fragmentation of social relations occasioned by the disappearance of a priori forms, Habermas defends as a releasing of man from the captivity of nature-bound relations and the acquisition of freedom and autonomy: the classical defence of modernity found in German Idealism.

As it transpires, we do not have to choose between these parallel but incompatible accounts. Lukács denies he is forwarding a universal philosophy of history; and he further scorns those who have idealised, praised and glorified the world of the Greeks.

We do not intend, nor are we able, to here elaborate a philosophy of history relative to this structural transformation of the transcendental loci. Nor do we intend to determine whether it was our progress or our decadence which provoked these changes, or whether the gods of Greece were driven away by other forces. Neither do we intend to chart, however approximately, the road that led to our own reality, nor to describe the seductive power of Greece even when dead and its dazzling brilliance which, like Lucifer's, made men forget again and again the irreparable cracks in the edifice of their world and tempted them to dream of new unities, unities which contradicted the world's new essence and were therefore always doomed to come to naught. (37)

Do the 'cracks' in the edifice of our world manifest Lukács's true allegiance to the past, regardless of what he says? Well, if the cracks are metaphysically irreparable, then they cannot *be* cracks; they can appear so only against the background of a unity metaphysically incommensurable with the structuring parameters of our world; this unity once it has been hypostatised from origin to *telos* becomes a mirage, a communal hallucination that falsifies the character or nature of the change from then to now. When Lukács says 'The circle within which the Greeks led their metaphysical life was smaller than ours: that is why we cannot, as part of our life, place ourselves inside it ... we cannot breathe in a closed world' (33), he is making a structural, metaphysical point about our situation; it is thus not simply a question of 'who would want to return to *Gemeinshaft* after having tasted the forbidden fruits of *Gesellschaft?*'[22] Nor is Lukács taking sides with Hegel and Benjamin who use man's fallen state, the dross and diamonds of historical experience, as the materials which will be redeemed in a *new* paradise, a paradise predicated precisely on the existence of a secular, fallen history. For that is a (universal) philosophy of history, a secular theology; and that, we have just seen, is not part of Lukács's project.

What controls Lukács's use of the past is not a utopian philosophy of history, but a methodology. And that methodology is, roughly, a dialectical (critical) hermeneutics. Because his critics have persistently ignored the methodological dimensions of *The Theory of the Novel* they have consistently been forced to attribute to Lukács positions which he was at pains to refute. He denies any desire to proffer a philosophy of history; and he explicitly criticises the idealist tradition for making the epic age into a Utopia. None the less, he must return to Greece for his analysis because the historical identity of the novel, an identity the novel provides for itself, is, in part, constituted by its connections with the ancient epic.

4 THE QUESTION OF TOTALITY

Surely though, Lukács's critics would not have been so persistent in their misreading if there was not something in *The Theory of the Novel* which seemed to justify their beliefs? The 'tone' of the work, to be sure, is nostalgic. But such pervasive mood of longing for better times, a better world, need not have its origins in a vision of a past world. Again, the evident Hegelian (Schillerian) inspiration behind the work – the comparison of naive and reflexive periods of history; the comparison of epic and prose worlds – provides some grounds for attributing a utopian philosophy of history of Lukács. But why would one hold on to this theoretical model in the face of explicit disclaimers?

The answer lies in Lukács's use and analysis of the concept of totality. A convenient, influential and mistaken account of his thinking about totality is given by Paul de Man.

A definitely post-Hegelian element is introduced with Lukács's insistence on the need for totality as the inner necessity that shapes all works of art. The unity of the Hellenic experience of the world has a formal correlative in the creation of closed, *total* forms, and this desire for totality is an inherent need of the human mind. It persists in modern, alienated man, but instead of fulfilling itself in the mere expression of his given unity with the world, it becomes instead the statement of an intent to retrieve the unity it no longer possesses. Clearly, Lukács's idealized fiction of Greece is a device to state a theory of consciousness that has the structure of an intentional movement.[23]

Note the uneasy tension of de Man's statement. On the one hand, totality represents an inherent need of the human mind; if this were *simply* so then there would be no need for Lukács to refer back to the Greek experience. So, on the other hand, de Man must speak of a desire (need, longing) of modern man 'to retrieve the unity [he] no longer possesses.' In all this the problem of form in its ethical/epistemological complexity is bracketed out for a dull psychological propensity. For all that, de Man catches something about the apparent logic of Lukács's argument. The integrated, closed character of the epic age appears to provide the conditions which makes its forms viable. And similarly, the closure of the Christian world – in Dante's heaven on the Day of Judgement – appears to be what allowed the Church to become a new *polis* (37), 'a new and paradoxical Greece' (38). Thus the only possible concrete, historical exemplifications of totality reside in past ages which either knew no history or through false belief provided closure for the chaos of history. For us, it seems, totality can only be had as the result of an intentional movement – concerned with form – through art.

Two questions merge here. First, is Lukács's account of the *shift* in the locus of form and totality true? The second, how are we to interpret and explain that shift? For the present the first question can be ignored since it is the burden of the whole of Lukács's theory to demonstrate that it is the shift of form from a social precondition to an intentional product of narrative that marks out the historical uniqueness of the novel. What remains ambiguous in both de Man and Lukács is the answer to the second question.

For de Man the 'post-Hegelian' element in Lukács's theory is his statement of a theory of form in terms of a theory of intentionality. As will become evident when we come to discuss the irony of the novel in Chapter VI, de Man construes this theory of intentionality in metaphysical rather than historical terms; thus he takes the historical experience of modern literature to be such as to allow us a privileged insight into the true metaphysical nature of literature generally. Nothing could be further from Lukács's own intentions. However, precisely because he refuses to provide any overt explanations, or explicitly to commit himself to any particular explanatory systems, his conception of totality does remain systematically ambiguous. None the less, there is, I think, a pattern to Lukács various statements about the causes of the collapse of form into an intentional movement. To simplify somewhat, he tends to run together two different explanations: the productivity of spirit as historicity on the one hand, and individualism as a product of reification and fragmentation on the other. Properly speaking, the problem of totality arises at the *intersection* of these two phenomena (both products of the rise of capitalism); but Lukács, working under the shadow of Simmel as much as of Marx, cannot see this because, although he does regard modern individualism as *essentially* problematic (92), he cannot see any alternative to it, and thus cannot see it as *the* effect of reification. More simply still, here, and not in *HCC*, Lukács tends to conflate objectification and reification, thus giving historical developments a more lasting and problematic status than would a Marxist analysis of the same phenomena. Because he does not (or cannot) disentangle the progressive from the regressive elements of capital, because he cannot distinguish between a historical development and its mode of manifestation in capital, all the developments of modernity take on the aura of being at once releases from captivity and new forms of enslavement. It is this systematic ambiguity as to the significance of modernity that makes Lukács's striking distinction between epic and novel so theoretically opaque. Yet we must be clear here that what is at issue is not what Lukács believed in 1915, but the actual premises and assumptions of the arguments he proceeds to give; that is, what presuppositions about the movement of history actually inform his argument and are required for its coherence. These, I shall argue, are throughout the theses of Marxist theory as interpreted by Lukács in *HCC*.

For example, in a passage already examined, Lukács appears to be identifying the productivity of spirit (conversely, the death of God) as the cause of the modern predicament. Well, does the productivity of spirit entail a loss in the self-evidence of form, and consequently a fragmentation of the totality, a dispersion of the communal and public into the idiosyncratic and private? Only if the grounds of self-evidence are considered on analogy with the natural and perduring. And the logic of this stance is Platonic. What is valid, true or worthy is that which escapes the ravages of time. The world of history and society is susceptible to the dual pressure of conditionality and conventionality: if X is in history, then X is a product of something else; if X is a product of something else then its validity (worth) resides in that which produced it; but if what produced it is also in history then its validity is also conditional on its antecedents, and so forth *ad infinitum*. Thus only what is not in history can be valid. As for conventionality, it suffers from circularity, that is, it allows us no way of distinguishing opinion from knowledge: we may all agree that X is true (worthy); but our agreeing that X is true cannot be what makes X true for agreement has been reached on propositions that are evidently false. Thus the true must transcend the conventional, it must have access to what is the case independently of say-so; but since society is regulated in part on say-so, then the norms of society cannot be self-grounding; the validity of social norms must reside in what is not itself social, namely, nature (God). There is inherent in the classical logic of truth and worthiness a force which tends to empty sociality and historicity of their constitutive and productive capacity. Thus it is not surprising that ideological production is often identified with naturalisation, and inversely that critique and deconstruction are identified with denaturalisation, demonstrating the historical specificity of what appears natural and eternal.

Lukács imposes this logic of truth and worthiness onto circumstances where it is inapplicable. We have discovered the productivity of spirit; this means that the classical logic of truth and worthiness is no longer valid. It is no longer legitimate to judge truth or worthiness by the classical standards of objectivity, for to do so would entail denying that history really is productive. Historicity raises problems of truth and value, but does not of itself entail the insoluble difficulties Lukács mentions, namely that we have found the only substantiality in ourselves (individually), or that there exist unbridgeable (metaphysical) chasms between thought and action, self and society, between us and ourselves.

On the contrary, each of these difficulties appears to have a different source: individualism as the collusive product of the Christian view of the self in the new secular setting of capitalism. Thus when Lukács says that 'only the ethical [i.e. creative, transcendental] subject is constitutive' (65) – the thesis that is the key to his view of the novel – he cites the logic of reification, the structural isolation of self from society, and the fragmentation (autonomisation) of the different domains of society from one another. As we have seen, under such circumstances totality is problematic for, on the one hand, the autonomisation of the economic from social control entails the dismissal of form from the essential processes of social reproduction; while on the other hand, individual constitutivity (the creative, ethical self) entails the denial that a form's legitimacy is in any way connected to anything transcending the self. Norms now can have only pragmatic, prudential force, and relations between selves thus become contractual in nature.

The concept of totality in Lukács does not represent the ideal state of affairs had by societies lacking a conception of subjectivity, for totality can be present even when subjectivity is present. Nor does the concept of totality designate a psychological propensity, although whatever it is totality does designate has become isolated in the intentional movements of art forms. The cause of the dissolution of totality cannot be blamed on the death of God or the productivity of spirit, although all previous examples of non-intentional totalities have been located in societies that did not share in the modern experience of historicity. Totality does figure what we have lost, as whatever it is which is lost with our being in the possession of the Kantian or Cartesian conception of subjectivity. Only the experience of the novel, the theory of the novel can fill in that figure.

5   THE ABSENT ORIGINS OF REPRESENTATION

Here is the central conclusion of the epic/novel, integrated/problematic comparison.

Henceforth, any resurrection of the Greek world signifies a more or less conscious hypostasy of aesthetics into metaphysics... an attempt to forget that art is only one sphere among many, and *that the very disintegration and inadequacy of the world is the precondition for the existence of art and its becoming conscious.* This exaggeration of the substantiality of art is bound to weigh heavily upon its forms: they have to produce out of themselves all that was once simply accepted as given: in other words, before their own a priori effectiveness can begin to manifest itself, they must create by their own power alone the pre-conditions for such effectiveness – an object and its environment. (38, emphasis mine)

The argument of this paragraph is radical. Lukács is claiming that the precondition for art's becoming autonomous, for art's becoming 'art' and nothing else, is the fragmentation (reification) of the social world. And while this thesis presupposes historicity and productivity as a necessitating condition, ideological individualism is its essence.

According to Lukács, modernity is in part constituted by the disappearance of 'formal a priori' structures regulating human action and self-understanding, by the disappearance of a 'marked convergence between ethic as an interior factor of life and its substratum (for action) in the social structures' (74). With the collapse, for whatever reasons, of the traditional theocentric universe came the demise as well of the *universally shared* value and order giving teleologies which shaped (figured) that world. Form is no longer experienced as intrinsic to experienced reality, or even as attainable in the ordering of the after world (Dante). Community and shared experiences of value and order are replaced by individual experience and volition. The primacy of individual experience and volition is an essential part of our practical ideology and of the modes of discursive validation in bourgeois philosophy. This generates the problem of form in two senses: the novelist can no longer rely on past history, fable, myth, traditional plots or religious and theological paradigms to structure his discourse *literarily because* these forms no longer carry *social* accreditation, that is, they are no longer constitutive components of a social ethic. Traditional art forms were given forms in accordance with which artists could narrate experience; but that very givenness, Lukács is claiming, entailed that those forms were not restrictedly art-forms. Rather, they were components of a social ethic, an ethos and tradition whose validity was available and recognised outside the domains we now designate by the terms 'art' and 'literature'. Hence, neither these domains nor their forms existed as fully independent and autonomous aspects of the social world in pre-capitalist social formations.[24]

As we have already seen, Lukács is not altogether clear about the causes and therefore the nature of this autonomy. Thus he writes: 'Art, the visionary reality of the world made to our measure, has thus become autonomous: it is no longer a copy, for all the models have gone; it is a created totality, for the natural unity of the metaphysical spheres has been destroyed forever' (37). To be sure, what is not given for use must be produced, but that alone does not entail that literary forms are produced for there is no reason why literary production should not be subservient to forms and totalities created and validated elsewhere in a social formation. It is, then, because there are *no models* produced and validated outside of literature that literary forms are (become) 'visionary'. Productivity is not problematic in itself, or need not be, but becomes so only when conjoined with the disappearance of community. It is the autonomy and not the created character of literary forms which makes them problematic.

Only when the forms which art deploys are no longer socially underwritten can they become *art forms tout court*. But art's autonomy signifies an emptying of the social world of meaningful complexes, social structures responsive to human needs and desires. Art's autonomy is coextensive with the autonomy (conceptual independence) of truth in, say, mechanistic science and value-free social science from ethics. The Good, the True and the Beautiful are no longer interrelated forms of universal articulation, no longer predicates of one God; they have been isolated and separated from one another, they have become autonomous domains of experience. They may experientially overlap one another, but the trend of modernity has been increasingly to reveal and demand their conceptual and social autonomy.

It is within this context that the Homeric epic has its significance. From our perspective the epic appears homogeneous and undifferentiated because the very categories and terms of classification which give us an access to the world are inapplicable, in their modern radicality and separation, to it. And this, I want to claim, is not a problem but a solution to the problem: to interpret the epic is to relate it to our categories; but because in its unity it denies or resists those categories in their irrevocable plurality, interpretation tends to freeze that resistance into an origin. This hypostatisation of the incomprehensible into an origin thus subtly inverts the problem; it affirms its weakness as the strength, the splendour of the other. But this move, premised on the reified understanding of understanding, the autonomisation of the categories of understanding, notoriously coerces us into seeking an escape from history, into recovering the origin in a non-historical telos.

I am thus joining Lukács and Auerbach in claiming that in

the last analysis we cannot *interpret* the Homeric epic. One way of defending this claim, tacitly endorsed by Scholes and Kellogg, is to argue that the ancient epic *is* homogeneous and un-differentiated. Lukács's argument is different: he is claiming, however indirectly, that the undifferentiated structural unity of the epic is an hermeneutical appearance, a historical effect. The origin of this appearance lies not in it (alone), but (as well) in the categories we have in our possession to appropriate it. Once, however, the legitimacy of those categories is challenged, once, that is, we recognise them as the products of a social process with progressive and regressive tendencies of which those categories are a part (the isolation of 'truth', for example, is essential to the secularising of experience, and thus to the production of a truly 'social' society), then we are no longer licensed in giving an interpretation to the uninterpretable.

The twisting of blindness into insight (origin) is essential to the recuperative analyses of (so-called) non-historical societies. Thus the fragmentation, reification and division of labour, language and culture – thought loosely, outside their theore-tical and historical specificity – become themselves the sign, the mark of a unity that once was. And because this unity appears through its resistance to all change and movement to reside outside history it can be imaged as the origin of history, its metaphysical source and therefore its goal. Thus for Benjamin the plurality of languages signifies an original unity of language which it is the task of the translator to begin to reanimate: 'an original unity of language in paradise [is] followed by the Fall (". . . as many translations as languages once man has fallen from paradise, which knew only one language."), thereafter by the tower of Babel, and ever since by the "yearning" for the "integration of the many languages into the one true one".'[25] Similarly, Benjamin compares historiography, remembered unity, which is the creative matrix of the various (like the colours of the spectrum) epic forms to a white light:[26] 'Such unrefracted light is,' Wohlfarth suggests, 'light which contains its own translation, light from before (or after) the fall into multiplicity; it is the *terminus a quo*, logical or chronological, and the *terminus ad quem*.'[27] But why should we assume that the products of unity are spoiled by their differentiation? Could not the diffuse unity of origin require differentiation for perfection?

Does not Marx argue that the production of purely social forms of sociality entails an increase in universality? Perhaps nothing can be seen in an unrefracted light. Perhaps nothing can be said in a language that denies all otherness. To assume the perfection of the white light is to assume that the blindness produced by pure illumination is really a form of vision – perfect vision. And cannot a pre-Babel language be as easily interpreted as a language in which nothing is said as a language in which everything is said?

Triadic dialectic is a form of historicism which denies historicity, the hermeneutic condition of all authentic historical reflection. In such theories history itself is used as the lever which justifies the claim to unlimited accessibility to the non-historical past. One way of doing this is to specify the categorial difference between historical and non-historical societies while bracketing the specificity of the constituting structures of our (historical) society, and thus bracketing the problem of limited versus total accessibility. (And it is only as a total claim of accessibility, epistemically proleptic as it may be, that the unity and perfection of the epic world can 'figure' in universal philosophies of history.) Once the constituting structures of our society are presented then the grounds for assuming an unlimited and total accessibility to the past are eliminated. As we have seen, there are no privileged historical locations where the meaning of history as such is revealed; whatever is salvageable from the past is salvageable only piecemeal, as history allows or necessitates.

Because there is no 'truth' to be recovered from epic societies (now), because epic narrative (now) resists the demands of our categories does not entail there are no lessons to be learned from our experience of the epic. For Lukács it is in the epic's resistance to interpretation that its meaning lies. The *apparent* condition of that resistance is the a- or non-historical character of epic meaning, for being outside history mythic truth *is*, and cannot be conceived of as other than it is. But the ground of this feature of epic or mythic thought is its belonging to an oral society, a society which knows no past or future because the practical means of fixing each present into a moment which can become a past which was open to a different future either does not exist or is insufficiently socially distributed to be effective as a continuous record of difference, of change and innovation. While oral

societies change, that change is unremarked, except in the
alternations it effects on traditional myths, but these alterations
themselves must go unnoticed for there are no means of noticing
them. Thus although myths and epics can refer to a past they are
about the present. It is in mythic thought's refusal or inability to
think a past or future as radically different from the present that
its authority lies. Conversely, writing and history ('Once the
story is written down, history begins.') of themselves generate a
problem of authority: because the new is unhallowed and
unsupported by tradition, a tradition which in oral societies is
unreflective, then writing cultures impose on their members a
burden of reflection, of critically appropriating past or present
in their recognised difference. When what is new is seen *as* new
than there is a need for justification. The passage from an oral
society to a culture of writing is the passage from *mythos* to logos,
from the unreflective singing of the tradition to the reflective
appropriation of it in prose.[28] It is, then, in their belonging to oral
societies and writing cultures respectively that the grounds for
distinguishing epic and later prose narratives reside.

None the less, there exists a continuity between the oral
tradition and its progeny which is not maintained into the age of
the novel. Oral societies, in virtue of their orality, do not appear
to possess distinguishable narrative genres. With writing came
a differentiation of narrative impulses; but this differentiation did
not bespeak an absolute autonomy of any one domain from any
other domain. Plato's construction of the Good as conditioning
the visibility of the Ideas, and the analogous role played by God
in Christian theologies approximate the 'totality' and objectivity available to the ancient epic. Hence the 'unity of the
metaphysical spheres' is shared, however differently, by writing
and non-writing cultures. With the novel that unity disappears;
the meaning of that disappearance, as the novel figures it,
concerns the place and character of form within society as a
whole. The independence but non-autonomy of post-epic
narratives can too easily be read in terms of the modern
autonomy of forms; the impenetrability of the ancient epic
forces us to question, to rewrite the history of written narratives.
In this way Lukács's conception of the ancient epic functions to
distinguish the novel from everything that preceded it as
opposed to distinguishing the epic from everything that followed

it. But it is the moment of dissonance provided by an experience of the ancient epic which (re-)awakens us to the otherness of this past, and hence to the dissonances of the present.

Through the understanding of what makes the ancient epic impenetrable to our categories, through, that is, the construction of a history in which that impenetrability can itself speak to us we begin the work of identifying our historical situation. Only by following the series of alterations which have befallen the epic, by discovering the points of identity and difference within the epic tradition can we locate the novel as both inside and outside that tradition. This work of identification requires us to locate epic writings in their social context, to note how belonging to an oral or religious culture affects the narratives of that culture; and further, to ask what features of a culture are really responsible for different narrative effects and forms. Lukács's point is not about a past unity which is forever lost to us, but about a present of separation which needs to be seen *as* fragmented in order to be understood correctly.

Lukács could not make his point in terms of our categorial system because it is about the status of that system itself. Literary form not only has a social and historical belonging, but as such has a social meaning; literary form speaks the place of literature in a society and by that very fact images from within the nature of the social world it belongs to as a whole. The social meaning of literary forms is something that shows itself only through social change and historical difference; the meaning of literary forms manifests itself only as an effect of historical consciousness, as, that is, an effect of the hermeneutical awareness of the present in its historical otherness. Effective historical consciousness is always a consciousness of dissonance. *In Lukács's theory it is the dissonance of the ancient epic which allows the novel to be brought to historical consciousness; the comprehension of that dissonance in the novel is the goal of his theory.*

As will be argued in the next chapter, Lukács's theory of the novel is an ethical (political) one because the question of form reveals itself to historical consciousness to be a normative question. The question of form can be normative only because literary form has a social meaning. To show that the problem of the novel is the problem of authorising its vision, its in-forming of the language of experience, is to reveal that it is the lack of a normative substratum which is constitutive of the novel. Against the backdrop of the epic, and what succeeded it, that the novel is literature and only literature suddenly looks suspect (problematic). But this backdrop, this problem, is something the practice of novel writing itself tells us.

When we see the novel in historical perspective the status and authority of its forms surface as what binds and dislocates the novel from its heritage. The cult of art, like the cult of the Greek world, turns aesthetics into metaphysics, giving to art forms an authority they do not possess, and hence equally doing violence 'to the essence of everything that lies outside the sphere of art' (38). Alternatively, to allow art forms to be just art forms, the sort of forms to which an 'aesthetic perception', say, would be appropriate, is to forget the history of form and capitulate to the emptying of art of its social and normative content. Only an ethics of the novel, a dialectics of form can negotiate these antithetical temptations.

Lukács ends the first chapter of *The Theory of the Novel* with these words:

A totality that can be simply accepted is no longer given to the forms of art: therefore they must either narrow down and volatilise whatever has to be given form to the point where they can encompass it, or else they must show polemically the impossibility of achieving their necessary object and the inner nullity of their own means. And in this case they carry the fragmentary nature of the world's structure into the world of forms' (38–9).

To volatilise the world demonically in order that form may encompass it is to fictionalise our experience, to fail to be true to the world (by being too true to the demands of form). Conversely, to respect the truth of experience is to admit the impenetrability of experience by form, the failure of form and one's lack of authority. Either form succeeds through a denial of the world, or form fails through a respect for the demands of experience. That is the antinomy of the novel; and the recognition of that antinomy is not aesthetic but ethical.

III
Categories : Abstract Forms

Form is what is fundamentally social about literature.... It is a kind of link, the only true connection between the creative artist and his public, and therefore the only category of literature that is both social and aesthetic.

(Georg Lukács)

Art is the negative knowledge of the actual world.

(Theodor Adorno)

1 FROM TRAGEDY TO THE CRISIS OF CULTURE

Culture was the 'one and only' thought of Lukács's life.

(Gyorgy Markus)

There can be little doubt that Lukács's conceptions of form and culture, and of the link between them, are largely derived from the writings of Georg Simmel, in particular from his *The Philosophy of Money*.[1] It is equally evident that Simmel's diagnosis of the tragedy of the culture is meant to be a generalisation of Marx's analysis of commodity fetishism,[2] an application of Marx's analysis to the social world generally. Lukács's Marxism, and his generalisation of Marx's procedures, were mediated through the writings of Simmel. Lukács was already applying and extending Simmel's model in the period 1906–9 while working on a history of the development of modern drama.

Simmel's concept of Form is a historicised, and so hegelianised, elaboration and extension of Kant's theory of categories. In Simmel, Kant's unsynthesised manifold of representation becomes the raw material of the cosmos (nature). Reality as such is unintelligible because it is a continuous and homogeneous process. Like Kant, Simmel believes that the principles or categories which define any form are properties of that form

77

itself and cannot be derived from experience (nature). Forms are constitutive of experience. In order for any phenomenon to become intelligible it must be brought under, constituted by the categories of some form. The kind of intelligibility any pheno-menon has depends on the kind or type of form it is constituted by. Different forms are constitutive of different domains of experience. Each form has the Kantian function of unifying and structuring a domain of experience. The work of bringing unity to a manifold of experience is accomplished at various levels; the lowest level of unification, what Simmel calls a prioris, is the concept. A prioris constitute manifolds into discernible objects. Thus each form or modality of experience – e.g. there are forms of art, religion, science, philosophy, ethics; but equally Simmel recognises 'adventure' and prostitution as forms of life – has nested within it lower level forms specific to it. Simmel never provides a formal or logical analysis of the unifying and structuring function of forms because he believes that each form establishes a different type of 'belonging together' among its contents. Each form, we might say, provides a different grammar of experience. Thus the categories of any form are not deducible from the categories of any other form, although the in-formed products of one domain may become objects for another form, e.g. art forms may become the raw material for history. Although materials from one form of experience may be comprehended from the vantage point of a different form, no form is reducible to another form; forms are irreducibly heterogeneous; no form has a privileged ontological or epistemological status. Finally, Simmel argues against Kant that all forms are historical; there is no such thing as art or science in general; there are only these forms in a particular social and historical configuration.

At this level of analysis Simmel's strictures against the classical Kantian conception of categories is not unlike Wittgenstein's later critique of his own project in the *Tractatus*. The dynamic element in Simmel's philosophy is provided by his theory of culture. All forms are cultural in the sense that they are originally extensions and expressions of natural needs and capacities which have reached a non-natural, social or cultural level of development. Forms are nature civilised; they are expressions and means whereby we cultivate our natural potentialities; they are the purposive and teleological replacement for natural, causal forces: 'culture exists only if man draws into his development something that is external to him. Cultivation is certainly a state of the soul, but one that is reached only by means of the use of purposely created objects.'[3] Culture, then, is always two-sided; objective (or material) culture is the world of objectifications created for the purpose of realising subjective culture; subjective culture is Goethean refinement and synthesis of the total personality of the individual. Subjective culture is the re-absorption of objective culture into the individual. The goal of objective culture is subjective culture. When objective culture is so re-appropriable by individuals at large, then there exists a harmony of culture. No such harmony exists in modern times.

Cultural value, and hence the logic of culture, is not derivable from or commensurable with the logic and value of any of the formal domains which compose a culture. As we have already seen, each domain of form possesses its own grammar and thus, by extension, its own scale of values. What counts as an achievement in art or science is internal to the categories constituting those domains. Hence each domain possesses an internal logic of development which is autonomous from that of every other domain. What counts as an achievement within a domain, however, may be of little cultural value because that achievement is not capable of being integrated into the psychic life of individuals generally: 'There are human products of almost ultimate perfection to which we have no access, or they no access to us, because of their perfect integration.'[4] Objective culture may become so refined and complex that it becomes generally the case that the goal of culture, subjective culture, remains unsatisfied. Simmel contends that a development of this kind has occurred in modern times, and that it was inevitable; the very means of subjective culture have become ends in themselves, thus inverting the cultural process. Since this inversion of means and ends is intrinsic to the logic of culture, since the nature of the culture process necessarily invokes its own undoing the cultural process is itself tragic. Cultural objectification inevitably and necessarily becomes cultural alienation.

Simmel's conception of the tragedy of culture is a metaphysical explanation for a particular, historical malady. Significantly, the metaphysical account of the tragedy of culture, which was forwarded in his 1911 essay 'On the Concept and the Tragedy of Culture', is not identical with the account offered in *The Philosophy of Money*. In his earlier work Simmel, following Marx and Tonnies, explicitly explained the divorce between subjective and objective culture through the division of labour, that is, cultural disintegration was caused by specialisation, rationalisation and, interestingly, the separation of the worker from the means of production.[5] Further, the general argument of that work depends on an appropriation of Marx's analysis of the inversion of use-value and exchange value in capital production; indeed, what Simmel provides there is a diagnosis of cultural inversion predicated on that economic inversion: culture becomes instrumentalised through the reign of money into a means for capital accumulation. Although Simmel does not concern himself in *The Philosophy of Money* with the systematic features responsible for the inversion brought about by the culture of money, and therefore remains either uninterested in or blind to the political and class aspects of Marx's thought, the theoretical distance between Simmel and Marx is far less in that work than it is often portrayed as being. Simmel's failure to consider those aspects of Marx's thought was doubtless conditioned by his preference for individualism; and that preference is what led him to finally subsume his social analysis in a metaphysical theory in which our historical fate became a metaphysical tragedy.[6]

History and Class Consciousness, we have argued, is an attempt to rewrite Marxist theory as a theory of culture; it can now be added that Lukács was also attempting to rewrite Simmel's theory of culture in Marxist, collectivist terms, reversing Simmel's drift into metaphysics through an account of the conditions for and nature of cultural renewal. In order for this latter rewriting to succeed Lukács had to rework the central terms of Simmel's cultural theory. Such a rewriting is most evident and explicit in Lukács's (1920) 'The Old Culture and The New Culture',[9] where his first alteration is to make room for the concept of class within the concept of culture. Culture, he argues, must be contraposed to civilisation; civilisation is the rule of man over external nature; culture comprises those products and abilities which are dispensable for the immediate purposes of sustaining life, that is, culture involves those elements of social life which are not *directly* in the service of species reproduction. There can only be a culture, then, when there is a freedom from strenuous labour. Culture is the prerogative of societies that create a surplus produce. From this it follows that the majority of old cultures were primarily the cultures of the ruling classes, of those who extract and live off surplus produce. It further follows that the goal of civilisation is culture, that is, the ultimate historical meaning of instrumental activity is the acquisition of a domain of objects and activities that are valuable in themselves; and, Lukács argues, the sociological precondition for culture in this sense is the recognition of man as end in himself.

Each of these refinements involves a complex series of theoretical cross-references. Lukács's use of the civilisation – culture distinction not only allows a class aspect to enter into the problem of culture, it further involves a Kantian rewriting of the Marxist categories of exchange value and use-value. On the one hand, the domination of use-value by exchange value involves a perversion of civilisation by reversing means and ends; on the other hand, use-value can escape the reign of 'utility' by taking on a possible, historically conditioned meaning by being identified with values that are 'categorical', that is, with objects and activities that are valuable for themselves and not for something else. In other words, the reign of freedom which is the escape from the reign of necessity now takes on a properly Kantian, non-natural, normative significance; and this can only be accomplished if the domain of value itself is subdivided. Conversely, what is hypostatised in Kant – for Kant *only* a good will is valuable in itself – is historicised and socialised by means of the concept of culture: culture, and not the categorical imperative, is man's internal domination over his environment.[8] Culture is a freedom for culture, a social autonomy from the reign of necessity expressed in economic activity. While Lukács's distinction between culture and civilisation has certain formal analogies with Habermas's now well-known distinction between systems of purposive rationality and symbolic interaction – both sets of distinctions play on the Kantian distinction between hypothetical and non-hypothetical forms of rationality – Lukács's analysis remains more Kantian in reading culture as a socialised expression of autonomy, and more Marxist by tying Kantian autonomy to the socialising of society on the one hand, and the creation of surplus produce on the other.[9] Lukács requires no transcendental arguments to ground his normative system since those norms are immanent products of history.

Having made these revisions, Lukács is in a position to give a quite different analysis of the crisis in modern culture, an analysis which can demonstrate that cultural crisis is 'a crisis of culture (in the strict sense of creations of the spirit) and a crisis of "man", of human existence,' and not, it should be added, a metaphysical tragedy of culture.[10] From the fact that every culture is primarily a culture of the ruling classes, it does not follow that the cultural process need be crisis-ridden. Indeed, it seems logically possible for history to be a continuing growth in the acquisition of culture by ever larger sectors of different social formations. In Simmelian terms we might say that there is no logical or trans-historical reason why the growth of objective culture should entail a diminution is subjective culture. Lukács provides two related explanations for the crisis of modern culture. First, he argues that the autonomy of the economy from extra-economic, cultural control has the effect of making all cultural goods into commodities; that is, the domination of exchange value over use-value can become complete only if all other domains are, in the last analysis, relativised to the needs of the economy. Since culture is the domain of ends in themselves, then, necessarily, capital production contradicts the very idea of culture. Following Simmel, Lukács argues that capital production, a monied society, involves the instrumentalisation of the rest of society. 'The moment cultural productions become commodities, their autonomy – the possibility of culture – ceases.'[11] Now the irony of the defeat of culture by commodity production is that capitalism, as the first truly social society, has as its only intrinsic ideological principle the freedom of the individual, the recognition of all men as ends in themselves, the recognition of each man as the 'owner' of his labour power. So long as the bourgeoisie was a rising but not a dominant class, so long as their ideology was directed against the constraints of a feudal estate society, culture in the traditional sense was still possible. However

as the bourgeoisie came to power . . . it could no longer seriously carry

through its ideology; it could not apply the idea of individual freedom
to the whole society without bringing about the self-negation of the
social order that brought this ideology into being in the first place.
Briefly, it was impossible for the bourgeois class to apply its own idea of
freedom to the proletariat.[12]

This gives us the second limb of Lukács's explanation of the crisis
in culture: bourgeois ideology is necessarily in contradiction
with the reality of the existing social order. The crisis of culture,
the commodification of the cultural world, *appears* as a crisis *in*
culture when the form (= ideology) and content (= social
reality) of cultural expression enter into contradiction with one
another.[13]

According to Lukács, and in this he has been followed by
Habermas,[14] pre-capitalist or traditional societies did not have
ideologies in the modern sense because civilisation always
functioned within the parameters dictated by culture, that is,
cultural forms themselves grounded the institutional framework
of the society as a whole. In this sense, Lukács argues, there was a
harmony between culture and economy. The existence of such a
harmony did not entail the non-existence of exploitation or of
the extraction of surplus value. Nor, it should be added, does the
affirmation of such harmony entail a sanctioning of the actual
values expressed by those cultures. All that such harmony
denotes is a congruence between cultural expressions and the
actual forms of social life. Since cultural or 'ideological' (using
the term broadly) forms possess a 'relative autonomy'[15] from
their economic foundations, these forms must be relatively
autonomous from the 'givens' that are formed by them. Thus
the cultural products of traditional societies can attain an
'organic unity' in the sense that cultural form and social content
are but different expressions of the same. Culture itself becomes
fragmented when there is a conflict between form and content.
It is equally at this moment that every non-economic factor
becomes ideological. But since ideology as such arises at the
moment when there is a contradiction in culture, between form
and content, ideology and the critique of ideology arise
simultaneously. It is for this reason, Lukács states, that 'the
culture of capitalism, to the extent that it truly existed, could
consist of nothing but the ruthless critique of the capitalist

epoch.'[16] There is, we might say, no place or space for the ideology of capital to penetrate the social order of capital.

The theoretical exposition of precisely this contradiction between cultural, ideological form and social content forms the dialectical centre of the *The Theory of the Novel*. The novel is immanently critical of the social world created by capital, and theoretically antinomic (problematic). The novel both expresses and *is* the crisis of the culture of capital. In pre-capitalist societies culture remained tied to civilisation; under capital the domination of use-value by exchange value is the rule of civilisation over culture, hence the destruction of culture in the traditional sense. Since the ideological premise for that domination, the universal recognition of man as an end in himself, is equally the tacit premise for the existence of all culture, then necessarily authentic or fully realised cultural expressions must be discordant, dissonant and antinomic in structure.

2   FORM AND LIFE

Lukács's account of the relation between form and life changed little between the writing of *Soul and Form* (1910) and *The Theory of the Novel*, with two exceptions. The relation between form and life is presented in the earlier work as a metaphysical verity,, while in the later work Lukács reverses the path traversed by Simmel from history to metaphysics by demonstrating that the contradiction between form and life is specific to the cultural world of capital. *Soul and Form*, then, is a metaphysical allegory of cultural production under capital, a work of cultural criticism despite itself. The lynchpin of that allegory is metaphysical individualism, while in *The Theory of the Novel* individualism is the appearance form of capital socialisation. If, as has sometimes been argued,[17] *Soul and Form* is a proto-existentialist work, then the historicisation of the schema of that work entails an implicit ideological criticism of existentialism.

The general thesis of *Soul and Form* is explicit in the essay on Kierkegaard, 'The Foundering of Form Against Life'. Following Simmel, Lukács throughout interprets form as that which unifies diverse elements, life, into a meaningful structure. Form is the structuring of life. Meaningful structures

(*Sinngebilde*) are formations of life. 'Life', Lukács says, 'is an anarchy of light and dark; nothing is ever completely fulfilled in life, nothing ever quite ends.... Everything flows, everything merges into another thing... everything is destroyed, everything is smashed, nothing ever flowers into real life.'[18] Life is both shapeless and meaningless; and it is these things because it is a heterogeneous process. The question, then, is: What is the value of form in life? We know that there are works, objectifications, which through their forms render the elements of life meaningful. But these are precisely objectifications, and as objectifications their meaningfulness is independent of the lives of their creators. For Lukács there exists no direct way, for us, in which the meaningfulness of an objectification, its capacity to bring life to the level of form, can be transferred from the product to the producer. On the contrary, the relation between the two is typically one of inverse proportion: the greater the objectified achievement the more formless is the life of its maker. The grounds for this claim lie in the logic of aesthetic production. Art can transcend alienation only by departing from empirical experience; only in a fictional world can form completely constitute experience. Thus a necessary condition for authentic art is the reduction of the world to the demands of the constituting self. Conversely, if aesthetic production is viewed as a form of self-activity, in contrast to logical and ethical forms, then the aesthetic self is one which can realise itself only by withdrawing from the plenitude of empirical experience and thereby restricting itself to what is immanent to the experience of the self as self. The price of attaining a pure subjectivity, of living, we might say, at the level of a Fichtean transcendental ego, is the demonic restricting of the self to where it can satisfy the totalising and holistic demands of form. However, at the very moment where the work achieves its form it departs from the constitutive activity of its creator; the work's totality excludes the artist for whom its production was inescapably a *life* project. The artist can never live the completed work as his activity, its closure makes him a reader. The project of objectifying meaning in a work is then a metaphysical adventure which succeeds on the basis of the defeat of the project as a life-project.[19] Artistic, literary meaning excludes empirical meaningfulness for its creator. Thus the problem of the Kierkegaard essay comes into focus: How can life be meaningful? Under what conditions can a life be absolute?

Form can enter life only if a life-act can be absolute; more prosaically, a form or mode of life must allow of taking on an unequivocal significance. Against Hegel Kierkegaard argued that a system cannot be lived; abstract philosophy leaves existence out of account. In response he contrived a philosophy which circumscribed possibilities or stages of life, a philosophy which stylised modes of life. These forms of life were the aesthetic, the ethical and the religious; and only the religious life could be absolute. Religious life could be absolute because God can be loved absolutely; and God can be loved absolutely because in the face of God we are eternally in the wrong. 'My love is sure and unquestionable only if I am never in the right: and God alone can give one this assurance.'[20] My love is unjustified if my beloved is unfaithful; to be proved right against my beloved is to dissolve the worth of my love. Only before God is my love justified for before Him I am always in the wrong.

Lukács measures the absoluteness of Kierkegaardian theory against Kierkegaard's life, but Kierkegaard's life as lived, that is, in its interactions with others. Lukács, that is, attempts to measure Kierkegaard's thesis·that there can be a 'teleological suspension of the ethical' against the facts of Kierkegaard's life. Can there be a teleological suspension of the ethical? Can what binds us to the flow of life be suspended or dissolved in the absolute? Between the poetic stylisation of life in Kierkegaard's theory and the absoluteness of his love for God stood the world of the ethical, marriage and dutifulness. What did Kierkegaard's 'gesture' of breaking off his engagement with Regine Olsen mean? Or rather, was the breaking off of that engagement a gesture, rounded and complete, which could free Regine for life and Kierkegaard for God? In life, Lukács argues, a gesture is never complete; actions are open to an indefinite number of interpretations. But then if action cannot be completed, then there cannot be absolute stages in life. Interpersonal life is always nuanced, problematic, without sharp contours. At the end of his life Kierkegaard wrote, 'I am struggling in vain, I am losing the ground under my feet. My life will, after all, have been a poet's life and no more.'[21] Only in poetry can there be life-defining gestures; life dissolves form into questions and possibilities, and renders experience subjective, private, isolated. If poetic experience fails because for it 'all life is merely raw material' which can be realised as form only by 'doing spontaneous violence to living matter',[22] religious life fails because it naively believes it is 'distinct' from the ethical and the poetic. Kierkegaard, despite himself poeticises life: 'Is not a stage a "higher unity" (in the Hegelian sense) too? Is not the denial of a life-system [= Hegel] itself a system – and very much so? Is not the leap (from one stage to another) merely a sudden transition? . . . . Can one be honest in the face of life, and yet stylize life's events in literary form?'[23]

Lukács concedes to Kierkegaard the thesis that significant communication is 'existential', while denying that existence can be absolutely subjective. Form can succeed only by being communicated, or rather, the problem of form becomes the problem of communication, but existential communication is form as life, ethical form. What Lukács discovered in *Soul and Form* is the ethical character and question submerged in aesthetic form. Form founders against life because life is not yet form ; form can render life meaningful only as ethical form. In 1910 this was for Lukács very much a Kantian insight. It becomes a Marxist insight when forms stop being spontaneous products of the soul and become elements of a social practice.

We have already seen how in *The Theory of the Novel* the notion of gesture is relocated from poetry into epic society; the hermeneutical significance of which is to transform directly the nature of aesthetic form into one of ethical action. The premise of that transformation must be, at least, the transformation of the metaphysical description of life into an historical description. To the question of why form founders against life a socio-historical answer must be given. In *The Theory of the Novel* Lukács presents reification as society becoming a 'second nature': 'It [society] is a second nature, and like nature (first nature), it is determinable only as the embodiment of recognised necessities and therefore it is incomprehensible, unknowable in its real substance . . . . This second nature is not dumb, sensuous and yet senseless like the first: it is a complex of senses – meanings – which has become rigid and strange, and which no longer awakens interiority: it is a charnel-house of long-dead interiorities' (62, 64). The world of capital is a social world naturalised into a Newtonian world of necessities, a world of regularities whose laws appear to have no connection with the activities of those governed by them. It is, we might say, because the social world has the shape of a Newtonian world of necessities that Kant can figure the whole of the objective, intersubjective world of 'things' under the law of cause and effect, and in consequence must restrict the domain of ethics to subjectivity. In such a world ethics can be objective only as art; art (or the 'aesthetic' as such) is constituted by the failure of ethics to constitute experience in its own image. Conversely, modern art can succeed, can realise its vocation, only by figuring this loss as its constitutive condition. In formal terms, only the novel among literary forms realises this constitutive condition.

Because the novel, as modern epic, must thematise life, and not only the meaning of life, it must confront the *conditions* for human actions as well as the meaning or sense of those actions. Other literary forms, notably drama, may address themselves to the arena in which human action takes place (Ibsen), and may, like the epic, focus on life as traversing those conditions (Miller), as an extensive totality. Lukács's contention is only that the novel as epic is formally constituted by these conditions. 'For the epic, the world at any given moment is an ultimate principle; it is empirical at its deepest, most decisive, all determining transcendental base . . . the character created by the epic is the empirical "I" ' (46–7). Therefore, only when meaning is already written into empirical experience, when 'right and custom are identical with morality' (= *Sittlichkeit* (65)) can epics proper be written. Drama, on the other hand, gives form to the 'intensive totality of essence . . . . The character created by drama . . . is the intelligible "I" of man' (46–7); and therefore even when meaning is no longer immanent in life essence can still 'crown itself with its own existence' (45). Lukács's thought here is that because drama is directed toward the moment when form becomes life, then irrespective of the fact that this genre could only come into being at a certain historical conjuncture, its nature is such that the historical disturbances which have forced the disappearance of the epic and the creation of the novel can be accommodated to it. Drama does change because what counts as essential and the accessibility of essence to life changes, but these changes are recognisably changes in drama, not changes of drama into something else.[24]

Having established roughly what Lukács intends by life, that is, something of how it is life is to relate to epic writing and the historical character of 'life' under capital, we now have available the inaugural terms of reference for his argument. Lukács's theory of the novel is an analysis of the form of the novel; since the form of the novel is a certain writing practice Lukács assumes he is entitled to analyse the novel as a set of *strategies* for coping with certain pervasive problems in realising or making good the project of that practice. So the form of the novel is *reconstructed as a set of practical deliberations in the execution of a project*. Since the premises of the reconstructed deliberation are 'social facts' conditioning the practice in question, each step of the deliberation comes to reveal analytically the social character or meaning of the practice. What the reconstruction shows is that the form of the novel is 'Kantian', and that the novel suffers antinomies analogous with the antinomies to which Kant's philosophy is subject. But the novel is not a theory; the practices of the novel give phenomenological expression to those theoretical antinomies. And those antinomies, we know, are the antinomies of bourgeois thought.

Lukács's argument is theoretical and not empirical or inductive (like, say, Watt's *The Rise of the Novel*). Beginning with premises about the social world and the project of epic writing, his argument reveals the conceptual connections among structuring elements of the novel; but because his procedure is practical, relates to a practice, the conceptual connections turn out to be the structure of practice. What we have in the end, then, is not the representation of an object (*the* novel), but the interpretation of a practice.[25] Like any interpretation of a social practice the result is very general. Further, since Lukács is interpreting the practice of novel writing, his theory is not such as would allow one simply to *apply* the theory in order to interpret any particular novel. The meaning of a social practice should not be confused with the interpretation of products of that practice. Lukács is not offering a recursive procedure for the interpretation of novels; nor is his work in any sense a work of literary criticism.

Because my exposition of Lukács's argument will be complex, it will prove helpful to provide an overview of the argument as whole. After which the remainder of this chapter can attend to the first two steps of the argument.

There are two premises to Lukács's argument: one relating to shifts in 'life', the other referring to displacements in the grounding of 'form'. Let us denominate the premise about life the 'second nature' or 'reification' thesis. It states that ten-dentially the social structures produced by capital are no longer adequate vehicles for meaningful experience; life under capital is experienced as being 'alienating' because the social world appears as an autonomous system. The premise about form can be called the 'secularisation' thesis: 'The novel is the epic of a world that has been abandoned by God' (88). Novel writing issues from a world in which forms of intelligibility and meaning are no longer given, they are not authorised by tradition or unequivocally underwritten by the 'community' at large (37–9). A corollary of the second premise is the 'individualism' thesis: 'We have found the only true substance within ourselves' (34).

Lukács assumes that the second premise and its corollary are causal consequences of the first premise. It is because of the socialising character of capital production (together with the rise of modern natural science, etc.) that traditional forms of meaningfulness outside individual volition have lost their authority. Further, the second premise only rarely functions as an explicit premise in the writing of the classical realist novel. In a writer like Jane Austen, for example, there is a presumption of communal authority for the proposed value-terms of her writing. When the second premise is explicitly recognised then typically we are no longer in the world of realist discourse. The premise only appears across different writings, and is assumed to be explanatory of shifts in explicit writing strategies. A similar disappearing bivalence – not quite explicit in classical realist writings and when it is explicit the writing is no longer realist – can be attributed to the first premise as well. It is because of the disappearing bivalence of the premises of novel writing that their effects are partly conditioned by their non-recognition, that the classical realist novel never appears as such. The novel, like its form, is always becoming: writing in anxious forgetfulness of the conditions constituting it (realism) or writing in denial of the project thus constituted (modernism). It is as if only by forgetfulness or transgression is novel writing possible; but that, as we shall see, is because the novel is essentially antinomic, an impossible or contradictory practice.

The validity of the premises is derived in part from independent theoretical analysis, in part from their explanatory power, and in part from a morphological analysis of the most highly evolved exemplars of the species. It is evident that the explanation of the shifts in strategy and for the different degrees of explicitness in the premises must be the development, the deepening of social reification. After all, the novel begins in a world in which the bourgeoisie is a rising and non-dominant class, and develops into a mature form in a world where contradictions or limitations in their ideology are becoming apparent. Thus a complete account of the form of the novel would necessarily be a history of the novel. None the less, since the form of the novel only appears comparatively, across or through changes and developments, an account of 'the' form of the novel is a necessary preliminary to producing the corresponding history.

Lukács's first thesis is not practical, but theoretical; it is a direct deduction from the original premises. In a naturalised social world since no forms of meaningfulness are present in that world, because that world is not ethically constituted, then the value terms in accordance with which we comprehend and make that world intelligible can only be regulative *vis à vis* experience. In other words, the world of the novel can be totalised only in abstract terms (70); the form or meaning of a novel must be 'ideological' in the sense given above.

Lukács's practical demonstration begins at this juncture. A practical deliberation asks what is to be done in particular circumstances in order to realise specific ends. The end in question is the writing of an epic appropriate to our social world. How is one to go on writing under these conditions? If the principle of epic writing is the empirical world, but no forms are constitutive of that world, then, thesis two, the novel must be a dialectic of form-giving and representation, that is, one must attempt through the use of abstract concepts to create a totality of empirical experience which appears to be, although is not, immanent to that experience. Since form is not evident in experience, the necessary means to creating the desired appearance is to allow form to be either discovered or created. In either case, thesis three, form can only appear as not abstract if schematised, if, that is, it is represented as the outcome of a process (72–3). The novel will be a temporal, and not merely a geographical, adventure. Time and temporality must be constitutive of the represented world of the novel (120–30).

Each of the first three theses involves general reflections on the relation between form and life. They jointly suggest a dialectic between abstract form-giving and mimesis represented through a dynamic or constitutive temporal sequence. Lukács's fourth thesis is that we can represent this dialectic only if we adopt a biographical form of representation. The outward form of the novel is biographical (81); the novel appears as the story of an individual's life. Biographical form, in strategic terms functions as a counterweight to abstract, conceptual form; it gives the conceptual system an anchorage in the represented world. In a novel, we might say, an individual life is both what is represented and a means of representation. Like time, the self belongs to both transcendental (form-giving) and empirical (life) levels, it belongs to the form of representation and to the represented world. Although a formal constituent of the novel, whose function is determined by the need for representability, biographical form can accomplish this function only because the regnant ideology so licenses the centrality of individual experience.

Thesis five is a straightforward deduction from theses three and four: if form must be represented as becoming in connection with an individual life, then what becomes in precise terms must be the self. The inner form of the novel is the journey toward identity. If becoming were extrinsic, then biographical form could be put in the service of truths transcending the self. Traditional religious or didactic biographies are of this kind. If process were constitutive but biographical form extrinsic, then we would have that as yet mythological form: the socialist 'novel'. When the grammar of epic representation prescribes both process and biographical form then the self becomes both the form and content of the story.

Now because the novel is a dialectic of form-giving and mimesis on the one hand, and a representation of an individual's search for meaning on the other, then novel narration implicitly repeats novel narrative. Thesis six states that biographical form in the novel is always implicitly autobiographical. One cannot, in other words, privilege self and process as forms, and hence as constitutive, without simultaneously including the becoming of meaning in the text as an example of that process. The novel is a reflexive/reflective genre. For Lukács the paradigmatic novel is not, as is often claimed, the realistic novel of education, the *Bildungsroman*, for it lacks the requisite reflexivity; rather only that special *Bildungsroman*, the story of a life which ends with the hero beginning to write the story we have just read, comes near to matching Lukács's model. But even it fails, for there is one further step in the argument. If the novel is constitutively reflexive and self-conscious, if, that is, the novel is a dialectic movement from empirical to transcendental levels and back, a dialectic where the meaning of the narrative refers to its mode of narration, then that movement itself must be represented, given form. Irony is the novel's self-consciousness of itself as a self-conscious genre. Objectivity in the novel requires an author's ironising of his own form-giving activity, thus both admitting and dissembling reflexivity.

This way of presenting Lukács's argument, while making clear some of the conceptual connections he wishes to establish, represses the antinomies of the novel form and so the social content of those formal elements. Equally, without an awareness of those aspects of his argument, an awareness of the way in which the novel's objectivity and coherence is always immanently under threat, some of the complexity of the deliberation itself is dissipated. The task of the following argument is to fill in those absences.

3 'THE SENSE OF THE WORLD MUST
   LIE OUTSIDE THE WORLD'

The principle of the epic is the existing empirical world. The 'happy' epic is one which can find in experience the meaning of experience, where experience is already reduced to homogeneity through the work of a cultural symbolic elaboration. Strictly speaking, the happy epic is in part productive of what it represents, it functions to produce and reproduce the immanence of essence. None the less, since that capacity does not belong to epic writing on its own, because the epic can only function in that manner in particular social circumstances, Lukács often speaks of happy epics as if they were passive recorders of social life, as if they were a pure mimesis. The *authority* of happy epics resides in the represented world rather than in the act of representation. This is why Lukács can regard Dante as the last great writer of a happy epic. 'The totality of Dante's world is the totality of a *visual* system of concepts. It is because of this *sensual "thingness"*, this substantiality both of the concepts themselves and of their hierarchical order within the system, that completeness and totality can become constitutive structural categories rather than regulative ones' (70; emphasis mine). If, as Kant has it, all judgement requires both a passive, intuitive element (the principle of empiricism) and an active, conceptual element (the principle of rationalism), then the world of the happy epic is empirical, passive and hence visual. In the happy epic conceptual activity is collapsed into passive perception because the intuitions of the epic world are already, as it were, conceptualised and totalised. The fiction of passivity, signalled by the primacy of the perceptual, registers the experience of a social system in which even economic domination, as distinct from alienation and exploitation, can be regarded as an obligation involving an element of reciprocity. As Marx says of pre-capitalist modes of production: 'Each individual conducts himself only as a link, as a member of this community, as proprietor or possessor. The real appropriation through the labour process happens *under* these presuppositions, which are not themselves the product of labour but appear as its natural or divine presuppositions.'[26] Epic passivity figures these kinds of presuppositionality.

Although the writer of a happy epic, Dante for Lukács is a transitional figure. His transitional status manifests itself in three ways:

(i) his characters are already individuals, consciously 'placing themselves in opposition to a reality that is becoming closed to them' (68);

(ii) as consequence there is no completeness in life itself, rather 'the immanence of the meaning of life is present...only in the beyond: it is the perfect immanence of the transcendent' (59);

(iii) therefore, the totality of Dante's epic is 'architectural' rather than 'organic' (68).

Dante's totality is systematic, and hence conceptual in character ('On the whole the system follows Aristotelian–Thomist ethics.'[27]); yet, the divine grounding of the system allowed it none the less to have the character of a *given* reality, and as given it could be visualised, made substantial. The placement and image of the individual in eternity is the figure and fulfilment of his or her complete notion or concept (to use a Thomist term of art). This is Dante's figural realism in which the appearance of the individual 'in the other world is a fulfilment of their appearance on earth, their earthly appearance a figure of their appearance in the other world.'[28] Because in the beyond God's design is *actively* fulfilled, Dante's hierarchy is one of 'fulfilled postulates' (68), as opposed to the merely regulative character of novel postulates and the 'postulate-free organic nature of the older epics'.

The world of the novel is, tendentially, a reified world from which God has departed. A reified world is one in which, first, there is a 'disharmony between the interiority of the individual and the substratum of his actions' (79), that is, a world in which the normative principles governing action have retreated into interiority, in which norms have become (regulative) ideals rather than customary procedures; a world in which *Moralität* has displaced and replaced *Sittlichkeit*. Secondly, a reified world is one in which the 'outside world, which is stranger to ideals and an enemy of interiority', is unable to achieve real completeness; it is unable 'to find either the form of totality for itself as a whole, or any form of coherence for its own relationship to its elements and their relationship to one another' (79). By this Lukács means two things: on the one hand, objects, things, are experienced as commodities whose relations to one another are quantitative rather than qualitative; on the other hand, institutions are experienced as being 'autonomous' from one another, and hence without intrinsic (= value intelligible) connection with one another. From the perspective of Enlightenment ideology these now alienating experiences were goals to be achieved: extirpating the 'sacred' from everyday life, replacing allegorical or magical forms of connectedness with causal connections, making social forms instrumental. Indeed, Lukács's point about the totality can be stated simply as the thesis that the external world more and more comes to be regarded as impregnated with causal connections and no other.

Of this 'decoded' external world Lukács claims that neither its parts nor the whole can be represented, they defy 'any forms of directly sensuous representation' (79). As stated this thesis sounds patently false. However, it is clear that Lukács intends here only the thesis that 'facts' as such are meaningless: there exists no intelligible totality to represent, hence the 'parts' of the world are not experienced as parts of a totality (they do not of themselves signify their belongingness to a totality). The external world is discrete and heterogeneous; the world is simply all that is the case. Only if this is so can it be claimed that we have found the only true substance in ourselves. (Such a subject, of course, is not *in* the world at all: 'The subject does not belong to the world: rather, it is a limit of the world. Where *in* the world is a metaphysical subject to be found?') Thus, after claiming that the external world cannot be represented, Lukács continues, 'They [the part and whole of the external world] acquire life only when they can be related either to the life-experiencing interiority of the individual lost in their labyrinth, or to the observing and creative eye of the artist's subjectivity: when they become objects of mood or reflexion' (79).

The heterogeneity (fragmentation; reification; autonomisation) of the external world destroys the conditions for epic passivity. The 'death of God' has destroyed the authority of all given forms; no forms *qua* forms are *given*. The form of fragmentation has created the appearance of the isolated subject; and only the isolated subject now can *give* meaning to experience. One further premise is necessary before the first of Lukács's theses can be established. He says, 'The novel is the epic of an age in which the extensive totality of life is no longer directly given, in which the immanence of meaning in life has become a problem, *yet which still thinks in terms of totality*' (56; emphasis mine). Totality is for us a normative postulate; the idea (ideal) of totality remains valid, if only as an ideal. To experience this life as one of loss, as inadequate, partial, haunted by what ought to be but is not is to think in terms of totality. More precisely, and more significantly, the principle of totality (or 'unity' – the difference is important for Lukács) is operative both in the practice of literary production and of literary consumption. In literary production the principle of closure governs the plot construction, symbolic ordering and the organisation of what Barthes calls the hermeneutic code.[29] As we shall see, the idea of a meaningful totality is implicit in the very idea of a narrative. It is the intelligibility of the empirical world which is at issue in the novel, not, of course, as lived, which is the problem connecting social theory with political practice, but as livable, as a world in which in principle if not in fact sense can be made of life. Because unreconstructed literary criticism (consumption) depends upon isolating the lived from the livable, by reading aesthetic meaning as an autonomous, non-social mode of ordering, it assumes 'that the text will establish in *internal terms* . . . relationships that focus one's reflections on the *quality and significance* of the specific actions presented.'[30]

The principle of totality functions as a premise and not a normative postulate in Lukács's argument because he is not claiming, in this place, that literary works ought to seek to make empirical discourse intelligible : rather, he is asking, given such a principle is operative in literary production, how can it succeed? What is its relation to empirical discourse?

The external world cannot be represented. Let us render this statement in the following terms. We operate day to day with a practical ideology which stipulates that objects are in themselves just objects, perhaps useful or beautiful in the eye of the beholder, but of themselves meaningless. Things in themselves ought to be described in value-neutral terms. Our relations with others are in external terms contractual and instrumental. Practical discourses relating to things, institutions and the external relations between individuals (the practical ideology is ambivalent here, but on the whole claims relations between persons are only 'external' relations, contractual and instrumental – see, e.g. Locke, Hobbes, Nozick, etc.) of themselves have no intelligibility in the formal sense. To claim that the novel is mimetic is to claim that the novel uses these practical discourses, that, in part at least, it accepts the fact that the protocols governing practical discourses generally stipulate the value-neutrality thesis. A work licenses itself as mimetic by (a) indicating its acceptance of the empirical world as its principle (which is accomplished precisely by its employment of the forms stipulated by theses three, four and five); and (b) tokening its acceptance of the conventions and norms for descriptive practices stipulated by our practical ideology. In technical terms, this tokening is accomplished by procedures for naturalising a narrative; for example, by presenting descriptions of objects, gestures or bits of dialogue which have no significant place in the formal (plot, theme) economy of the work; by relativising descriptions to a presumed empirical observer, or by validating an observation by referring to a general presumption ('as everyone knows').[31] Such gestures authorise the mimetic level of a text.

Lukács states his first thesis in these terms.

In a novel, totality can be systematised only in abstract terms, which is why any system that could be established in the novel – a system being, after the final disappearance of the organic, the only possible form of a rounded totality – had to be one of abstract concepts and therefore not directly suitable for aesthetic form-giving. (70)

If intelligibility is not written into the extensive totality of the world, if the world is heterogeneous, then that which gives the world intelligibility must be abstract or conceptual in character. The world of the novel is Kantian: the manifold of intuitions is unsynthesised in formal (normative) terms; nothing is valuable in itself. What makes the world intelligible are abstract, a priori concepts. Every account of life, every way of ordering empirical discourse which would make it intelligible is an interpretation of that discourse in terms *of* a conceptual, theoretical system not immanent to empirical discourse. Meaning is active and conceptual; as such it is not 'visual' or 'perceptual'; what does not belong to the perceived world as such must therefore be abstract.

The autonomisation of the economy, the instrumentalisation of the political, the domination of use-value by exchange value, the removal of religious and ethical beliefs into a 'private' domain and, finally, the development of a cultural positivism separately and jointly mark a neutralising and/or naturalising of experience. When Lukács claims that form is abstract he does

not mean that we lack normative beliefs, he means only that
these are merely *beliefs*, they are not constitutive of the empirical
world. These beliefs state what ought to be or what should be or
what we would desire (wish) things to be; but as such, as oughts,
they equally state how things are not. Now if things are not as
they ought to be, then what are the grounds for these beliefs?
Whatever we take the grounds for belief to be – a priori reflection, conscience, intellectual intuition, faith – these grounds
are not validated in or by our practical ideology, or rather,
are validated as having significance and 'objectivity' only for the
individual concerned. Further, in so far as that practical
ideology is itself normative, e.g. one ought to interpret experience in causal, value-neutral terms (because 'naturally' the
world just is – is constituted as – causal), then value-beliefs not
only do not but they cannot (ever) constitute experience. More
precisely, the practical ideologies of modernity naturalise the
naturalistic interpretation of experience and thereby positively
exclude the possibility of formal, ethical or normative constitution. Consequently, if a novel were to claim that the world
could be different, could be empirically intelligible, then it
would have to forfeit or dispense with its mimetic intentions and
authority: it would be a utopian 'epic', an 'epic' of desire or
dream, a *pure* fiction. 'Any attempt at a properly utopian epic
must fail because it is bound, subjectively or objectively, to
transcend the empirical and spill into the lyrical or dramatic'
(46). Conversely, it is not surprising that 'serious' fiction often
ends with defeat, accommodation (marriage and domesticity
when the family could still be regarded as a 'natural' site, a
haven in a heartless world), submission. These tokens of mimesis
are equally verifications of the practical ideology which requires
defeat, which names its own inexorable necessities as natural.

4   FORM-GIVING AND MIMESIS:
    DIALECTICAL FICTIONS

What makes the novel important for Lukács is that it cannot
avoid the formal imperative: let life be intelligible. Since the
novel is epic in its ambitions it must both uphold the denial of
form sedimented in our practical ideology, and yet somehow

discharge its aesthetic obligation to render life whole. To deny the denial of form would entail forfeiting the novel's mimetic ambitions; to deny the place of form altogether would be to deny the novel's aesthetic ambitions. The aesthetic problem of the novel is just the problem of modernity, modernity's contradictory self-conception (as played out, for example, in Hegel's state and civil society doctrine) from within the confines of epic narrative.

The principle of totality governs the novel's aesthetic ambitions on the formal level. What, however, legitimates the operation of this principle? It is, I have suggested, the idea that we *presuppose* the *in principle* intelligibility of experience; that is, if not in fact then at least in principle life should be intelligible. In life, *counterfactually but in principle life is intelligible.* This is the principle behind aesthetic form-giving which gives it its weight; it is the principle that makes the aesthetic ethical, but the aesthetic can be ethical only because the ethical itself has already been rendered aesthetic (fictional). By this I mean the following. In Kant the objective, empirical world, the world of objects, desires, inclinations and ordinary psychological experience is governed by the principle of cause and effect. As constitutive of empirical experience nothing is allowed to escape the dictates of this principle. Since right action presupposes freedom, Kant must transpose the will and the law governing it – the Categorical Imperative or Moral Law – into a non-empirical or noumenal domain. Because for Kant space and time are forms of intuition, are the forms under which anything can be presented to us for cognition, then the ethical domain is outside of space and time. Kant's system images an almost complete reification of the social world; nothing outside the self corresponds to the ethical will; indeed, not even psychological life corresponds to the will since it too must submit to the reign of causal determination. Yet reification is not quite complete since we are still aware of ourselves as free beings through our awareness of the categorical imperative, that insuperable fact of reason which registers to us our absolute worth as ends in ourselves. As free and moral beings, however, we are confined to the noumenal world, that is, to a non-empirical existence.

Now, that Kant's two-world theory raises as many problems as it solves has been often noted.[32] Not only would all categorical demands be vain since they could not alter events in the phenomenal realm, but further, the moral world itself becomes implausibly attenuated since 'moral volition is ineluctably temporal. The will is tempted in time, decides in time, and . . . feels guilty or satisfied in time.'[33] Finally, the autonomy of ethics from the empirical sets sensuousness as such in opposition to morality, and hence renders happiness wholly external to moral right and worth. Kant provides a kind of recognition of these difficulties in his practical postulation of the immortality of the soul and the existence of God. These postulates are practical, negatively, because they do not extend our knowledge of the (intelligible or noumenal) world; positively, they are necessary for us to affirm for the sake of the categorical imperative which is itself taken as supremely authoritative for us as reasonable and rational beings. The postulate of the immortality of the soul, by legitimating the possibility of an infinite moral progress against sensuous temptation, allows us to image the possibility of sensuous (empirical) nature being brought into harmony with the demands of morality. The postulate of the existence of God allows us to image the possibility of the external world coming to harmonise with moral ideals so that ethical merit may be rewarded with happiness. In fine, the two postulates image the possible correspondence of morality with nature within and without.

What is significant here is that it is only with the assumption of these two postulates that ethical life becomes possible, coherent and intelligible: while the very necessity of the postulates affirms the impossibility of ethical life here and now. Reason makes these postulates because without them the principles of reason, the principles governing moral action, would place us in a practically or ethically intolerable situation were we to attempt to follow them. Roughly, we would have to pursue moral ends we knew to be in principle unachievable; but this is unacceptable since we cannot be obligated to do the impossible ('ought implies can'). Further, if we were to reject the postulates then we would have either to reject the moral law, and so become egoists; or pretend that the goals of ethical life were achievable here and now, thus becoming deluded visionaries.[34] Reason, then, is drawn into making the postulates in order to preserve coherence with itself: they are postulates of and for reason.

Moral life can follow the dictates of reason only by taking up an 'as if' stance: we must act as if moral perfection were possible, and as if morality will be rewarded with happiness if we are to act under the moral law; but we must act under the moral law in order to be reasonable and rational beings. This double 'as if' places moral reason into an imaginary space: since moral action presupposes the double 'as if', which in its turn projects an imaginary space where moral reason can be realised, then the inside of moral reason itself becomes a projection of the imagination. The imaginative supplement to moral reason thus becomes internal to it.

Because moral reason requires imaginative supplementation in order to harmonise with itself moral life comes to depend upon the imagination for its intelligibility. Hence an inversion occurs: because the ends or goals of moral life are possible only counterfactually, moral reason must be guided by imaginative projections – projections for which there are no sufficient empirical or rational guidelines – in its tasks of planning and legislation. Since we cannot have or conceive of the shape and structure of a moral life except through imaginative projections, projections which are given in only the vaguest outlines in the postulates, the task of rendering ethical life intelligible falls to the imagination. In fine, to say that the highest good is a necessary object of moral volition grounded in reason alone comes to mean that the essential ends of moral action are available only as fictions of reason. Since these fictions are necessary for reason, then the reasonableness of these fictions are alone capable of validating reason.[35]

Reason becomes contemplative when it finds itself unable to determine empirical reality. Positivism is an example of the effect of contemplation on cognition. In the ethical domain the effect of contemplation is to force reason into a beyond (*ein Jenseits*); in cultural terms the beyond finds a social place for itself in socially accredited and controlled acts of imagination. It is because ethical reason must imaginatively supplement itself that novelistic form-giving is weighted with the task of ethically and rationally authorising itself. Bereft of access to the empirical world via collective political action, the demand for the in principle intelligibility of life can only be met through aesthetic form-giving; the ethical figuring of empirical existence. The novel is the crisis of modern culture because it is the space, and the only space available to contemplative reason, where ethical reason and empirical reality can meet. It is then neither through accident nor arbitrary ideological assumptions that contemplative consciousness has so often chosen literary culture, and in especial the novel, as a site for ethical argumentation and ideological debate. That site is predetermined by the implicit confinement of ethics to an intelligible realm unspoiled by reification. That the realm itself is a product of reification goes unnoticed. The result of this confinement and the consequent inversion of the relation between reason and imagination, ethics and aesthetics, is to make an adequate analysis of the novel require the eliciting of those formal features of novel writing which reveal the ethical interior to what are overtly 'aesthetic' questions. The dialectic of form-giving and mimesis is the primary thematisation of that ethical interior.

Form, we have said, operates on two levels in Lukács's theory. On the one hand, form denotes meaningful coherence, what informs, gives order and meaning to experience. It is this sense of form which leads Lukács to emphasise the notion of totality since the opposite of totality is discontinuity and rupture, unreason and relativism. Form can only provide meaningful order if it collects and relates the discrete moments of experience to one another. On the other hand, form denotes those features of a discourse or domain which remain stable through variations of content. In this second sense genre conventions are aspects of literary form and syntactical structures are aspects of linguistic form. When Lukács claims that the novel is a dialectic of representation and form-giving he is using the notion of form in both senses.

If forms are not given by tradition, God or nature; if we have found the only true substance within ourselves; and if we have invented the creativity of spirit; then community and shared experiences of value and order are replaced by individual experience and volition. The primacy of individual experience and volition is an essential part of our practical ideology, and of the modes of discursive validation in bourgeois philosophy. This generates the problem of form in both its senses : the novelist can no longer rely on past history, fable, myth, traditional plots or religious and theological paradigms to structure his discourse

literarily (form in its second sense) *because* these forms no longer
carry social accreditation (form in its first sense). Form (in its
first sense) is for us a creature of creative subjectivity, of
individual volition. We, in our choices and actions, give
meaning to reality for according to our practical ideology there
is nothing transcending the individual will which could, in
principle, give meaning, significance or value to experience.
(The very use of the term 'experience' tokens this first person
prejudice.)

When it is said that novel is form-less, is not quite really a
genre, what is being referred to is the novel's acceptance of the
disappearance of form in its second sense. But this disappearance is explained by the disappearance of form in its first
sense. Conversely, because the disappearance of form in its
first sense entails (the relation between the two is conceptual
as well as causal) the disappearance of form in its second
sense, the aesthetic conventions which allow a writer to write,
the *problem* of form in its ethical sense is inscribed within
the novel as a genre from its beginnings. Aesthetic form in the
novel is ethical because it must compensate for the normative
slack in literary form brought about through the double
disappearance of form in its traditional sense.

The creation of form is the most profound confirmation of the existence of a dissonance. But in all other genres ... this affirmation of a
dissonance precedes the act of form-giving [e.g. in tragedy and comedy]
whereas in the novel it is form itself.... In the novel ... ethic – the
ethical intention – is visible in the creation of every detail and hence is,
in its most concrete content, an effective structural element of the work
itself. (72)

The *giving* form to the language of experience is the novelist's way
of 'going on', but it is a problematical way of going on because as
literary forms, as forms that lack validation from elsewhere, the
act affirms its inner lack of authority. To write, to go on writing,
there must be forms with which to write; the writer must give
form to the discourse of experience; but this act of form-giving
must register, overcome and re-register the lack of authority
intrinsic in these forms. The novel is an unstable and impossible
dialectic of form-giving and mimesis because the conditions
which require a writer to (internally) authorise his/her vision

deny that such authority can be had. (Of course, the literary modes of distribution, our practices of reading, learning to read (education), criticism and the like, are there to compensate this lack of authority, to recuperate the failure of form through, for example, a liberal, humanist ideology which promotes value pluralism, that is, the valorisation of subjectivity and the individual choice of values.[36] What the structure of the novel laments the culture of the novel exalts. It is as if only as aesthetic items, drawn into a sphere of their own, that ethical forms can find a kind of social validation. It is as if instead of 'literary' forms being parasitic on extra-literary, communal values, as was the case in pre-capitalist social formations, now the authentication of values is literary upon which the non-literary is parasitic. Could not this reversal be called the fictionalising of meaning? Is it not the dark underside of Phillipe Soller's easy statement that 'the novel is the manner in which society comes to conceive of itself. Our identity depends on the novel, what others think of us, what we think of ourselves, the way in which our life is imperceptibly moulded into a whole. How do others see us if not as a character from a novel?'[37])

Form may be manifested in the novel in a variety of ways: through plot, imagery, symbolism, or conceptual schemata governing the narrative (e.g. 'Pride goeth before the fall'; 'The just get their due rewards'; 'Love and death beat together').[38] However manifested in a text form is essentially conceptual and abstract in character; and this for the simple reason that form necessarily transcends the protocols of the practical ideology which the novel must adopt if it is to claim verisimilitude for itself. Thus there is inevitably and always a shift from constitutive to regulative, from judgement to imperative: 'It ought to be that pride goeth before the fall'; 'The just ought to get their due rewards'. The demands of mimesis revoke the imperatives of form. But this distance between form and life is more than defeat, a normative ellipsis; it is also an enabling condition constitutive of novel writing. The novel, unlike any other genre, thrives on its essential impossibility. 'The objectivity of the novel', Lukács tells us, 'is the mature man's knowledge that meaning can never quite penetrate reality, but that, without meaning, reality would disintegrate into the nothingness of inessentiality' (88). The energy and creative impetus of the novel derives from the attempt to negotiate this unfillable space. Indeed, according to Lukács, the practices of the novel, the imperatives of form, reproduce of themselves the conditions precipitating their defeat: 'The incapacity of ideas to penetrate reality *makes reality heterogeneous and discrete*' (80; emphasis mine). The writer's quest for immanence turns on itself to become inventiveness, prolixity and rhetorical excess.[39] Each threat of formal closure, each moment where the fact of form imposing itself on life might become manifest is countered by the invocation of heterogeneity, by swerves in writing or narrative which reassert the unassimilability of life to form.

Now an assumption running through this argument, an assumption upon whose validity the soundness of the argument turns, is that form requires an 'immanence of meaning', that only as fallen, inadequate or defeated are forms 'ought to be's'. Kant marks this sense of the fallen character of categorical imperatives in his distinction between holy wills and finite wills (a metaphysical hypostatisation of the distinction between *Moralität* and *Sittlichkeit*). It is only because form requires immanence that the creation of forms is the affirmation of dissonance; it is only because form requires immanence that dissonance is a crisis of authority. While the substantiation of this thesis would require an elaborate defence of the Hegelian critique of Kantian ethics, we can glimpse these normative contours to the practices of the novel in Lukács's adumbration of an ethics of the novel.

We have already seen how the refusal of the demands of mimesis and too firm a desire to see form as immanent produces 'utopian' fiction; nor is it any accident that we contrast utopian (idealist) with realist. We also recognise another route to dissolving the resistance of reality to form, namely the relativisation of world to mood. The lyrical novel dissolves the world in order to realise form, not of course as an extensive totality, but now as an intensive totality. Form becomes insight, illumination, lyrical moments and spots of time. Satiric fiction refuses dissonance by presupposing the authority of form, but the presupposition is here empirical, 'it narrows down the objective form to a subjective one and reduces the totality to a mere aspect of itself' (75). Finally, Lukács argues, the novel alone has a caricatural twin nearly indistinguishable from itself, namely, the entertainment novel. The difference is only that in the entertainment novel nothing is at issue. In the novel 'because of the regulative, hidden nature of the effective binding and forming ideas, because of the apparent resemblance of empty animation to a process whose ultimate content cannot be rationalised, superficial likeness can almost lead to the caricature being mistaken for the real thing' (73). Lukács's point here is that since form is, in part, ethical *intent* it is possible with the novel to produce an appearance of the real thing which is different only in the intent not being present. More generally, Lukács's thought here is that we can come to appreciate the normative nature of the rules governing the novel practice of writing by noting how deviations from those formal norms produce subgenres that are recognisable as deviations. As in all other things, deviations affirm the norm. While we may have extra-formal grounds for evaluating the subgenres of the novel differently than does Lukács, since those sub-genres are formally best understood as formal strategies for traversing and closing the gap between form and life, and thus 'solving' the question of authority by dissolving the problem, his analysis does confirm and discover the locus of the novel, the aspect of form which is written in and by the social totality: that form ought to be immanent to life and form cannot be immanent to life. By calling this an ethics of the novel I mean that it is a formal procedure for identifying and analysing sub-genres of the novel which because of the ethical meaning of form in the novel gives evaluative weight to the different kinds of practices.

The novel is a dialectic of form-giving and mimesis, where form demands immanence and the world mimetically transcribed resists form. Edward Said, in his *Beginnings*, reworks Lukács's dialectical analysis, beginning with the Koran instead of Homer, in terms of a dialectic between authority and molestation.[35] Authority in Said corresponds, roughly, to form-giving; it is the author's capacity to create a fictive world capable of augmenting the real one, of controlling and maintaining that world. Molestation corresponds, roughly, to mimesis (life); it is the author's awareness that his authority is a sham, that his world is fictive, 'a consciousness of one's duplicity, one's confinement to a fictive, scriptive realm ...'. Like Lukács, Said regards the interaction of his two categories as enabling conditions and restraints on inventiveness. Further, Said clearly believes his analysis to be social, to be a reading of the novel as the model *secular* narrative.[36] Where Said differs from Lukács – there is, I think, throughout Said's analysis of the novel a continuing 'formal' resemblance – is that his two categories are (socially conditioned) forms of awareness rather than social categories proper. As such Said either cannot explain *why* a writer (a character) should feel molested, or he explains the awareness of molestation as the inevitable consequences of secularisation, of the death of God and the productivity of spirit. But, as I argued in the previous chapter, productivity (authority) is not necessarily problematic, we need not suffer molestation. In order for molestation to be comprehensible one requires on the one hand, the Marxist analysis of life, that is, some account of reification, institutional autonomisation and the 'non-representability' of the external world; on the other hand, one must explain the authority of authority, that is, show how form requires immanence, and thereby speaks its own, non-present, conditions of validation. Fictiveness, in the specific sense Said rightly attributes to it, namely a sense of confinement and inadequacy (illusoriness) in relation to reality, is not a function of secularity alone, but more, the isolation of form in 'fiction' which is the institutional corollary of the ethical frozen in the contemplative. Only categorial contemplation can explain molestation.

IV

The Novel's Schematism : Binding Time

narrativity and temporality are closely related – as closely as . . . a
language game and a form of life.

(Paul Ricoeur)

1 SCHEMATISM

If form in the novel is abstract and conceptual while the world of
the novel is secular and causal, then in order for conceptual
forms to attach themselves to empirical life they must be
schematised, that is, they must be routed through a temporal
sequence which can be matched to empirical events which
possess a different order of determination. The novel, then shifts
between form-giving and mimesis by shifting between two
different forms of determination: a causal order of events and a
narrative (formally figured) order of events. The reified dualism
between cause and form has been theoretically legitimated in
formalist and structuralist narratology as the distinction between story and discourse, *fabula* and *sjuzhet*.[1] Story corresponds
to the sequence of events and actions apart from their manifestation in discourse; the level of story in the novel is governed
by the practical ideology and naturalising techniques governing
novelistic mimesis generally. Discourse is the in-formed narration of those events. In their discursive presentation events are
bound together as parts to a whole; initially, or at its lowest
level, this binding occurs at the level of plot where earlier events
generate later events, and later events fulfil or complete earlier
events. Progressive binding ties together the action – consequence – action pattern of human action with our epistemic
capacity to follow stories in their movement through time.
Retrospective binding ties together the recollective ordering of
the past into intrepretive sequences with our capacity to have

109

followed a story (see the point of the story, get the joke, see the figure in the carpet).[2] In this latter mode we reinterpret beginnings from the perspective of the end, eliciting from this totality a theme, thought or meaning. For us, since the causal order of event determination is quasi-autonomous from the levels of plot and theme, then narrative activity is precisely the redemption, recuperation or transformation of succession into meaning. Given the quasi-autonomy of causal succession, however, the novel inevitably remains torn between the causal and extra-causal modes of ordering, with the effect that writers, sometimes, explain a meaning as both a causal effect and as an appropriate conclusion to a discursively grasped sequence of actions.[3] (Might realism be just this attempt to satisfy the demands of both orders of event determination simultaneously?) Thus, the more reified the represented world of the novel, the greater will be the distance separating event and plot, which is to say, the more difficult it will be to make a plot (and hence a theme) out of the presented events; and the more difficult this primitive narrative act the more meaning will come to reside at the level of form alone, and hence the more questionable will be the authority of the narrative or, at least, the less versimilitude will be a possible source of authority.

For example, the most direct way of authorising a conceptual scheme is to have the attunement between story and discourse be sufficiently precise that form appears to emerge from the story itself. Such is the goal in so-called novels of plot, where actions and events appear to connect of their own accord (naturally) to yield thereby the appearance of a meaningful but concrete life. The more strained, artificial or melodramatic is plot the greater will be the distance separating form and life; the finer their attunement the greater will be the coherence between ideology and its empirical substratum. Tendentially, the history of the novel manifests a decline in the novel of plot.[4] As a consequence, we would expect to find modernist writing emphasising rather than concealing (or figuratively closing) the gap between form and life, discourse and story; plot to be minimised, theme to be taken as dirempt from events, and the activity of writing (imagination) valorised. Between these two extremes (somewhere), between the novel of plot and the modernist opening of the gap between story and discourse, stands the realist novel.

Now to claim that the novel can be properly thought of as an attempt to come to terms with time, to say that novels are somehow uniquely concerned with the struggle against time is not to claim that time or temporality, the passing of time and the movement of history were not issues for previous genres. Rather, it is to argue that time enters the world of the novel in a unique manner. This uniqueness can be located at the intersection of two theses: (i) time in the novel is divorced from eternity so that the meaning of a temporal sequence can no longer be referred to (necessarily) unchanging models or paradigms; and (ii) empirical time tendentially comes to be governed by simple causal connections between series of events. At the level of temporality itself thesis (ii) can be restated as claiming that tendentially temporal ordering becomes divorced from non-quantitative considerations. Thesis (i) is about an alteration in the locus of forms, and corresponds to the productivity of spirit; thesis (ii) is about modifications to life, and is a direct product of reification. Thesis (i) without thesis (ii), I have argued, is not in itself problematic; thesis (ii) without thesis (i) would sanction, for example, some type of theological fatalism. Only the two theses together, working within a horizon of individualism, yield time as a specifically modern phenomenon.

The ideal or optimistic fusion of the two theses remains *Robinson Crusoe*, where nature is tamed by a 'free' cultural labour, and time triumphantly ordered and mastered through the prospective and retentive strategies of prayer/calculation and inventory/justification.[5] More generally, the satisfaction of the 'genealogical imperative' occasioned by the union of (i) and (ii) is achieved by finding schemata which can give a conceptual system temporal correlates. Prayer/calculation and inventory/ justification as prospective and retentive strategies do not themselves bind time; they are narrational schemata, and hence narrational strategies for giving temporal form to antecedently assumed conceptual systems. None the less, the invocation of those systems can be legitimated only to the degree to which some schemata can be discovered for them. Their applicability to experience as schematised is their legitimation, or in Kant's terms, to have a schema for a concept is to give a pure or abstract concept empirical value. (Does it need to be said here that the need for verification is itself a symptom of the two theses, of the divorce of form from life?) Kant states his schematism theory thus: 'Thus an application of the category (= abstract concept or form) to appearances (= life) becomes possible by means of the transcendental (= belongs to the level of discourse as opposed to story) determination of time, which, as the schema of the (pure) concepts of understanding, mediates the subsumption of the appearances under the category' (B 177 = A 138). Kant's thought here is that one might possess a concept without knowing how or being quite able to apply that concept to experience. Such a possibility is common enough in cases where the concept in question is theoretical (e.g. the concept of a 'neutrino'), or carries a more than usual theoretical burden (e.g. 'tadpole'). Now certain concepts, categories, are not empirical in origin according to Kant; they are a priori concepts which we employ in synthesising (ordering) experience; and they are necessary concepts for us because without them experience would not be intelligible. Since the categories are necessary for experience and all experience is temporal, a result Kant argues for in the Aesthetic, what the categories and empirical phenomena necessarily share is time. Therefore, the categories will be the fundamental modes of temporal organisation; and the schema of each category will be its specific way of structuring time. Schemata are transcendental determinations of time (where transcendental means 'necessary for the possibility of experience').[6]

For the novel schemata are narrational strategies for rendering normative or evaluative concepts empirical. Since we take the concepts in question (justice, meaning, salvation, happiness, etc.) to be constitutive of our moral life, without them the meaningfulness of life would evaporate, then the schemata for these (theoretical/ideological) familiar concepts will be transcendental determinations of our moral experience through time, or so the novel wagers. (Our suggestion of the place of time in the novel, thesis (i), is the Lukácsian equivalent of Kant's argument in the Aesthetic that all experience is necessarily temporal, and therefore it is time alone which can and must play the mediating role between pure concept and empirical experience.) Of course, for Kant the non-empirical purity of the categories is guaranteed by their a priori origin. For the novelist the non-empirical character of these concepts is an historical result (of reification), a social fact; it is as if these concepts had suddenly lost their grounding in experience and could find no way back in. The practice of novel writing is the way back in, as if the novel itself were a vast schematising procedure, a search for modes of temporal ordering which would give our normative concepts access to the world; not just access, though, but a constitutive role in our comprehending experience. Only as transcendentally constitutive, as more than individual desires or views, are those concepts at issue. Our earlier point about the decline of plot in the novel can now be reformulated: the more the divorce of form from life becomes manifest in the novel the more fragile, artificial or purely literary will novelistic schemata appear. The schematism procedure of the novel, which is but a more precise characterisation in terms of narrative strategy of the dialectic between form and life, is the 'imaginary' core of novel fictions, the space or site of the peculiarly novelistic imagination. Given what was said in the previous chapter about the respective roles of reason and imagination, and the inversion in their relation brought about by the reification of reason, Kant's locating of the schematism procedure underlines this result in a way that could have been anticipated: 'The schema is in itself always a product of the imagination.... This representation of a universal procedure of imagination in providing an image for a concept, I entitle the schema of this concept' (B 179–80). Only through the transcendental imagination can our a priori concepts have temporal form, and only as temporalised can our a priori concepts be granted empirical status. The transcendental imagination stands between and unites the pure categories of the understanding with the pure manifold of intuition (sensibility) by rendering the former into modes of time consciousness; thus, transcendentally understood, all forms of synthesis are forms of temporal synthesis. If we were to read this claim metaphysically it would be tempting to regard the imagination as the common root of our passive sensibility and our active intellects, for if these two disparate faculties necessary for knowledge are to be united then there must be a third thing which unites them and which can ground their difference (as active and passive) without itself being subject to it.[6a]

If we do not follow this metaphysical speculation it is not

because we wish to deny the artificiality of the active/passive distinction as Kant formulates it, or deny that the distinction so formulated needs overcoming. Rather, we wish to insist that such an overcoming is premature until we have located the *historical* sources of the separation in question, that is, until we have grasped the historical meaning of the separation of sensibility and intellect as formulated by Kant and thereby recovered the historical meaning of the claim that it is the *imagination* which mediates between the two. From this perspective our earlier contention that Kant requires an imaginative supplementation to legislative reason in order to preserve and make possible the rationality of legislative reason takes on a slightly altered sense.

The restriction of the Categorical Imperative to *discrete* acts of legislation now becomes the sign or mark of its inability to determine the external world for as discrete each act of legislation may be regarded as atemporal; but this atemporality, this indifference to past or future, except in so far as the usual consequences of an action are part of what is considered in judging its moral worth, is what makes *intentions* the objects of moral legislation. Discrete acts of legislation, imaging a kind of ethical atomism, reduces legislative reason to the unreason of ethical worth 'at a moment', making acts (or intentions) as such the ultimate objects of moral evaluation. This, however, would lead to the view that ethical life as such is pointless above and beyond what is revealed or produced by any particular action. Kant's 'Postulates of Pure Practical Reason', then, can be seen as righting ('writing') this state of affairs by providing the will with an end or goal, a *telos*, which provides a principle of selection for various life projects and simultaneously images this relating of our different actions and policies to one another in terms of a progress towards both autonomy (self-mastery) and happiness (a world adequate to the autonomous will). The imagination here gives duration and purpose to legislative reason, returning and offering to the Categorical Imperative the reason of its rationality, by inscribing the discrete acts of moral legislation within a temporal *whole* which thus becomes the rational substratum of those acts.

The incapacity of Kantian reason, or our reason, to determine empirical experience, the meaning of the retreat of form into interiority, is its incapacity to determine a life as a whole, as moving through time to some end. Conversely, we can project the image of our life as a whole only through an act of imagination, as an 'as if' possibility; but that imaginative projection itself forms the true foundation for the rationality of our particular acts of moral legislation. Ethical time, time from the perspective of pure practical reason alone, that is, time from the perspective of contemplative reason, is atomistic, its discreteness negating the presumed rationality or worth of particular acts. The imagination binds the temporal atoms of ethical legislation together by giving it a temporal form, a protentive – retentive structure, which makes possible the image of life as a whole. On this reading the 'Postulates' just are the transcendental schema for categorical legislation. None the less, this thesis is ambivalent between the claim that the Postulates' provide only the temporal form, the protentive – retentive structure for moral legislation, and the claim that they provide themselves an image of the whole. Read either way, however, the point remains that categorical legislation must be 'imaginatively' supplemented, and this supplementation involves making categorical legislation into a form of temporal synthesis in virtue of which the whole of a life becomes the integrator and foundation for the worth of its parts. The fictions of a moral god and the immortality of the soul do indeed offend our desire for theoretical purity when we read Kant, yet, I want to argue, the rational impulse behind those fictions is precisely what novel fictions, the institution of the novel preserves. This feature of Lukács's argument was correctly grasped by Benjamin in 'The Storyteller' where he asserts that we read novels in order to learn or gain a sense of 'the meaning of life' (see section 4 below), a meaning that is not available to us empirically (non-imaginatively). On this view the meaning of life is a conception of an individual's life as a whole, a whole which gives meaning (worth) to its parts through an act of temporal synthesis. Of course, there is no a priori reason why the concept of a life as a whole should be temporal in character; that it is so for us, and for the novel, is demanded by the secularity of our world.

We can only temporalise the concepts constitutive of our moral life as an act of imagination, where imaginative activity just is the giving of temporal form to the abstract concepts of 'reason'. Part, then, of the 'fictionality' of the novel derives from the fact that the binding of form to life is a narrative act, an imaginative diagram (A $142 =$ B 181), the producing of a certain kind of narrative form which can anchor conceptual forms in the represented world; but narrative form here is temporal form. Thus the novel is the literary form of our time because it takes up the burden of the temporalising of form which the secularity of the modern world simultaneously demands and refuses. (I shall explicate the constitutive character of this refusal in the next chapter.) The novel's schematising operations render concepts temporal. The productivity of the novel is its adding to abstract concepts a temporal meaning; but that productivity is the productivity of an imagining, providing a temporal schema for a concept. The so-called 'other life' which novel fictions provide is not a life meaning which invokes terms or concepts different from those we ordinarily employ; rather, it is those same terms used as temporal synthesisers which make novel lives appear as different from our own.

Only through recognising how the fragmentation of ethical life, the contemplative reduction of ethical life to interiority (*Moralität*) effects an atomising detemporalisation of normative subjectivity can we come to understand why novel acts of imagination are fundamentally temporal in character. If moral life requires imaginative supplementation in order to preserve and ground its rationality, then in cultural terms the institution of the novel becomes a kind of societal transcendental imagination. Thus the distance between the novel and its world becomes the distance between transcendental and empirical, the parts of moral life and their now displaced substratum. What distinguishes Lukács's account of the novel from all others is his unequivocal recognition of its transcendental function together with its separation from empirical life. That separation is what makes the temporal 'whole' of life an imaginative production.

Despite his reputation for having specified the problem of time in the novel, Lukács is generally uninterested in either the genealogical imperative or the schematism procedures specific to the novel; rather, he focuses his attention on a moment of deviation from the general procedure where the problem of time becomes manifest, and the obstacles to binding life to form are revealed in their historical specificity. More charitably, one might even say that he focuses on that moment where the schematism procedure manifests itself for the first time as a textual operation (an act of imagination) which thereby reveals the problem of time in the novel. To read him this way will take some effort on our part. Still, our approach to the topic will have to be indirect because Lukács's analysis of time occurs in Part II of *The Theory of the Novel* in the course of his discussion of Flaubert's *Sentimental Education*, and the methodological approach he takes there is at odds with the methodology of Part I which we have been following.

In the 1962 Preface to the work Lukács states that it was composed of a left ethic and a right-wing epistemology, that is, from his emergent Hegelianism and the fashionable neo-Kantianism of the time. The left-wing elements of the book dominate the analyses of Part I; the employment of neo-Kantian ideal types dominates the argument of the second part of the work. While it is tempting to consider 'the novel' of Part I an ideal type construction, we have argued that this is not the case. The analyses of Part I are interpretations of a practice. Lukács's left ethic is nothing but a recognition of the precariousness of form-giving in a world resistant to meaningful forms; it reflects the novel's own essential unhappy consciousness as a genre. 'The objectivity of the novel is the mature man's knowledge that meaning can never quite penetrate reality, but that, without meaning, reality would disintegrate into the nothingness of inessentiality' (88). Elsewhere Lukács states: 'The creation of forms is the most profound confirmation of the existence of a dissonance. But in all other genres . . . this affirmation of a dissonance precedes the act of form-giving, whereas in the novel it is the form itself' (72). Not all novelistic enterprises self-consciously exemplify this thesis; we know, for example, that Balzacian realism was premised on the assumption that writing was a re-presentation of the social world in which the interpretative elements stood outside the recording, representational project. No matter how deeply the conventions of realism have become embedded in our anticipations of how the world looks, it is none the less the case that the fictional forms of realism belie the conditions for the production of the novel:

the distance between form and experience. For Lukács, the production of novelistic totalities is necessarily a self-defeating process. Social theory totalises reality historically and structurally, explaining the nature and origins of the dualisms which permeate our lives. The novel must take these same dualisms not as structural features of reality, but as strangely contingent absences that the mediation of form is capable of overcoming; yet, and at the same time, by taking the given world seriously, the novel should show the real impossibility of that formal overcoming. Because of its distance from both theory and action the novel is inevitably tempted to underplay the intractability of reality or to divinise the powers of language and imagination. Ironic structuring, so pervasive in modernist writing, represents a way of avoiding these extremes without abandoning novel writing altogether; but this is no more than a recognition of the limits of the novel, it is not a real solution to the world's fragility.

2   THE RIGHT-WING EPISTEMOLOGY

Part II of *The Theory of the Novel*, which is an 'attempt at a typology of the novel form', is a disaster for precisely the reason Lukács notes in his Preface; its employment of a right-wing epistemology. He there describes this methodology as involving the formation of 'general synthetic characteristics – in most cases only intuitively grasped – of a school, period, etc., then to proceed by deduction from these generalizations to the analysis of individual phenomenon, and in that way to arrive at what we claimed to be a comprehensive overall view' (13). The proposed typology is governed by the question of whether the soul of the protagonist is incommensurable with reality because, either, the 'world is narrower or it is broader than the outside world assigned to it as the arena and substratum of its actions' (97). The first sort of incommensurability, where the narrowness of the protagonist's vision leads him to forget the space between vision and reality, and to treat reality as if it corresponded to his vision, is exemplified by *Don Quixote*. Lukács's second type, where the soul is felt to be 'wider and larger than the destinies life has to offer' (112), is supposedly typified by *Sentimental Education*.

It is hard to conceive of why Lukács ever had any faith in this proposal. First, while it might appear as analytically true that if the soul and the world are incommensurable this must be because the soul is narrower or wider than what the world has to offer, this is not a valid deduction. Normally, the lack of commensurability between the soul and the world is not a function of the general characteristics of the protagonist's vision, but rather is a question of particular desires and visions being defeated by specific social circumstances. Frédéric and Quixote differ in that Quixote takes the world to correspond to his vision of it while Frédéric, whose responses to the world are every bit as inappropriate as Quixote's, does not attempt to impose his desires on a recalcitrant reality but rather retreats from the world into fantasy and dream. It is what these characters do with their visions which distinguishes them. Visions themselves may differ in terms of breadth, but in this sense Quixote's vision may be regarded as richer and more complex than Frédéric's. Breadth of vision compared with the breadth of the world seems too metaphorical a basis on which to build a typology.

Second, why should Lukács suppose that although the novel must be characterised in historico-philosophical terms, particular types of novel may be phenomenologically distinguished on the basis of an analytic schema which is both historically and theoretically underdetermined? Third is the curious fact that Lukács simply drops from his account in Part II all the complex distinctions developed in Part I. Why should the distinction between the novel of 'abstract idealism' (*Don Quixote*) and the novel of the 'romanticism of disillusionment' (*Sentimental Education*) cancel all the differences among lyrical, satiric, essayistic and entertainment novels? Moreover, what of other traditional distinctions among the novel of manners, the adventure novel, the picaresque novel, and so forth? The fourth problem is directly related to the preceding point. Genre represent conventional functions of language which generate particular word – world or word – thought relations that guide the reader in his encounter with a text. If genre, then, create the conditions for coherent readings of texts, how can any typological scheme legitimately bypass them completely? Lukács's purpose in drawing up his typology might be such that considerations of genre are irrelevant; but then we should want to know more about what his purposes are exactly. Fifth, the ironic structure of the novel entails that the form of the novel must contain a kind of openness, one which allows for unprecedented development. Yet Lukács's polar typology anticipates its own systematic closure, viz. the synthesis of the two analytically-determined types. Lastly, the typological procedure itself, which produces only analytic classifications, stands methodologically in direct opposition to the totalising movement of Part I. In brief, the theoretical values immanent in the dialectical procedures of Part I are ignored in the analyses of Part II. It is for these and associated reasons that the analyses of Part II are unsatisfactory; their unsatisfactoriness reflects not at all on the achievements of Part I.

3   THE ROMANTICISM OF DISILLUSIONMENT

Although Lukács's typology is theoretically inadequate, his account of the romanticism of disillusionment works well as an account of a type of novel in which the divorce between form and life becomes the overt theme around which the novel turns. In Lukácsian terms, such novels are exemplars of the novel form itself.

The historical premise for romantic disillusionment is a state of the world in which desire is displaced both from it and from any imagined version – past, present, future or mythical – of it. 'The utopian longing of the soul is a legitimate desire, worthy of being the centre of the world, only if it is absolutely incapable of being satisfied in the present intellectual state of man, that is to say, incapable of being satisfied in any world that can be imagined or given form' (115). While it is difficult to judge whether this curious specification of the conditions necessary to legitimate a certain kind of novel has ever been fulfilled, it is true to say that with the defeat of the revolutions of 1848 the world could be imaginatively reduced to this from the vantage point of a Flaubert, that is, the post-1848 world of France was no longer a challenge to the 'l'idiot de la famille'. Revolutionary failure provided the conditions for a writing which derealised the world of praxis or, what is the same, lets writing show itself to be the only praxis. This is why, I shall argue, that just as it is often said that Emma Bovary's death was the result of the fatality of

Flaubert's style, it is even more pronouncedly the case that the revolution of 1848 was a victim of his style.

Lukács continues his argument by claiming that the immoderate elevation of subjectivity involved in the romanticism of disillusionment has defeat as its precondition, 'the abandonment of any claim to participation in the shaping of the outside world' (117). This statement is no more than an elaboration of the original premise. It is, however, important to note that Lukács considers these theses to apply to the protagonist of the novel. There should be no question here that they describe authorial and not protagonist values. To say: 'Life becomes a work of literature, but as a result man becomes the author of his own life and at the same time the observer of that life as a created work of art' (118) comes much closer to describing Flaubert's reduction of reality to writing and the consequent god-like perspective he is allowed over his fictional realm, than it does to the ill-fated, inconsequential dreams of Frédéric Moreau.

What makes Frédéric's dreams, plans and schemes ill-fated and inconsequential is not the resistance of reality, but the ironic contours which Flaubert's writing gives to them. Two examples must suffice. In the first Frédéric has just left a dinner at the end of which Madame Arnoux has held out her hand to him to say good-bye. He is in transports of ecstasy. In this mood he feels his soul swelling, a greatness in him blossoming.[7]

He had been endowed with an extraordinary talent, the object of which he did not know. He asked himself in all seriousness whether he was to be a great painter or a great poet; and he decided in favour of painting, for the demands of this profession would bring him closer to Madame Arnoux. So he had found his vocation. The object of his existence was now clear, and there could be no doubt about the future. (61*)

We know Frédéric will not be a painter not by our foreknowledge of his abilities, but by the circumstances and manner in which Flaubert has Frédéric make his decision; as if one could decide to be a great painter or poet; or indeed, one could makes such a decision on the basis of the proximity it will allow to a woman. Similarly, we know from the following account the Frédéric will fail in his plans to be a statesman.

The banker was definitely a splendid fellow. Frédéric could not help thinking of his advice; and soon he was dazzled by a vision which made his head swim. The great figures of the Convention passed before his eyes. It seemed to him that a magnificent dawn was about to break.... Now was the time for him to throw himself into the movement.... He already saw himself in a waistcoat with lapels and a tricolour sash; and this longing, this hallucination became so strong that he confessed it to Dussardier. (297*)

Frédéric does not know that all dreams must succumb; nor does he attempt to fashion his own life by making it a work of literature. That is for Flaubert. Frédéric is a mediocre man; the content of his mediocrity is the ironic style which permeates the generation of his projects.

The moment of the romanticism of disillusionment is conditioned by the conditions for the novel in general together with particular historical circumstances. The creative self, which forms a constitutive moment of the novel, becomes the whole of reality, the only thing of worth when fictional forms themselves no longer contain the possibility of transfiguring the discourse of experience. Two features of this situation call themselves to our attention if we ask what is involved in this elevation of the creative self. First, the reduction of reality to illusion: the Second Empire is an illusion, just as the Emperor is an imitation Napoleon. Once this illusoriness of reality is grasped, the reality, the authority of art can assert itself. One critic makes this point nicely in connection with Emma Bovary's beauty. 'Like the novel, she is a made object whose express intention is to spite her "natural" failure as a mother and wife.... [When describing her] Flaubert uses words to create an altogether nonvisual, hence literary impression: Emma is a beautiful verbal object...'[8] The efficacy of writing replaces and triumphs over nature and society. And in the verbal universe the creative self is God: all-powerful, malign or malicious as he pleases.

4   Time as Form

Lukács clearly grasps the artistic problems of the kind of writing Flaubert engages in. If writing itself is to dominate, then nothing in the writing must give solace to the reader: the claims of the protagonist's soul and the demands of reality must be equally dissolved into nullity. But this leads to the possibility of a work having only 'the ineffective, monotonous brilliance of a surface in the process of decomposition.... The novel remains a beautiful yet unreal mixture of voluptuousness and bitterness, sorrow and scorn, but not a unity; a series of images and aspects, but not a life totality' (120). In fine, we are faced not with the problem of the unity of representations – this can be accomplished by formal means – but with the representation of a unity. It is here Lukács begins his famous discussion of time and the novel.

Lukács correctly perceives why it is that in the novel alone is 'time posited together with form' (122). 'Time', he says, 'can become constitutive only when the bond with the transcendental home has been severed' (ibid.). In less ornate terms, time becomes constitutive when all that resists the powers of time has been eliminated; and the thesis that we have invented the productivity of spirit entails just that: forms, meanings, essences, all are products of time, and all are subject to the laws of disintegration and decay ordained by time. This same conclusion might have been anticipated from a different angle. The standpoint of the Kantian philosophy and the standpoint of the novel are almost formally identical. Now it is central to Kant's system that all knowledge, all representation is temporal. By paying attention to how we come to represent the world we come to recognise the simple fact that experience comes to us *seriatim* in a stream of transience, and yet it must be capable of being held together in a unity of representation. Forms of understanding, what the creative self creates, function to hold together in a single mental image, a complex mental act the temporal string of events present to consciousness. Thinking, representation, knowledge for the Kantian philosophy is a wholly temporal affair. As Lukács must have known, for Kant's system it is necessarily true that time and form are posited together. The duality within time, time as essential to thought and to the object of thought, explains why psychologistic novels emphasising the self's journey to meaning, and the more plotted novel with its largely biographical contours are equally temporally constituted.

If, for us, time provides the conditions for any possible meaning, it also contains the conditions for the corruption of all meaning. 'In the novel, meaning is separated from life [we cannot find the Kantian 'schemata' by which we can attach moral form to experience], and hence the essential from the temporal; we might almost say that the entire inner action of the novel is nothing but a struggle against the power of time' (122). Generally Lukács concedes that time is the corrupting, disintegrating agent against which the novel's protagonist wages. In a remarkable passage, however, he argues that in *Sentimental Education* Flaubert conquers time with time, and thereby generates a represented unity.

The unrestricted, uninterrupted flow of time is the unifying principle of the homogeneity that rubs the sharp edges off each heterogeneous fragment and establishes a relationship – albeit an irrational and inexpressible one – between them. Time brings order into the chaos of men's lives and gives it the semblance of a spontaneously flowering, organic entity; characters having no apparent meaning appear, establish relations with one another, break them off, disappear again without any meaning having been revealed.... The atmosphere of thus being borne upon the unique and unrepeatable stream of life cancels out the accidental nature of their experiences and the isolated nature of the events recounted. (125)

Lukács also explains this victory over time, in terms which contradict those of the passage just quoted, as made possibly by the experiences of hope and memory; 'a synoptic vision of time as a solidified unity *ante rem* and its synoptic comprehension *post rem*' (124). Hope, he lamely explains, is what tries to conquer life by embracing and adorning, even though it is continually repulsed by life. True to say, hope does adorn life with figures life rejects; but such a figuring is precisely what creates the novel's inner unhappiness: the imposition by subjectivity of a form on experience which is incompatible with the possibilities of experience. Hope, then, is subject to the same difficulties as the novel's enterprise itself, and does exactly what Lukács argues should not be done: it offers a false solace to the reader by legitimating aspirations ungrounded in reality; as if we should all take our cue from Frédéric and hope only under the proviso that those hopes cannot be fulfilled. What is worse, hope does not possess this pre-figuring power for Flaubert. Flaubert's ironising all Frédéric hopes and dreams as they arise creates an immediate discontinuity between them and anything which might follow from them.

Whatever the inadequacy of hope, there is still the question as to why Lukács places such faith in time's powers to unify life. The answer is as simple as it is inadequate. Time, as an uninterrupted flow, 'is not an abstract concept, not a unit conceptually constructed after the event ... but a thing existing in itself and for itself, a concrete organic continuum' (125). (This too is a Kantian thesis: time is a unique intuition, that is, an individual and not a concept.) Time unifies because uninterrupted time is a unity; therefore, a faithful representation of time will create a representational unity. Two questions must be asked of this thesis: (i) Is time such a unity, and does it possess the organic, unifying qualities Lukács ascribes to it? and (ii) Does Flaubert have or present such a conception of time? The first question points to a weakness we have already noted in Lukács's procedure in Part II: he fails to subject the categories he uses, here 'time', to the same sort of historico-philosophical treatment he provided for the categories of Part I. While I would not presume to present such an analysis here, let me suggest the direction I would expect such an examination to take with respect to time.

Experience is temporalised in many ways: there is psychological time, the daily biographical rhythms of waking and sleep, the cycle of life from birth through adolescence and maturity to old age and death; there are the natural cycles of day and night, and the passing of the seasons which order the rhythms of the growth and decay of vegetable life. Cyclical time has about it an inevitability and necessity: we cannot avoid the coming of night, winter or death. Linear time is for us experienced in terms of past, present and future; typically, the past appears as an order of necessities, the present as actualities, and the future as possibilities. The modal shape of our lives will inevitably be experienced temporally. Since meaning, in Lukács's sense, is what shapes experience, then all meaning must posses a temporal dimension. Meaning without time is the domain of vain hopes. And time, nature's times, are nothing too until they have been mediated by our meaning – giving forms.

Time without form is either empty, or, as we shall see, the time that kills. The important thing is to realise that time and meaning must function together.

I shall call the fusion of time and meaning dialectical time, and time without meaning non-dialectical time. The difference between dialectical and non-dialectical time is everything. Man is a part of nature; but human nature is more than nature. Human nature can negate, alter and transform given nature through the efficacy of desire and work. The transformation of given nature (including ourselves) through desire and work creates history. Man is a part of nature, albeit an intensely historicised part of nature; as historical he works on given nature making it part of history. This relation between man and nature Marx calls the labour-process: 'a metabolic and formative relation between men and nature'. One aspect of the historicising, the humanising of nature is the humanising of natural time. The festivals and rituals, sacred and secular, surrounding birth and death, seed time and harvest time, are part of this process. Similar ritual care has traditionally been taken with the celebration of historical and mythical events; occasions in which the community asserts links between its members – past, present and future. Now even when such activities did no more than harmonise man with nature, letting history, which is naturally the domain of novelty, become absorbed into the cyclical rhythms of nature, the process of renewal through repetition is none the less dialectical: time is here full and meaningful. Central to any dialectical conception of time is death. Death is the mark of temporality on our individual existences. To take cognisance of death is to take cognisance of the flesh; it is our bodies (or the bodies we are) which make us part of the natural world and hence subject to death. A repression of death is then a repression of time. Temporal systems which have no room for death are non-dialectical. While we can easily imagine temporal systems which have no place for history – primitive societies often fall into this category – we cannot conceive of any temporal system which represses death and yet maintains a dialectical sense of history. The reason for this is that the recognition of dialectical history requires a recognition of finitude and so death. We must be able to conceive of desire and work cancelling out the present and its endless repetition. But this is to imagine a world in which we have no place. Thus a dialectical conception of death (natural time) is a necessary condition for a dialectical conception of history. Although the possession of the former does not entail the possession of the latter.

Now that we have examples of this fusion of time and meaning does not yet explain how such a thing is possible, thus one might still wonder how such a fusion is to be carried out. The schematism procedure of Kant and the novel is less an explanation of the fusion in question than a denial that an adequate explanation can be provided. That the schematism procedure is a mysterious power of the imagination tokens a primordial diremption of concept and succession which the procedure's 'imaginary' character only serves to heighten. If succession and concept possess no characteristics which would allow them to be joined, then their union in imagination must be a pure fiction; thus, the real possibility of their union necessarily entails a potentiality of each for the other: meaning must be temporal and temporality must be a potentiality for meaningfulness. The premise, then, of any convincing analysis must be that human time, broadly conceived, is not analysable in terms of sheer succession, a linear series of 'nows' where the line of time moves from the past through the present into the future, or through any causal or physicalist equivalent of the simple succession model. If meaning is a temporal affair, then a non- or a-meaningful analysis of time will force meaning into eternity, thus making all temporal meaning allegorical: time will be a moving image of eternity, and temporal experience fallen from and parasitic on eternity. Further, if we were to press forward with a simple (causal) succession model of time, we would be making the reified conception of time and history, the transformation of qualitative temporal experience into quantitative items, into the norm as opposed to some kind of deviation from the norm. There must be, then, some original or primordial belonging together of time and meaning, indicating thereby that human time can be grasped only through some form of existential analysis which ties together the experience of time to fundamental features of human existence. A successful account of this kind would reveal the existential structure of time, and from the fact that we have already noted various levels of event determination we would expect such an account to reveal a variety of existential levels of temporal organisation.

Such an account is well beyond the scope of this essay. Further, even if we possessed an account of the required kind we would still be left with the task of relating existential time to narrative; and to deal with that question adequately we would have to argue for a thesis which lingers just below the surface of all Lukács's mature writings, namely, that narrativity generally is the structure of language in which existential temporality achieves expression. That thesis, however, is important for our argument, and it would be worthwhile to at least catch some glimpse of its contours. Because, however, the thesis cannot be argued for here, since that would presuppose a completed existential analysis of time, I shall insinuate the thesis by working from fairly evident structural features of narrative or narrative experience to plausible or possible existential correlates.[9] If the general hypothesis is correct, if narrativity is the linguistic retrieval of temporality and human existence is temporally constituted, then at the limit one might expect to find narrativity and existential temporality merging, narrative language becoming itself an existential modality.

At their lowest level narratives are composed of events, actions, happenings. No such events, actions or happenings can become parts of a narrative unless they can be meaningfully connected with other such items of the same kind, that is, unless they have the potential for entering into the appropriate kinds of relations with other such items. To be part of an intelligible sequence an event must simultaneously meet two conditions: (i) it must be qualitatively distinct from surrounding events (or significantly repetitive); and (ii) some part of its distinctness must be attributable to its temporal connection with other events. The combination of qualitative distinctness together with connectivity guarantees from the outset that narrative sequences escape from the anonymous repetition of 'nows'. Descriptions of events that meet these conditions are 'story statements'. Story statements describe events as, e.g. outcomes, beginnings obstacles or turning-points. Not any or every death is an end, or birth a beginning. While it is true to say that not every narrative event is actually so described, none the less since in learning how to follow a story we learn how to regard the narrated events as forward-looking (story following involves anticipating what happens next), we learn how to regard such events as potentially so describable. Story statements describe events either as contributing to the plot or reveal them as potentially so describable. Plots are significant sequences of events; since, however, the termination of the sequence, the end towards which the process is moving, is never *simply* deducible or predictable from the antecedent events, that what makes a conclusion meaningful or appropriate is that it be acceptable, then the events themselves can never be properly described in naively causal fashion. Events for which there were available only causal explanations under general laws connected by such laws to other similar events would be mere bits of behaviour, not even fully human actions.[10] In fine, significant action in a narrative is always a response to a situation in order to realise some desired end or project.

Temporally, because the past is condensed in the situation to be responded to, the epistemic and ontic conditions for action, and the future no more than the end in view, time becomes the merely taken for granted horizon within which the agent operates; it is the time of clocks and calendars, time needed and time lost, time enough or too little for what is to be done. And this time, of course, can be flattened into a recurrence of 'nows'. Yet, on the existential level it is clear that, first, the sense of chronological time is parasitic on the public structure of engagements. It is because the promise must be kept, someone is waiting, the crops need to be brought in, the bank about to close that we reckon with time, that we become exposed to what is not now and needs to be made present. Taking this thought a little further, it is clear that it is intentional action itself which possesses a temporal structure through its conceptual character-istics. Intentional action is action under the appropriate description; thus the meaning of an action in part depends upon conceptual relations, relations not in the agent's control, which have implications which are both backward- and forward-looking. The backward-looking element comes in via the agent's beliefs about what has occurred and the relevant factors conditioning any possible course of action. To feel insulted or accept an offer, for example, is to have certain beliefs about what someone else has said or done. Equally, to make a promise (date, offer, insult) is to place oneself in some particular relation to the other which binds one's future actions. One can withdraw or make good an offer, revise or clarify it, but the range of (future) options available is determined by the kind of thing done. Present action necessarily, if it is action, stretches backward and forward. In his account of intentional action von Wright goes so far as to say 'that the behaviour's *intentionality is its place in a story about the agent.*'[11] To understand an action (one's own or someone else's) to grasp fully the intentional character of an action is already to be engaged in storytelling, using story-statements, constructing a plot; the purpose, point or goal of any action can be made intelligible only when seen against the backdrop of past events and the agent's beliefs about those events; and the intelligibility of beliefs and purposes may themselves require a larger context of more general purposes and so an understanding of a more remote past; the story is underway. Thus story-following and story-statements, the anticipations evoked in following a story, correlate with the intentional structure of human action inscribed within a public realm where the sense of those intentions is grounded and realised.

Secondly, the temporal perspectives relevant to the understanding of action are themselves reflections of the temporalising character of action itself. Intentional action as a response to what was for the sake of some future state of affairs is a synthesis of past, present and future. In acting the past and future are present in our beliefs and purposes. But it is more than beliefs which make the past present; a social situation is a sedimentation of the past in the present. It is not just a question of, for example, their being old injuries that cannot be forgotten, but equally it being the case that our clothes (house, factory, language, etc.) are old, that we are painting after Picasso, which structures the world in which we act. Intentional action takes up the past, but takes it up in just one of many possible ways; and the way the past is taken up comments upon or articulates it. It is in this sense that we can say that action is a synthesis of the three temporal moments. If one is inclined to regard labour as the authentic form of human action, as the later Lukács was tempted to do, then Marx's analysis of labour as a temporal synthesis will be found satisfying: 'It is already part of the simple production process that the earlier state of production is preserved by the later, and that the positing of the higher use value preserves the old, or, the old use value is transformed only to the extent that it is raised to a higher use value.'[12] Labour and intentional action have a prospective – retrospective structure which provides the existential basis for all further elaborations of human temporality. More precisely, the basic temporal characteristics of action open us up to a variety of levels of temporal organisation and understanding, themselves further characteristics and elaborations of the intentionality of action, which come to expression in narrative.

Human action reckons with time, and can and must do so because of the public structure of engagements which give sense to when an action occurs; and action itself is temporalising as a synthesis of the three moments of time. At this level time only succours or constrains; it is not yet manifest in its own right. Nor, at this level, would narrative do more than function against the background of time. Yet this public prospective – retrospective movement of time is brought into view in narrative when the agent is forced to decide and act, when the agent is called upon to *intervene* in some process (if there is no calling then there is no story, nothing to tell). In that moment, when the agent finds him- or herself abandoned to circumstances not of his or her own making but for which he or she is somehow responsible and thus must act upon, in that moment the agent comes to be bound to the world order. The act of intervention by binding the time of action to the world provides one of the conditions for the revelation of the historical meaning of action, and thus for the revelation of the historicality of action as such. Intervention is the locus where the within time of ordinary action joins with historically specific social structures through the figure of abandonment and responsibility which calls all intervention forth. Put another way, the narrative figure of intervention correlates with and reveals the social parameters within which all action occurs; intervention figures the conditioning of action, the givenness of the world to the agent, and the demands (call) of the world on the agent. The moment of having to choose shows the past as throwing the agent into the future, where the past is not his past but a past which he makes his own by assuming responsibility for it through present and future action. Thus the narrative characteristics of story following, anticipation, story statements and intervention align themselves with the Marxist concepts of desire and labour which correspond to the temporal experiences of acting in time and the joining of action to the time of the world order.

Intervention itself, however, neither necessarily reveals the joining of domains or the domains joined; thus it does not fully exclude the possibility of time being reduced to recurrence. A further condition for excluding this possibility occurs with the closure of action in the completing of the story, in the transition from story following to having followed the story, where discourse fully takes over from story. In having followed a story we view all that has preceded from the point of view of the end, we view the sequence of events as a pattern, as parts belonging to a whole. Narrative understanding involves the cancelling out of the contingency of events and actions as revealed in the following of the story, and their retrieval in a whole which by fully coordinating them renders their meaning determinate (even if that determinate meaning is the indeterminancy of all meaning).

In what has come to be called 'configurational understanding', the form of understanding provided by narrative, we learn how to submerge events in discourses whose meanings are not derivable from their constituent elements or from any other mode of understanding.[13] Existentially, the configurational act of understanding, itself corresponding to the plot as a completed and closed sequence of actions, corresponds to the work of memory. Paul Ricoeur has put the thesis this way:

It is as though recollection inverted the so-called natural order of time. By reading the end in the beginning and the beginning in the end, we learn also to read time itself backward, as the recapitulating of the initial conditions of a course of action in its terminal consequences. In this way, a plot establishes human action not only within time . . . but within memory. Memory, accordingly *repeats* the course of events according to an order that is the counterpart of time as 'stretching-along' between a beginning and an end.[14]

Hence the unifying act of narrative ordering is to be identified with the rehearsal of action in memory, and thus with a form of recollection. At this level, the assumption of an end appropriate to human action, and so an order of meaning for those actions, is funnelled through a posteriori reflection on what has occurred. If the joining of individual action to the world order through intervention raises the possible significance of action to the level of historicality, realising thereby the meaning of intentional actions beyond the agent's horizon of awareness, the reflective ordering of action in memory takes the whole sequence of 'intentional action – (unintended) consequence – (new) intentional action' out of the purview of the prospective understanding typically associated with action and tacitly raises it to the level of the social or collective understanding of action.

Hence the significant polarities of narrative structure and experience – the open and closed, contingent and determinate (necessary), story and discourse, episodic and unifying aspects of narrative – are to be read off of the intention – reflection, prospective – retrospective ordering of time which mark the primordial relatedness of human action to time in the first instance. Thus the existential problem of extension in time reaches understanding in the doubling of time in narrative. Further, only through the double time of narrative does the social dimension of action, and hence the full intentional character of action, become manifest. The plotting of action, we have seen, is intrinsic to the conceptual determination of action ; the work of memory is to raise the implicit past of all action to a level where the retrospective character of action as plotted can be thematised. However, since retrospection is but one moment of a synthesis which each action achieves, a synthesis opened up to view in narrative, memory becomes an end of action. The purposefulness of action as plotted is conveyed in memory, where the end must succeed in binding the heretofore always forward looking sequences. As plotted, however, actions have a significance which calls into question the extension of life through time, life as a sequence of temporally multilayered actions. Narrative's double time reflects the social comprehension of extension or, more simply, the general ends appropriate for the understanding of all action : happiness, justice, salvation, etc. Even the double time of narrative, though, reveals only the problem of extension in time and not the existential correlate of that doubling ; that is, even if the prospective – retrospective structure of human action grounds the need for the doubling of time in narrative, that doubling itself appears to be a textual artefact without existential meaning.

For this we are required to move to another level of narrative experience, namely, where narrative experience is the existential experience of historicality. In order to clarify this puzzling idea let us contrast two distinct kinds or poles of recollection. On the one hand, a recollection may be a mere repetition of what has occurred in memory. In such cases the recounting is as much geographical as temporal; or rather, the adventure is geographical but displayed in time. Paradigmatic amongst narratives of this kind is the *Odyssey*; but any narrative which remains rooted to the level of within time, where change or transformation is either not developmental or not analogously 'geared' to time explicitly, will tend toward this pole of recollection. On the other hand, a recollection may be the very process by which the present comes to self-identity, so that the recollecting is the recognition and recovery of lost (forgotten) potentialities whose narrative relating is (the condition for) their realisation. For narratives of this kind, like Augustine's or Proust's, the return to beginnings, the repetition of beginnings recovers the past and in so doing retrieves and deepens the original temporal movement. Of course, a narrative of this kind may be only a representation of a developmental process in which past potentialities are retrieved and actualised; equally, however, the writing of such a narrative may be the retrieval of those past potentialities and the completion of the narrative their actualisation. In the latter case the writing of the narrative becomes the appropriation of the past which makes the narrative written possible. In modern times it is tempting to take this latter narrative possibility as a limit case where life meets art, where the art of living is inverted in the life dedicated to art. A hint as to why we should not limit narrative repetition to this special modern instance is provided in an argument of Hannah Arendt's.

The real story in which we are engaged as long as we live has no visible or invisible maker because it is not made. The only 'somebody' it reveals is its hero, and it is the only medium in which the originally intangible manifestation of a uniquely distinct 'who' can become tangible *ex post facto* through action and speech. *Who* somebody is or was we can know only by the story of which he is himself the hero – his biography in other words; everything else we know of him, including the work he may have produced and left behind, tell us only *what* he is or was.[15]

This hint about the connection between narrative, the existential deepening of the movement of time through repetition and identity, might remind us of what was said earlier about the nature of class consciousness. I shall explore the hint and the connections in the final chapter when we come to examine modernism's rejection of narrative.

In repetition, then, the historicality of action is fully realised and thematised, action becoming what it always, tacitly, is: the taking up of the past as the sole locus of potentialities for future action. The extensiveness of human life as stretching between birth and death is gathered together in order that these natural boundaries of action become constitutive horizons for action, the meaning of action being the gathering and relating of beginning and end. Said otherwise, without repetition the extension of life between birth and death becomes a sheer extension, a process which takes time but to which time itself remains externally related.

In his 'The Storyteller', Benjamin calls the above diagnosed modes or poles of recollection reminiscence and remembrance, correlating the former with the story – the post-epic form of narrative dedicated to the life of conventional psychological man, playing the same role in Benjamin's schema as the epic does in Lukács's – and the latter with the novel. Of the storyteller he says, 'Death is the sanction of everything [he] can tell. He has borrowed his authority from death.'[16] Death provides the (natural) closure to life, thus giving to the transience of experience a fixity the living cannot possess. It is this fixity which makes a life available for reminiscence. Since, however, for the storyteller history and nature are not yet separated, all history is natural history (which is precisely what chronicles are for Benjamin), then the authority of death is, just, 'borrowed from' and not thematised. Because the age of the novel lacks the secure order of a natural process, it cannot tolerate the unbound diffuseness and diversity of experience which is the object of the storyteller. Novelistic remembrance must elicit from experiential heterogeneity a meaning by means of an act of unification. In this way novel narrative ordering in recollection becomes the practical analogue of the synthetic unification of the manifold in perception. For Benjamin it is death in the novel which plays the role of the ultimate 'one' which the transcendental unity of apperception plays in theoretical cognition according to Kant.

A man – so says the truth that was meant here – who died at thirty-five will appear to *remembrance* at every point in his life as a man who dies at the age of thirty-five. In other words, the statement that makes no sense for real life becomes indisputable for remembered life. The nature of the character in the novel cannot be presented any better than is done in this statement, which says that the 'meaning' of his life is revealed only in his death. But the reader of a novel actually does look for human beings from whom he derives the 'meaning of life'. Therefore he must, no matter what, know in advance that he will share their experience of death: if need be their figurative death – the end of the novel – but preferably their actual one.... The novel is significant, therefore, not because it presents someone else's fate to us, perhaps didactically, but because this stranger's fate by virtue of the flame which consumes it yields us the warmth which we never draw from our own fate. What draws the reader to the novel is the hope of warming his shivering life with a death he reads about.

As we shall see, the novel is too prolix a form, miming thus its materials, to be unified in only this way; or rather, the heterogeneity of the field of the novel is so resistant to unification that even the interlocking categories of the novel, its forms, are not fully sufficient for this task. None the less, Benjamin's thesis is not unjust: without at least a figurative death memory's work would remain incomplete; indeed, without at least a figurative death there would be no place for recollection to begin, and thus no way to retrieve life from within time, to double time and raise it to the level of historicality. But if an author is to borrow more than his authority from death, then death must do more than close the sequence, it must signify in its own right. It is the recognition of death, and death as the locus of recognition (of individual identity and human finitude), which novel deaths (real or figurative) elicit. Because modern life has no natural *telos*, no unequivocal (transcendent) end or ends, then our finitude becomes the condition for all our ends and thus our proper end. By this latter I mean no more than that the recognition of the absoluteness of death is a necessary condition for comprehending projects and plots in a world from which God has departed; and consequently only death can, finally, draw the meaning of the extension of life to an end. Only death we might say, can raise life to the level of fate. Still, like the transcendental unity of apperception, death as a unifier is a formal and not an empirical condition for meaning in the novel. The point can be put this way: 'the figure of the meaning of life revealed in a death borrows its unifying power from death, but death must borrow its content from the figure revealed. It is a comment on the novel and not on narrative generally that in the novel form and life, transcendental and empirical are joined only in death.

From what has just been said about different forms of recollection a final, rather general point about the relation between time and narrative emerges. Each aspect of narrative structure or experience, of narrative production and con-sumption, we have mentioned can only feature as a deter-minable which is made determinate through the social and historical determination of its corresponding existential mo-dality. For example, in the case of the 'within time' feature of action we must ask about the nature of the horizon which is taken for granted: is it the time of clock or calendar, the time of daylight and darkness, or the seasons of the year. For each of these phenomena themselves we must ask after their social determination. As Benjamin reminds us, the calendar, whether religious or revolutionary, was itself a fusion of time and meaning, of quality with quantity, and thus a rejection of the empty counting of time.[17] And the seasons of the year are not natural, given clocks; on the contrary, as Carol Gould has nicely stated the point, 'the choice of the seasons as ways of marking time is itself made on the basis of the activities of planting and harvesting. The external reference is therefore an external-ization of a condition of the labouring activity itself or its objectification.'[18] In intervention since the within time of human action joins the world order, we must query the world order joined. Is intervention like, to use a random set of analogies, a sabot in a machine, the rebuilding of a house, the watering of a plant, or a vote in an assembly? Or, as a commentary upon narrative itself, could the moment of intervention be mere simulation, a gesture signifying nothing, engaging nothing but the motes of light enveloping it? For each type of intervention we can imagine we are confronted with a specific form of human action and a specific kind of temporal organisation into which it can intrude. When we consider plot as a whole we need to ask what sanctions its closure: nature, God, man, society, history, etc.? Is the recollection of construed as collective or individual? Finally, at the level of repetition we are faced with the two polar forms of recollection and their social determination; and, from a different angle, we must reconsider the conditions governing plot. In fine, the forms of narrative ordering are conditioned and mediated by the social and historical determination of the existential structures of time. All narrative acts face the task of making the features of narrative structure and experience commensurable with the socially determined existential structures of temporality. Given the mimetic ambitions of the epic tradition those socially determined existential structures reach narrative enunciation in the first instance via the language of experience which forms the basis for mimetic acts. Thus the social coding of those existential structures determine narrative from within and without.

From this vantage point we can see what went wrong with Lukács's account of time. His view of time as a 'concrete and organic continuum' is itself wholly non-dialectical and, what is worse, is presented undialectically, that is as not itself the result of historical mediations which have rendered time non-dialectical. Hence Lukács's account of the flow of time doubly mystifies it. The first mystification proceeds on the basis of the view that if time can be rendered a 'living and dynamic thing' producing for us, the novel's readers, an experience of continuity, then the contingency of the lives represented will have been cancelled. But, as Lukács admits, it is only the 'semblance' of an organic unity without any meaning being revealed (125). Which is to say, time is meaningless unless and until it has been historically mediated. Lukács can avoid this insight because he has already accepted organic unity as a value. But this is just a play on the word 'organic'. In coming to understand the non-alienated character of, say, early Greek society we call the unity we find there 'organic' in order to distinguish it from the mechanical and architectural unities later generations have discovered. It is the unity of form and life we value, a value expressed in terms of 'organic unity'. But an organic unity which does not involve a unity of form and life is valueless. Lukács simply transposes the evaluative term to a new phenomenon without considering the appropriateness of that transposition. Moreover, a 'semblance' of unity is not the representation of a unity, but an illusion of unity. Flaubert, we shall see, is carefully attempting to create such an illusion; his purpose in so doing is to keep our teleological anticipations activated without providing teleological resolutions or satisfactions. The inner dynamic of *Sentimental Education*, in fact, is one which denies the possibility of teleological satisfaction; a point Flaubert defiantly makes by ending the work with two codas temporally disparate from the rest of the narrative which define, if you will, Frédéric's mode of existence as one of continual displacement of the real for the imaginary. The novel does not end; rather it concludes with a statement of its inner inconclusiveness. *Sentimental Education* is an artful unity of representation, but not the representation of a unity.

The second source of mystification, Lukács's taking the flow of time as given, explains how the first mystification was made possible. Throughout Lukács assumes that the novel includes 'real' time. Real time, however, cannot be represented except through either the language of experience which preserves within itself the social experience of time, or through the figurative language of fiction which attempts to shape the language of experience to its own ends and goals. The social experience of time Flaubert represents, the language of experience he appropriates, is not that of 1848 but, if anything, the 'time' of the constitutional republic which lasted from 28 May 1849 to 2 December 1851 – which is, of course, the very day on which the continuous narrative prior to the coda ends. (The 'truth' of the narration, not the narrative, is, shall we say, the installation of illusion for reality.) Flaubert transposes the 'time' of the defeat of the revolution and the republic into the revolutionary period itself. It is Marx who gives us, with uncanny elegance, the social experience of the 1849 to 1851 period. It contains

wild and empty agitation in the name of tranquillity, the most solemn preaching of tranquillity in the name of revolution; passion without truth, truth without passion; heroes without deeds of heroism, history without events; a course of development apparently only driven forward by the calendar, and made wearisome by the constant repetition of the same tensions and relaxations; antagonisms which seem periodically to press forward to a climax, but become deadened and fall away without having attained their resolution...[19]

But *Sentimental Education* is not written from the perspective of the period of the constitutional republic; it is written from the perspective of the empty time following the republic when even the rhetoric of action has been dissolved. We might put it this way: for Flaubert 1848 was never a time of revolution; properly speaking, it was, at best, a period mimicking revolutionary history (1849–50), whose truth was a period in which action, change, history were impossible (post–1851). What examination of the temporal structure of *Sentimental Education* shows us is a world in which, through the repression of death and history, action, significant, transforming action has become impossible.

5   THE TIME OF 1848

We have already seen how Flaubert ironises Frédéric's projects in order immediately to undermine them, depriving them of efficacy in the very manner in which they are proposed. Frédéric's dreams are passions without truth. Flaubert intensifies this impossibility of action, still at a crude level, by plotting his scenes so that whenever Frédéric is about to act or about to contemplate a meaningful action he is cruelly interrupted. The overall effect of these continual interruptions is undeniably comic. Three brief examples will give you an idea of how this ironic plotting works.

Madame Arnoux sat motionless with her hands on the arms of her chair...her clear-cut profile stood out in pale relief in the dusk.
  He longed to throw himself on his knees. There was a creaking noise in the corridor; he did not dare. (201*)

it was on the point of falling into the water when Frédéric leapt forward and caught it. She said:
  'Thank you Monsieur.'
  Their eyes met.

'Are you ready, my dear?' Arnoux called out, appearing in the hood of the companion-way. (19*)

In spite of himself, he glanced at the bed in the depths of the alcove, imagining her head on the pillow; and he pictured the scene so clearly that he could scarcely refrain from clasping her in his arms. She closed her eyes, soothed, inert. Then he drew nearer, and, bending over her, gazed greedily into her face. The sound of boots echoed along the hall; it was Arnoux. (172*)

Sometimes this kind of plotting is more elaborate. For example, Frédéric has finally got Madame Arnoux to agree to go out with him; he takes a room specifically for the occasion in the hope of luring her into it and seducing her. On the day of the outing – the first of the 1848 revolution – Madame Arnoux's child falls dangerously ill and she forgets about her plans to meet Frédéric. Only later, with her son's recovery, does she remember. She takes her son's illness as a sign from God that her love of Frédéric is not to be consummated. 'Jumping to her feet, she flung herself on the little chair; and sending up her soul with all her strength, she offered God, as a sacrifice, her first love, her only weakness' (281*). We might want to say, against the background of defeats, that it is Flaubert who exacts this sacrifice from Madame Arnoux, not God.

For all that, we could be reading the story of star-crossed lovers. What makes us so confident that neither a tragic finale nor a happy ending await Frédéric? It is here that Flaubert's temporal scheme must enter our analysis.

Flaubert does contrive to present to the reader the impression of a continuous flow of time. As is well known, there are three places in the narrative where Flaubert surreptitiously advances the time of the action.

The first instance is at the end of Part One, when a whole year, from September 1843 to September 1844, is casually dropped; then, at the beginning of Part Two, the year 1846 mysteriously disappears, and Frédéric, returning to Paris in December 1845, throws a housewarming party in January 1847; and finally, in the third chapter of Part Three, the reader is taken swiftly and imperceptibly from August 1848 to May 1850, within the space of a few pages. (11*)[20]

What is significant about these instances is that they are extreme instances of Flaubert's usual practice; they do not represent in any way a departure of approach or technique. The movement of Flaubert's narrative is radically discontinuous and only provides for a semblance of continuity; this semblance of continuity produces the effect of a continuous narrative, of a developing story in a fictional realm where stasis and repetition reign.

The crux of Flaubert's approach to time is to relieve as much pressure as possible from the story as the conveyor of continuity and place the onus of continuity onto the story's narration.[21] As a result, the story, Frédéric's life, can remain radically discontinuous and non-dialectical while we continually receive the impression that the story is progressing. Central to Flaubert's procedure is the alternation of temporally non-dynamic expanses of inwardness and subjectivity, or ironised events leading nowhere, with occasional explicit statements of date.

Let us consider the period of March 1842 to August 1842 (60–70*). Throughout this short stretch from the words 'About the middle of March...' to 'August came along...' six pages later, the story progresses not at all; there is one inconsequential evening in Frédéric's flat, a few interchanges between him and Deslauriers, and Frédéric's dreams of Madame Arnoux. The impression that the story is advancing is achieved through the use of narrational devices that give all the dreams and events an ambiguous temporal shadow. Typical is Flaubert's use of verbs designating repeated processes or habitual actions ('He *worked* at Pellerin's place...', 'He *chose* days for calling on her...'; 'Yet there *were* occasions when he met her.'), which can be followed by or conjoined with non-productive reveries (non-productive because only habitual), both of which allow for easy transitions to non-specific times ('One evening...'), or, what is a very condensed version of the same process, the gradual modulation from a habitual event type to a specific event (from Deslauriers' taunting game with Arnoux's name presented as an action type to 'Finally Frédéric could stand it no longer...'; which event is followed by a 'But three weeks later...'). It is this process of employing non-specific time attribution and verbs designating habitual actions together with exact dating (or the mentioning of specific historical events), repeated and expanded, which works throughout the novel to generate an impression of there being a progressive movement while at the same time we experience the radical discontinuity which exists between moods and events.[22] The pressure of time being moved along in this way confirms rather than cancels the nonproductivity of events and dreams. As Marx puts it, the tensions (events) and relaxations (moods) come to appear to have no motive force *except* the calendar, hence the clock's ticking comes to represent the meaninglessness of dreams and events.

To put the same point another way: events have no importance except as the subjects of moods; there is no space where events and moods can interpenetrate. If time penetrates neither consciousness nor events, doing its proper work of mediating the two, then death, which is the mark of time on us, also must stand outside of life. And a life conceived of outside death's domain is incapable of being lived dialectically. And a non-dialectical life, a life subjected to the meaninglessness of repetition, is a life without history. As Frédéric thrice confronts death in the opening moments of the Revolution we can perceive immediately why the Revolution had to fail.

Frédéric, caught between two dense masses, did not budge: in any case, he was fascinated and enjoying himself tremendously. The wounded falling to the ground, and the dead lying stretched out, did not look as if they were really wounded or dead. He felt as if he were watching a play... People slipped in the mud on clothes, shakos, and weapons; Frédéric felt something soft under his foot; it was the hand of a sergeant in a grey overcoat who was lying face down in the gutter. Fresh groups of workers kept coming up, driving the fighters to the guard-house.... Frédéric was suddenly shaken by a man who fell groaning against his shoulder, with a bullet in his back. This shot, which for all he knew might have been aimed at him, infuriated him; and he was rushing forward when a National Guard stopped him.

'There's no point in it. The King has just left. Well, if you don't believe me, go and see for yourself.'

This assertion calmed Frédéric down. The Place du Carrousel looked peaceful enough. (286–7*)

Event and mood shuttle back and forth here, but nothing is born of them. The first deaths are unreal; Frédéric's stepping on the dead man's hand, an obvious moment for some kind of recognition, is reduced to nullity through the pressure of Flaubert's writing: Frédéric's brief moment of anger on the occasion of the third death is ironically cancelled, 'There's no point in it.' Mood, narrative pace, irony; each serves to remove death's reality, the recognition of which would permit Frédéric to engage with his world, and allow the events of the world to become meaningful for him (or anyone). Recognition and transformation are what are excised from this world; and what can a revolution be in a world where all change is repetition? Is this not but an inverted image of the period of the republic: events without history, and deeds of heroism without heroes?

We cannot warm our shivering lives with the deaths we read about in *Sentimental Education* because those deaths fail to signify, and thus do not resolve the beginning of things. The represented world remains unredeemed, the extension of life ununified. There is no repetition, or at least no repetition which might raise life from being merely in time. In the two codas following the completion of the main narrative (or pseudo-narrative), Flaubert comments upon the fictions of memory, on memory without repetition. In the first, occurring in March 1867, Frédéric surprises the now old and white-haired Madame Arnoux with his precise memory of the events they shared together. But these memories strike no chords, rekindle no flames; they involve a re-presentation of events without re-petition. In a typically Flaubertian gesture, in order to compensate for the lack he feels, Frédéric falls to his knees; the speeches he and Madame Arnoux then offer to one another surround the past in the well-worn conventions of romance. Only a pure fiction, these wholly artificial conventions can redeem experience. In the second, occurring a few months later, Frédéric and Deslauriers reminisce about the past. The moment they single out for attention, the best moment of their lives when their ideals had not yet been vanquished, was an unconsummated and vaguely humiliating visit to a brothel. Significantly, the visit occurred three years before the novel's beginning. So beginning and end are detached from action, and the action cut off from true beginnings and appropriate ends. For Flaubert these scenes perhaps bespeak the transfiguring power of language as such, as the potency derived from the mere naming of things. For later critics Flaubert is the hero who notices the real disparity between 'genealogical continuity and novelistic continuity'.[23] Flaubert announces, they might say, the fictionality and textuality of all narrative ordering. Lukács knew better; narrative becomes a fictional unification of experience when repetition becomes impossible because the appearance forms constituting the represented world do not permit of unification; because appearance and reality are not distinguished, the potentialities latent in the world remain unobserved and the wrong hero (an individual as opposed to a class, say) attempts to act. Reality colluded with Flaubert's project, allowing him thus to explore and reveal the world of the novel, a world (or the appearance form of a world) in which only a fictional unifying is possible. As a social form, however, the unhappy consciousness of novel fictions should remind us of a different alternative reality.

6 DIALECTICAL READING: A CODA

The 'truth' of Frédéric's life, like the events of 1848, is that it leads nowhere; his life leads nowhere *because* it is conditioned by the failures of 1848. This 'because' is what separates dialectical from undialectical readings of *Sentimental Education*. *Sentimental Education* may be 'a novel about nothing', but it is written from a determinate perspective which makes its very meaninglessness, its denial of meaning, significant. Not to take this step outside the experience of the novel is to accede to Flaubert's ideological perspective, to treat the moment of 1848 and its failure as nature's givens rather than as moments of history.

Since Flaubert's time novels whose order resides in their telling and not in what is told have become more common. Now these modes of narration – which create orders which are not dependent on any previously existing orders – vary as much amongst themselves as do representations of different objects. Orders of narration are as susceptible to interpretation and explanation as representational orders. To individuate orders of narration one from another involves interpreting and explaining. To stop at interpretation results in mystification. If one cannot recuperate (through the totalising movement of theory) the conditions for Flaubert's narrational programme, then one is left with it as the truth of one's interpretive activities. It is disturbing, for example, how closely Jonathan Culler's critical programme aligns itself with Flaubert's narrational programme. We have agreed that Flaubert's project involves something like a reduction of reality to illusion, and the assertion of the reality of writing. His writing possesses no more than a formal unity conjured from the treasure trove of grammar and syntax. The conclusion of *Sentimental Education* asserts, with irony, the vacuity, the non-education which has gone before: Frédéric was and will be someone whose sentiments fail to mesh with reality. His is a world in which teleologies play no part. And so is Culler's critical universe. 'Criticism', Culler says, 'exists to make things interesting. If one thus avoids foreclosure at the cost of vacuity, that is, I believe, a necessary operating expense... [we must] try to see that the final recuperation to which we are subject is not a premature foreclosure but allows us room for play and includes an awareness of its own process under an abstract and formal heading like "the difficulty of making sense".'[24] A criticism which replaces truth with 'making things interesting', and whose mode of self-consciousness proposes only the difficulties of making sense as opposed to the critical awareness of one's historical position and how difficult it is to transcend that position through theoretical totalisation and praxis, is a criticism which simply colludes with its object. Culler's critical values, like Flaubert's literary values, yield a tacit rejection of death and history, for this is all the denial of anything but formal recuperation implies. As I shall argue later, praxial totalisation, a dialectical criticism, is one which submerges textual meaning into a larger context, namely, the narrative we are making that transcends the conditions of novel production, distribution and consumption, the conditions behind the novel's essential unhappiness.

V

Paralogisms : The Self as Form

Throughout centuries of subjectivity there will never be any other I than the I withdrawn from his own discourse, and who will recite his fables, saying 'I am the State', or 'Ego, Hugo', or 'I am Madame Bovary', or even 'Good Lord, why is it that I am I?'

(Jean-Luc Nancy)

1 THE DELIBERATION

The central aesthetic problem of novel writing is synthesising the heterogeneity of life in accordance with form, where life and form, parts and whole, are considered as originally dirempt from one another, and as categorially discontinuous, as inhabiting different domains or levels of experience. The schematising procedure of the novel, whereby conceptual systems become temporal forms, is one strategic response to this difficulty. Of itself, however, the schematising procedure is an inadequate synthesising device for it can place no limits on the expanse of the represented world. More precisely, the operation of schematising procedures itself presupposes a logically anterior restriction on the possible kinds or range of contents to which it is applicable. In the epic, Lukács argues, all events come before us as always-already formed; thus because of the always-already formed character of epic events the closure of the epic world is guaranteed from the outset. Closure, then, is an internal correlative of there being an epic world *überhaupt*; the epic world is an infinite but bounded domain. Such is not the case in the novel; the novel lacks limits because the range of events which might be relevant to its validity, the range of events which might or might not correspond to its forms, is not supplied by either the world or the forms. A 'bad infinity' thus threatens the world of

147

the novel (81). In order to counter this threat the novel must possess forms, in the grammatical or structural sense, which can give form (ethics) a possible world in which to operate. Lukács believes there are two such forms, and he denominates them the 'outward' (or 'outer') and 'inner' forms of the novel. The outward form of the novel is biographical, while the inner form is 'the process of the problematic individual's journeying towards himself' (80).

Biographical form specifies in advance the kind of process and thus the kind of temporal ordering relevant to the world of the novel. The meanings or forms provided by the novel must be internal to a life history, with birth and death being constitutive limits on the meaning of the forms imposed and not simply contingent constraints on their revelation. If this requirement were not recognised then nothing about the novel's form would token its placement in a secular world. Allegorical narratives, of course, may employ biographical form as a vehicle for the representation of meaning, but the meaning revealed will not necessarily belong to the individual whose life story occasioned its manifestation. In the epic 'what is contained between the beginning and the end escapes precisely the biographical categories of process: it is the eternally existant becoming in ecstatic vision' (82); what is thus revealed reduces to absolute inessentiality the very life-events which are the objects of novelistic reflection and structuring. As we noted in our discussion of Benjamin, in both epic and the novel life and death function as boundaries, but in the former they are an external border, a frame, while in the latter they become constitutive horizons signifying in their own right. Beginnings and ends signify in the novel: beginnings must 'give birth', must be procreative, lifting the passing of time into becoming, genealogy into genesis; ends must be allowed to signify by revealing the meaning(s) offered as available within a finite existence, as, somehow, conceptually consanguineous with human finitude. Thus even when the births and deaths of a novel are figurative, even when the beginning and end of a novel do not relate to natural births and deaths, none the less the biographical form of the telling signifies that 'the development of a man is still the thread upon which the whole world of the novel is strung and along which it unrolls' (82).

If biographical form is to fulfil its constitutive function it must be further specified. The inner, or interior, form of the novel is such a specification or categorial predication on outer form. Biographical form can function constitutively just in case the meaning revealed by a life history does not escape, in principle, the extension of one life; and this will be the case if the terminus of the process is a form of self-recognition. Problematic individuals – women, children, orphans, criminals, madmen, etc. – are precisely persons who do not know who they are, who must discover or creatively become themselves. The social marginality of the problematic individual is the condition for the writer to author their life, to provide an alternative to established social identities or, at least, to reveal the recalcitrance, necessity or worth of existing forms of life. Form-giving would entirely transgress the demands of mimesis if a 'space' could not be found within the represented world for authorial interpretation to intrude; the marginalised character of problematic individuals provides such a space.

'While the self-recognition of problematic individuals provides a focus for authorial interpretation, the fact that it is a life extended in time that provides the possible raw materials for interpretation binds authorial form to a 'natural' form, a form within the represented world. It is for this reason that Lukács regards biographical form as a mediating term between conceptual system and experiential heterogeneity: 'The fluctuation between a conceptual system which can never completely capture life and a life complex which can never attain completeness because completeness is immanently utopian can be objectivised only in that organic quality which is the aim of biography' (77). It is because character in the novel is a compositional mediating device between form and life that literary theory divides its allegiance in the analysis of character: formalists subsume character into system, while representationalists continue to regard characters as fictional persons. Martin Price's rhetorical questioning of the place of character in the novel can be answered only through a consideration of how it is that dualism in character originates.

Is a character a person living a free and spontaneous life or part of a plot, and can any plot fully resemble the untidy actuality of real life?

Does the person dissolve into an agent of plot, or does the plot seem, at some level, the working out of the characters' inherent natures? Again, how shall we comprehend in one novel characters that are clearly seen as schematic or archetypal with characters whom seem full and substantial?[1]

Because characters are the focus of authorial interpretation they must be relativised to the conceptual system of the narrative; because that conceptual system would remain merely a system, abstract in the Hegelian sense, if it could not be attached to experience, then characters must be presumed to be elements of the empirical world prior to novelistic reflection. The fluctuation between conceptual system and life necessarily invades their point of mediation. The practice of novel writing, thus, must both relativise character to system and simultaneously furnish characters with sufficient empirical predicates for them to be mimetically engaging. None the less, as we shall see, the duality of character is more deeply embedded in the form of the novel than its compositional delineation anticipates.

By regimenting biographical form to the end of self-recognition novel writing relativises the world to the self and meaning to identity. Together these two theses represent the novel's 'Copernican turn' in the history of the epic: all experience is the experience of some subject, and a necessary condition for that experience to be intelligible is that the subject be able, at the end of the day, to answer the question 'Who am I?' Now, while Lukás clearly intended inner and outer biographical form to represent categorial features – constitutive rules – of the practice of the novel, it is equally clear that his motivation for separating out the aspects of biographical form into 'inner' and 'outer' was the gradual transition in the history of the novel from a search for meaning carried out in the world to a search for meaning carried out in the psyche of the hero, from action and plot to desire and mood as the proper carriers of narrative meaning. Once these historical correlations for the two aspects of biographical form have been made, one can readily perceive how they might be regarded as underwriting the analytical distinction between 'abstract idealism' and the 'romanticism of disillusionment', and how it might then be thought that these two categories in their analytical and historical placement provide a typology of the novel form.

Although the history of the novel does instantiate a journey inward, premised on the increasing reification of the social world, that transition does not validate Lukács's typology, for the outer and inner features of biographical form do not in fact correlate in the historical way which Lukács appears to suppose. Both aspects of biographical form are as applicable to *Tom Jones* as they are to *The Ambassadors*. The transition from empirical to psychological realism is a modification in biographical form as a whole and not a movement from one aspect of biographical form to another. Lukács's naming of the categorial forms 'inner' and 'outer' instigates a conflation between constitutive rules for a certain kind of writing with a spatial topography, a conflation aided by the simple transposition of concept into metaphor, inner and outer form thus becoming a conceptual metaphor. Thus it is that categorial dialectic becomes analytic topography, and analytic topography gestates into a spatial topography.

Now because biographical form in the novel is the search for self-recognition, biographical form is incipiently autobiographical; autobiographical form is the 'truth' of biographical form. In psychological terms the point can be rendered thus: the transition from the epic, broadly speaking, to the novel 'is the transference of the need to name the world to the prior need of naming oneself. To name the world is to make the representation of the world coincide with the world itself; to name myself is to make the representation that I have of the world coincide with the representation that I convey to others.'[2] This statement by Alain Grosrichard occurs not in a discussion of the theory of the novel, but in an account of the transition in Rousseau's work from theory to literature. None the less, it is not difficult to recognise in this passage the transition from dogmatic biography (or autobiography) in the service of some truth beyond the self to an autobiographical ontology in which naming the self becomes paramount. If self-recognition is the *telos* of biographical form, then biographical form naturally evokes autobiographical form, the novelist's reflection on the story and discourse of his hero. Autobiographical form is manifest in the novel as irony. For Lukács the meaning of the practice of novel writing can never be the hero's search for meaning, whatever its result, for that search is always only a shadow of authorial practice, the authoring of meaning through the novel form of writing. Irony binds the dialectic of form-giving and mimesis with biographical form; it thus brings into focus as practice and strategy the secularity and productivity which premise the novel form as a whole.

Lukács summarises the double function of biographical form, as both inner and outer form, in the aesthetic economy of the novel in these terms:

> On the one hand, the scope of the world is limited by the scope of the hero's possible experience and its mass is organised by the orientation of his development towards finding the meaning of life in self-recognition; on the other hand, the discretely heterogeneous mass of isolated persons, meaningless structures and meaningless events receives a unified articulation by the relating of each separate element to the central character and the problem symbolised by the story of his life. (81)

Biographical form gives limits to the world of the novel which permits the formal figuring of empirical discourse to achieve closure without transgressing the premises which constitute the problematic of the novel in the first instance. The common claim that the primordial discovery of the novel is the self must, according to Lukács, be understood in formal terms, as a strategic response to exigencies conditioning the production of a modern 'epic' narrative. The problem of the novel is the connection between form and life; the schematising procedure of the novel cannot establish the sought after connection directly, but must (as a matter of form) traverse and stay within the limits of a life history (or histories) which terminates in self-recognition. Of course, that biographical form can play the formal role it does in the novel is conditioned by the presence elsewhere in modern social formations of the ideology of individualism; further, the deployment of the self as form is properly part of the novelist's work of commensuration, of joining the novel to other social practices. To be sure, the self as form evokes, and must evoke if the work of commensuration is to succeed, the other individualisms of modernity; but this is not to say that our understanding of the self in the novel is reducible to its analogues in other social practices. Each social practice – economic, political, legal, religious, moral, etc. – articulates the self in accordance with the exigencies of its domain specific history in its relation to other domains. Hence, we can only comprehend the meaning of individualism in the novel in terms of the meanings effected by the self as form. Only by examining the concepts governing the practice of the self as form and noting the antinomies to which they give rise can the meaning of the ideological figure of the self be revealed. Biographical form gathers to itself three distinct but closely related forms of practice, namely, the novel, modern autobiography and modern philosophy as premised by Descartes' 'Cogito, ergo sum'. Now there is a moment prior to the novel, prior to Rousseau's *Confessions*, and prior to Descartes' *Meditations* which in a startling moment of indifference to institutional differences inaugurates and installs the modern self that, in their different ways, all these later practices of writing will attempt to recover and thematise. This is the moment of the *Discourse on Method*. Now if Lukács is correct in his thesis that the novel instigates a 'Copernican turn' in the epic tradition, then in noting the moment of the narrative installation of the self we are equally noting the moment of the emergence of the novel. The *Discourse* is the first novel; its (novel) narrative defines the problematic self which will dominate all that follows.

My strategy here is to provide a historical correction to Lukács's own argument in *TN*; I wish to displace *Don Quixote* as the founding moment of the novel, and to replace it with Descartes' *Discourse*. We have already seen how the history of the novel in Part II of *TN* is generated on the basis of a slippage of an analytic typology into a conceptual metaphor. What is worse for our purposes here, Lukács uses his simple typology of 'abstract idealism' and the 'romanticism of disillusionment' to define the incommensurability of self and world, and hence, by extension, to define the nature of the problematic self (97). Let me be clear. Lukács's overall strategy in Part II is to define hermeneutically the historical specificity of the novel through a characterisation of the nature of the self in *Don Quixote*, which itself narratively argues to its historical difference from the traditions of narrative preceding it. My overall strategy will be the same, except that I shall substitute the *Discourse* for *Don Quixote*. We have already canvassed one possible explanation for the failures of Part II, namely, Lukács's adoption of the unhistorical, neo-Kantian methodology of constructing ideal types. The question now arises, could Lukács have done otherwise in Part II? *If Don Quixote is not a novel*, despite the arguments it provides and which appear to be the source of Lukács's own arguments, then it is not clear that he could have provided a properly historical analysis. If *Don Quixote* is not a novel then any attempt to delineate rigorously the form of novel based on it will necessarily have to generate hopelessly abstract and unhistorical categories to account for the real historical heterogeneity of the phenomena at issue. This thesis I take to be true, whether or not it directly explains Lukács's particular failures.

Don Quixote is not a novel; of course, a novel can be excavated from the bulk of *Don Quixote*, and this because it does contain numerous novelistic features. It is these features which explain the influence of *Don Quixote* on the novel tradition; influence, however, neither requires nor entails sameness of genre. It is equally true that from the perspective of *our* practices of reading there is almost nothing to halt its reception *as* a novel; but the point has already been argued that it is illegitimate to define literary products from the perspective of their consumption alone. What hints, then, and hints are all that can be offered here, are there that might lead us to believe that *Don Quixote* is not a novel? First, and most evidently, there exists a tradition of literally history which locates the founding moment of the novel in *Robinson Crusoe* rather than *Don Quixote*. It is significant in this regard that the only theory I am aware of which attempts to locate the historical specificity of the novel in both texts, rather than in one as opposed to the other, must employ the non-literary and ahistorical categories of Freudian theory to collect the two into a distinct genre.[3] The problems facing such a reductive programme were discussed earlier. A second and interrelated problem concerns the fact that the apparent privilege accorded to *Don Quixote* ignores the recognised historical development of the novel, that is, Cervantes' text is used indifferently as a paradigm of literary realism and as a paradigm of literary modernism. What historical and textual sense can be made of this practice?

In his aptly titled essay 'The Example of Cervantes', Harry Levin offers a catalogue of Cervantes' literary techniques which have proved to be, he believes, constitutive of the novel. Cervantes, Levin contends, wanted to demonstrate in a book the difference between 'verses and reverses, between words and deeds, *palabras* and *hechos* – in short, between literary artifice and the real thing which is life itself.'[4] Since the only means at a writer's disposal are literary means, then Cervantes could achieve his end only by discrediting those means. His techniques for discrediting the literary means available to him are all versions of but one: parody. By having Don Quixote emulate, pedantically and fanatically, the literary models of the time those models are reduced to absurdities. By having Sancho Panza echoing Don Quixote's visions in a 'realistic' key the abstractness, the bookishness of those visions is revealed. And so it goes. Cervantes' realism, we might say, is the product or the result of his parodic reductions. His 'modernism' refers to his devotion to parody, his self-imposed confinement within the models and traditions he wished to discredit.[5] Cervantes' realism, then, is a product of his 'modernism'. It is, I believe, *as a literary 'modernist' with respect to the models and 'canons' of the chivalric romance*, together with other fading literary models and conventions, that Cervantes can be best understood.

The novel, Lukács claims, is a product of a world in which all the models have disappeared, hence the sign of the novel is the productivity of spirit. The world of Cervantes, however, is one in which there is a superabundance of models, models which no longer inform or have a basis in the social 'a prioris' governing institutional life and action. Don Quixote is a man without any *usable* models in accordance with which he may construct and narrate his life. Because he does not know this, because there is no direct way in which he can know this, he is doomed to use *all* the models at his disposal, his 'experience' overflowing their boundaries at every point. He lives a crisis and a comedy of identity; his crisis is illustrated by his inability to narrate his life; his life becoming, thus, a series of discrete adventures framed at either end by bookish abstractions; chivalric romance at the beginning and pastoral romance at the end. His hapless comedy derives from his innocent assumption that all the old models are in working order, in accordance with them a life can be narratively structured, that structure allowing him to say who he is. As the 'self' is no longer able to find itself in the old models it *begins* to stand apart from those models, it *begins* to resemble a 'self', our 'self'; as the models wane the 'self' grows reflective, its art self-conscious. *Don Quixote* is a transitional work, poised at the very (imperialist) end of the fedual era;[6] it rehearses, recollects and self-consciously writes the end of that era. In so doing it presages the arrival of our world, the world of the new science, a new realism, the world of capital, without, however, delineating the structural features of our world.

Many of Descartes' narrative gestures echo and resemble the gestures of Cervantes; but Descartes will give these gestures a new grounding and meaning. For example, as Levin rightly comments, Don Quixote's descent into the Cave of Montesinos marks a reversal, or halt, in the book's movement where the critique of fiction suddenly becomes a critique of reality. Perhaps, Cervantes is suggesting, Don Quixote is right and the rest of us are wrong; perhaps what we take to be reality is nothing but a dream. The chapter reads as a speculative commentary on the thesis 'life is a dream'; and because of the absence of witnesses, certainty as to what the truth of the matter is must be left in abeyance.[7] Conjecturally, we may argue that Cervantes' procedure of parodically 'de-coding' the old models points to a conception of 'reality' without being able to supply any criteria by which that real may be established; and that is the reason why he feels constrained to consider the alternative, to construct a 'model' reality that can vie with our disenchanted world for the title of 'reality'.[8] In contrast, when in the *Meditations* Descartes wonders whether life is a dream, whether 'all these things, and speaking generally, all things that relate to the nature of the body are nothing but dreams', his strategy is guided by the existence of a criterion of reality. Indeed, for Descartes the ordinary world of perception *is* like a dream, but that is not to the credit of romantic visions; true awakeness for Descartes is scientific knowing, and what is real is defined by the methods and assumptions of the new science.[10] The novel belongs with this vision of scientific knowing and not with a worried vision of a golden age (even if it is such a vision which normatively underwrites the new science).

As yet I have said nothing which would justify this chapter not being about *Robinson Crusoe*. If my 'novel' reading of the *Discourse* is correct, it will explain why *Robinson Crusoe* has been assigned a privileged place in the history of the novel. Again, one might wonder why, if my conjecture is correct, the novel is not Cartesian rather than Kantian in form? Only by noting the limits of Descartes' conception of the self can this question be answered. To begin with, however, I must justify my contention that the specificity of the novel is narratively given by the novel in the history it constructs for itself. Descartes' *oeuvre* places a rather obvious obstacle in the way of this procedure for it is usually assumed that the meaning of his various writings should be relativised to a reading of his central metaphysical work, the *Meditations*. But if it is the metaphysical theses of the *Meditations* which define the self for Descartes, then, for the purposes of my argument, it will turn out that the self is defined extrinsically or externally, hence making a nonsense of my deliberative procedure. Thus, either the Discourse cannot be given the position I wish to assign it, or the *Meditations* must be relativised to the *Discourse*. The latter option can, I think, be defended.

2   THE CARTESIAN NOVEL

The *Meditations* begin with two clear presuppositions: (i) the natural sciences require, and presently lack, secure foundations; and (ii) reason persuades Descartes that he 'ought' to doubt not only what he knows to be false, but equally 'matters which are not entirely certain and indubitable'.[11] Neither presupposition can go unquestioned. Why should it not be the case that the sciences require no foundation outside themselves? That is, why should it not be the case that the rationality of mathematics, and hence of mathematical physics, be internally available, that truth, to use Spinoza's phrase, be its own standard? In fact, Descartes appears to accept precisely this view of mathematics. In the *Discourse* in his review of his educational experiences Descartes says of mathematics that he was pleased with it 'because of the certitude and clarity of its grounds' (8*); he was further astonished that on 'such firm and solid foundations' nothing more substantial had been built.[12] It is implausible that in a text where the controlling metaphor is the discovery of 'foundations' that the writer would attribute foundations, solid foundations, to phenomena he believed needed foundations. If, as is widely agreed, Descartes' method is but a generalisation over the procedures of mathematical analysis, then the solidity of the foundations of the latter would naturally pass over into the new method. Finally, it is perspicuous in the *Discourse* that Descartes developed and employed his new method prior to securing for it any metaphysical grounding (15–18* ; 25–6*). Thus in the *Discourse* Descartes attributes secure foundations to mathematics independently of any philosophical or metaphysical grounds; his new method is a generalisation over a domain which already possesses secure foundations; and he saw no difficulties in developing and employing his new method without metaphysical foundations. In the light of the *Discourse* the programme of the *Meditations* to provide foundations for the sciences thus appears equivocal.[13]

Descartes' second presupposition is equally problematic. Why should one doubt beliefs lacking certainty? Reason's persuading 'ought' is not itself self-evident, for, prima facie, that one is not certain it is going to rain, say, is not sufficient grounds for doubting the sun will shine. Descartes' classification of beliefs into the certain and the 'manifestly false' traverses the philosophically benign and commonsensical thesis that one ought only to doubt those beliefs for which one has independent reasons for doubting. Systematic or philosophical doubt, then, is not rational in and of itself, but rather must be grounded in a pre-systematic of pre-philosophical crisis of reason, that is, only a pre-philosophical crisis of reason can legitimate reason questioning beliefs for which there are no independent grounds for doubt. More simply, since reason giving and the justification of beliefs always occurs within a conceptual framework, then the fact that most beliefs are not certain is also a part of that framework. There is no reason to believe within our belief system that non-certain beliefs are out of order. Thus to think that ordinary, non-certain beliefs are out of order is to suppose that our conceptual system itself is out of order, that is, that there is something fundamentally wrong with our modes of justifying and accepting beliefs generally. Only this belief could justify embarking upon systematic doubt as the founding moment of systematic reflection. Thus the rationality of Descartes' systematic doubt depends upon his pre-systematic beliefs. Some philosophers now believe that knowledge does not require a 'certain' foundation in order to be rational; consequently, they believe that no crisis of reason could provide sufficient grounds for embarking on a sceptial questioning of reason in general. The argument here, however, is that such a pre-systematic crisis of reason is a necessary condition for Descartes' systematic doubt. Again, Descartes appears to agree, for the very first sentence of the *Meditations* harkens back to the pre-philosophical crisis of reason recorded in the *Discourse*. The *Discourse*, then, is both temporally and logically prior to the *Meditations* for it provides, in pre-philosophical terms, the grounds and reasons necessary for reason to engage in the systematic questioning of the grounds of reasoning which alone, in Descartes' view, can terminate the crisis of reason.

Now if it is the case that the rationality of systematic doubt must be established pre-systematically and further, that pre-systematic reason is perhaps unreliable, then how can the rationality of the need for systematic doubt be established? If the argument of the last paragraph but one is correct, then it would follow that Descartes never directly faced this dilemma. Confirmation for this can be found in the final paragraph of the second part of the *Discourse* where Descartes confronts the need for philosophical principles to ground the application of his method to the whole domain of the natural sciences. Instead, however, of embarking directly upon the construction of a philosophical system, he argues that the proper course of action is to use the method in order to establish the truths which the new philosophical system can then ground; in fine, the method turns out to be self-grounding, which is what one would expect from a method which is but a generalisation of the methods of mathematical (algebraic and geometrical) analysis.[14] None the less, the dilemma of reason remains for two obstacles directly threatened Descartes' self-grounding method. First, there existed the theological challenge to the autonomy of reason represented by the Thomistic subsumption of reason to faith, a challenge directly thematised in the final, hyperbolic doubt of the First Meditation where God or some evil demon brings reason to the highest pitch of self-doubt.[15] Secondly, there existed the general challenge to reason represented by the Pyrrhonian scepticism of Montaigne and his followers.[16] Thus, even if one accepts the radical hypothesis that Descartes' mathematical physics was both temporally and logically prior to his metaphysics, the dilemma of reason stated at the beginning of this paragraph would still be a problem for the theoretical antecedents of Cartesian philosophy questioned the autonomy and validity of reason presupposed and operative in the putative self-grounding of Cartesian method.

What sort of text is the *Discourse* that would allow it to ground the self-grounding of method? What is there outside of certainty which would provide reason with a space where it could reveal itself as autonomous? Descartes states that his intention in the *Discourse* is not to teach his method, which would be pointless since teaching presupposes authority and it is precisely the authority of the teaching of the method which is at issue; rather, he will 'show' the paths he has followed, presenting his life 'as in a painting, in order that each may judge of it' (5*). A few sentences later we read: 'I am proposing this work as, so to speak, a history – or if you prefer, a fable...' The text of the *Discourse* is an autobiography and a fable, the fable of autobiography in which the self reveals itself as absolute, as prior to and determinate of all other truths. The *cogito* installs what might be termed an autobiographical ontology, that is, the primacy of the self, but not the truth of myself as opposed to yours, but truth as dependent on the self as such, a transcendental autobiographical truth. Descartes' autobiographical fable, then, is intended as The Fable of Autobiography.

A rhetorical adumbration of the dissolution of personal authority necessary to establish the transcendental authority of the self is rehearsed in the opening sentences of the *Discourse*. In the first sentence we are presented with an ambiguous piece of proverbial wisdom: 'Common sense is the most equitably divided thing in the world, for everyone believes he is so well provided with it that even those who are hardest to please in everything else usually do not want more of it than they have' (4*). One is led to suspect the truth stated in the first clause by the evidence adduced for it; the appeal to a self-evaluation grounded in self-regard invites a consideration of the original evaluation. Without a consideration of the pervasiveness of individual vanity, and hence the extent of self-deception that natural vanity promotes, the claim for equity itself appears to become an instance of self-deception. If the evidence for equity is based on self-deception, then the assertion supported by it must be self-deceptive. The reality of what is asserted directly contradicts its surface meaning. Most naturally, then, the sentence as a whole calls for an ironic reading: human vanity being what it is, people are naturally disposed to deceive themselves into regarding themselves as, at least, the equal of those around them. Those who miss the irony of the statement are so self-deceived; 'we' know better. Irony divides the readership into 'us' and 'them', aligning the knowing reader with the author in a space of truth, a space free from vanity and self-deception. With the readership thus divided we, the knowing readers, having aligned ourselves with the author, thrust the narrating 'I' thereby into a position of authority. Generally, the epistemic effect of a stable irony is to establish a community between author and reader, a community of the undeceived, a community of truth whose authority is the authorial separation of appearance and reality which only the knowing can recognise.

Neither the authority apparently assumed by Descartes nor the truth of the inequality of human intellects generated by his ironic statement survives what follows: 'It is not likely that everyone is mistaken in this matter...' The authorial voice suddenly sides with them against us, dissolving both the original hierarchy and the authority presupposed by it. If we are to share in the flattery to our rational capacities that follow, then we must be amongst 'them', those deluded in the first instance; but this move cannot be accomplished without occluding the question of self-deception originally raised. The vanity of 'them' becomes our hubris, the locus of self-deception spread evenly between the two groups, their differential placement with respect to the truth thereby lapsing, as we only half-shift our reading of the first sentence from irony to serious assertion. Instead of a firm 'us' and 'them' there comes into existence a many, indistinguishable in intellect because equally susceptible to the vanity and hubris which occasions self-deception. The authoritative 'we' has been dissolved into many 'I's', each, now responsible for itself. Finally, and most significantly, Descartes' narrating 'I' has withdrawn from the position of authority we originally attributed to it, transferring the place of authority outside any community and into the now unsure hands of the individual reader.

Descartes' unreliable narration is not, as might be supposed, a dissimulation of authorial responsibility; on the contrary, in a text in which the question of authority is at issue stable ironies beg the question by rhetorically instituting a community of truth before the locus of truth has been established. Indeed, in any text where the question of the authority of the narrator is the issue around which the text turns, then since the epistemic effect of stable ironies and reliable narrators is to institute a community of truth, a community formed through a sharing of the truth through a capacity to distinguish appearance and reality, then it must be the rhetoric of irony which dissimulates textual responsibility. Since the ethics of the novel turns on authorial authority, stable ironies can only be regarded as evasions, as ideological recuperations of community by rhetorical means in texts which structurally and normatively assume the priority and autonomy of the individual from society (community). If irony assumes community, then the use of verbal irony cannot be used to establish authority; within an individualistic context verbal irony can have only ideological uses. Conversely, unstable ironies and unreliable narrators allow texts to enact or perform truths, to show truths that depend upon the reader's solitary re-enactment for their validation; that is, such forms of rhetoric establish indirect communications between author and reader which neither assume nor establish any form of community, except perhaps the quixotic community of solipsists. Lukács's conception of irony, the kind of irony he thinks constitutive of the novel, is like this latter kind. It is a conception of irony that owes as much to Kierkegaard as it does to German Idealism; but its origin is in this text of Descartes' which performs the original dissolution of the reading public.

Descartes' opening paragraph rhetorically suspends his narrative authority, generating thereby a neutral epistemic space where the reader becomes individually responsible for validating whatever he takes to be the truth of the authorial performance. (Equally, it could be added, by explaining the apparent differences in subjects by the diversity of objects experienced, and further, by thus making the central quality of a 'good mind' that it be applied 'correctly', Descartes quietly installs the need for an objective and anonymous 'method' as the only possible normative constraint that can be placed on the now epistemically isolated subject.) In the first instance, Descartes' autobiographical fable is but a discursive extension of his original rhetorical suspension of authority. Each term of Descartes' narrative operation serves to support and modify the other. In a context in which autobiography was traditionally conceived to be in the service of some truth beyond the self the idea of narrating simply 'my life' would be incoherent. So the autobiography must be like a fable in having a truth or moral; but this moral must not supposed to be something completely apart from the self. Fable lifts autobiography into generality, while autobiography binds the validity of the fable to the experience of the isolated subject. There exists, then, an un-resolved tension between the anonymity and universality of the fable and the singularity of the autobiographical narrative. Against this background Descartes' continual reminders to the reader that he is writing primarily for himself (5*, 34*, 49–50*, 55–6*) can be seen as serving a threefold function having little to do with conventional expressions of modesty. As markers for the autobiographical character of the narrative these ex-pressions bracket the putative universality of the fable forcing the reader thereby to question the fable's exemplarity. In so doing they maintain the original withdrawal of narrative authority accomplished in the opening paragraph. Finally, since the tension between fable and autobiography is resolved in the *cogito*, these declarations come to appear as indirect communications which rhetorically insist on the reader adopt-ing the Cartesian, first person stance.

None the less, one may still wonder how this intermediary and ambiguous narrative form can be useful and suitable for a discourse seeking to found a method of truth in the sciences, or, more modestly now, the autonomy of 'reason'. We have already denied that the *Discourse* as a whole, and hence its narrative format, might be construed as a mere literary covering for Descartes' metaphysical system; on the contrary, systematic doubt requires a pre-systematic justification. The difficulty with this is that the pre-systematic justification can neither employ given standards of truth and reason, for it is they which are in question, nor legitimately assume the validity of the yet to be established new criteria. Descartes' narrative form can best be understood as the analogue or equivalent in narrative terms of a presuppositionless starting point. The narrative of the *Discourse* is a movement from natural or existential doubt to systematic doubt as a narrative event precipitated in the wake of existential doubt. Because the systematic doubt is narratively embedded, is couched in terms of a narrative of personal crisis, the narrative as a whole can become system because it includes system; and it can include systematic doubt and its resolution in the self because both doubt and the self are originally pure narrative operators without systematic import.

Now it is obvious from this that the narrative in the first instance need only be judged *qua* narrative, as plausible; literal truth and falsity are irrelevant to the inaugural movements of the narrative. If truth and falsity are irrelevant to the narrative's fundamental gestures, then so must be the distinction between truth (empirical history) and fiction. Autobiographical fable not only stands mid-way between universal teaching and individual experience, it equally straddles the divide between history and fiction. *Only* as a movement of indifference amongst these narrative possibilities can the *Discourse* succeed; a collapse into any one of the four would vitiate Descartes' project by undermining the presuppositionless character of the starting point. Autobiography would reduce Descartes' teaching either to nullity, his truth alone, or circularity, that is, Descartes cannot presuppose his autobiographical ontology before it is validated, and thus he cannot employ a pure autobiographical approach in order to establish the systematic priority of the first person. Fable as exemplary teaching and fable as story (fiction) thus serve to bracket the presuppositions which might be thought to be entailed by the adopting of an autobiographical scheme. Yet as fable, the *Discourse* would be unable to arbitrate the question of authority; and as fiction it would have no authority. Finally, if the *Discourse* were an empirical history, then its validity would lie outside itself, and the movement from narrative to system would appear as arbitrary.

One might wonder at this juncture whether this cataloguing of narrative possibilities is altogether accurate. While it might well be the case that subjectively, that is, for the reader the *Discourse* must be a systematically ambiguous text with respect to genre, objectively there seems no reason for not regarding it as a fiction, a novel or novella. There can be no reason for not accepting this proposal so long as two points are kept firmly in mind. First, if the *Discourse* is a novel then it must be a realist novel obeying socially acceptable standards of verisimilitude; indeed, part of the generative capacity of the *Discourse* with respect to the novel and autobiography is its installing of truth-likeness, as opposed to empirical truthfulness, as evidentially sufficient for making certain types of claims about the nature of subjectivity. Secondly, and more importantly, in classifying the *Discourse* as a novel we cannot be thought to be even proleptically assigning the text to the domain of pure fiction for in the context of the *Discourse* the distinction between truth and fiction can have only a secondary and derived status.[17] Since, however, this is a result or achievement of the Cartesian programme, a programme whose inaugural narrative gestures are categorially indistinguishable from those of the novel, then it will prove a useful theoretical heuristic to treat the *Discourse* as an ur-novel in which we can trace the coming to be of the space the novel will be assigned.

3 THE PROBLEMATIC INDIVIDUAL

If the novel is a palimpsest through whose surface radiates the epic past, Descartes' ur-novel is less the discovery of that past, of a world no longer present, than an act of distancing, of constructing a past for this different present. The *Discourse* constructs a present from which the past will henceforth appear as the absolutely other. On the assumption of the equality of all individuals Descartes rejects the classical hero, the great-souled man, for 'the greatest spirits are capable of the greatest vices, as well as the greatest virtues' (4*). Myths and history, that is, all previous models of exemplary action, all that was ever thought worthy of imitation, are equally to be rejected; the former for its reliance on fabulation, portraying 'many events as possible when in fact they are not' (7*); the latter for its omission of the 'basest and least worthy of circumstances'. Were we to attempt to follow these past models we would 'fall into the excesses of the knights of our romances'; the forms of the past thus come to appear as fictions, as romances in contrast with a new realism. What makes these forms fictions, however, is not that they come from the past but rather than they are models to be imitated, that they have or appear an authority outside the self. No other evidence is ever adduced for their fictionality by Descartes. Implicitly, the same line of argument is at work in Descartes' rejection of theology whose 'revealed truths' are 'above our intelligence', and the understanding of which would require 'some extraordinary assistance from heaven' (8*). Descartes' world is a secular world in which nothing outside the self is worthy of imitation because the authority of what transcends the self is essentially problematic. In the very act, then, of constructing a past of romance Descartes makes implicit reference to the self whose unequivocal authority he has yet to establish. The crisis of reason engendered by the fictiousness or transcendence of all past models can only be a crisis for a self already dislodged from the security of traditional identities, a self 'bent and staggering', buffeted by a mysterious wind which left those around him 'erect and steady on their feet'.[18] Even if Descartes' autobiography is but a fable he still requires a narrative reason prior to the *cogito* which can isolate his self from the world and so legitimate the original autobiographical gesture.

Two related narrative reasons provide the clue to Descartes' isolation: a promise and a desire. The promise is the promise of learning: 'I have been brought up on books since my childhood, and because I was persuaded that through them we can acquire a clear and certain knowledge of all that is useful in life, I had an extreme desire to learn from them' (6*). Since we may assume that the opposite of what is clear is unclear and incomprehensible, and the opposite of what is useful is the useless, what is of no use, then these criteria of adequacy, criteria whose true meaning is the method of truth for the sciences, require no antecedent justification. Further, since 'letters' are the mediators of the tradition, the repository of cultural meaning and identity, then the promise is the promise of a culture to provide a clear accounting of what is useful for life. And how could a culture promise less and still be a culture? But since all culture must make such a promise, what is it that demarcates Descartes' experience of that culture from everyone else's? It is an 'extreme' or excessive 'desire to learn to distinguish the true from the false' (10*). In narrative terms Descartes' excessive desire is the effect of the promise broken, of the failure of learning to provide a model in accordance with which he could 'walk with

confidence in this life' (10*). Yet, since the promise would not
have been broken without the excess of desire, the palpability of
the cultural promise and its subsequent failure come to appear
as figures of a desire without narrative antecedents. While
narrative reason and plausibility are satisfied by the original
conditions of contract and promise, narrational strategy is
governed by an excess which the narrative itself does not
initially resolve.

The failure of learning to fulfil the promise of culture
precipitates the autobiographical form of narration by its tacit
cancellation of the validity of previous modes of identity
formation; the crisis of reason recorded in Descartes' account of
his education is equally a crisis of self and identity. Unless this
identification between reason and identity is made here neither
the putative resolutive power of the *cogito* nor its inadequacies
are comprehensible.[19] The self-recovery of the *cogito* will be not
only a recovery of reason from doubt but equally, and more
importantly in narrative terms, a recovery of self; the significance of the crisis of reason can only be captured in its
implications for self-understanding and social identity in general, in its power to dissolve previous modes and models of
social identity and thus render one's self problematic, unable to
answer the recurring question 'Who am I?' What has prevented
Descartes' readers from appreciating this double identity – an
identity of a crisis of reason with a crisis of self, and a
simultaneous resolution to the two crisis – has been the habit of
reading the *Discourse* as somehow merely (instead of really)
preparatory to the reading of the *Meditations*. But are the
Meditations themselves free from this identity of reason and self?
Is it an accident that Descartes' systematic work is a set of
'meditations'? Are not meditations spiritual exercises which re-
form the reader and thereby make him able to accept or see new
truths? Further, if the real point of the *Meditations* is not to
establish a foundation for the sciences, since they need none, but
to provide for and defend and autonomy of reason (from faith
and scepticism), then Descartes could not secure his end without
invoking or deploying mechanisms for transforming the reader.
Thus, even in the *Meditations* systematic doubt is not merely or
only systematic or epistemic in import, but possesses as well a
therapeutic, pedagogic and finally a cultural significance; it

paves the way for us to be transformed *into* Cartesian selves.
Descartes' literary forms, his novel narrative and his meditative
format, are the mechanisms which create the indissoluble bond
between reason and self; the first enacts Descartes' own transformation, while the second re-forms its reader in order that he
may pass into the new world of the new science.

Once we recognise Descartes as a problematic individual in
search of self-recognition we can understand why the introduction of the method in Part II of the *Discourse*, an evident
response to the crisis of reason, neither prematurely closes the
narrative nor satisfies the desire, whatever it is, which figures the
narrative in the first instance. On the contrary, rather than
resolving narrative tensions the method introduces a new
question, namely, what is meaning of right reasoning, of reason
as such for me? The question is not about the nature of reason
but about the meaning of reason; the question is ethical rather
than epistemological. Although, then, Descartes' provisional
moral code is announced as only provisional, as intended only to
facilitate the practice of the method in order that the conditions
for philosophical reflection on it may, in time, be satisfied, in
reality the code provides an original inscription of the place of
the problematic self.

As opposed to what might have been expected, Descartes'
moral code offers no form of self-recognition in the traditional
sense, that is, if offers no rules for locating or forming a stable
social identity; rather, it extracts the self permanently from all
binding social commitments, 'all promises by which one gives up
some of his liberty' (21*), and thus renders all relations to the
social order tentative or provisional, although this tentativeness
is now itself permanent. The claim that one should regard as
excessive promises which might bind one's liberty in any way is
equivalent to placing one's relations to oneself as ethically prior
to one's commitments to community and the social order.
Ironically, this statement occurs in the first ethical maxim whose
primary thesis is that one ought to obey the laws and customs of
one's country, and practice the orthodox religion of the time.
Descartes prepares the reader for the subordination of this thesis
by reminding him that 'in the corruption of our customs there
are few people who are willing to say everything that they
believe' (20*); since it is our customs which are corrupt there is

no reason to believe that Descartes will say everything he believes. The corruption troubling Descartes' writing was the Church's condemnation of Galileo, an act which led Descartes to suppress his own scientific treatise *Le Monde* (49–59*). It is no accident that Descartes spends ten pages in the concluding Part of the *Discourse* ambiguously explaining his reasons for not publishing his scientific treatise. What surfaces from beneath his declarations of modesty and philanthropic intention, however, is an evident fear of censorship, a fear that his fate would be the same as Galileo's.

But I feel that much the more obliged to manage the time left to me, the more I hope to be able to use it well; and doubtless I would have many opportunities to waste it, if I published the foundations of my physics. For, although, they are almost all so evident that it is necessary only to hear them to believe them . . . nevertheless, because it is impossible for them to agree with all the diverse opinions of other men, I forsee that I would often be diverted by the opposition that they would awaken. (54–5*)

When Descartes comes to explain his reasons for finally publishing his scientific results, with the *Discourse* itself serving as an introduction, fear again appears as the primary motive : 'And because I have been unable to keep from acquiring some sort of reputation . . . I thought that I should at least do my best to avoid having a bad one' (59*). The literary practice of the *Discourse* is one of indirection occasioned by anxiety, an anxiety for his self as comprehended through the new science. The literary form of the *Discourse*, then, is as much a function of censorship as it is a function of the new conception of the self entailed by the new science; the procedures and content of the new science, we might say, necessitate a new account of the relation between man and nature. To put this point another way, the self of the *Discourse* was precipitated prior to its full manifestation there by the new science as it intruded into the decaying world of feudalism. In part, the self of the *Discourse* is formed directly, as it were, by the way in which the new science 'writes' man and nature; in part, the self is also formed by its need to create a space or meaning for itself as the image offered it by the new science is culturally (albeit, physically) refused and threatened. What is the image offered by the new science as seen by Descartes?

As opposed to the 'speculative philosophy of the schools', Descartes sought to provide a practical philosophy which would make us 'masters and possessors' of nature (50*). Instead of revelation and salvation, the promise of the new science is that we should be afforded 'the fruits of the earth and all the commodities that are found there, but especially also for the conservation of health, which is without doubt the primary good, and the basis of all other goods of this life.' The new science does not reveal man's place in the cosmos; it is an objective picture of the natural world which of itself is neither good nor bad. The new science is to be useful, a means towards ends about which it has nothing to say. Those ends are primarily those of the body; narrowly speaking, the good of the body is health strictly speaking; more broadly, however, all goods are bodily goods because in naturalistic terms what is good is what 'I' desire: the fruits of the earth and all the commodities found there. Because mathematical physics is purely mechanistic there is not room in it for any account of ends or goals; what is good or bad is neither true nor false since everything that can be said objectively can be said by the new science. Since, however, what is good or bad is relativised to my body, my desires, then what is good or bad is, broadly speaking, relative to each, private, self. Finally, since the only limit on what is properly desirable is that our desires themselves should not contravene our fundamental liberty, then the actual scope of human desire is limitless.[20] It is this excessive or extreme desire, an infinite desiring, which instigates the excessive desire to know truth from falsehood, to know all that would allow Descartes to enjoy health and the fruits of the earth. The narrative of the *Discourse* is a figure of this original and infinite desiring as constrained by the threat of censorship.

Prudence and egoism together dictate that in such a setting it is wise to offer one's allegiance publicly to Church and state. For the new self of Cartesian theory, however, such allegiances can only be contingent. Although accepting the norms of the reigning social order entails holding opinions which, in accordance with the method of doubt prescribed by the first rule of method, Descartes has already found doubtful, these opinions no longer are a form of prejudice and blindness to him. Rather, the declaration of such opinions is now to be regarded as *expedient*, and this expediency is itself the new hallmark of all relations to state and religion. Within the new secular individualism conformity and expediency come to replace ethics as the regulators of personal affairs; ethics proper thus comes to turn upon one's relations to oneself and to nature. The apparently paradoxical combination of outward conformity and unlimited desire is stated concisely at the end of the fourth maxim: 'And finally, I would not have been able to limit my desires, nor to be content, if I had not followed a path by which I thought I should be assured of acquiring all the knowledge. . . [and] all the true goods which would ever be in my power' (24*).

The second and third maxims, anticipating the new ethics in terms of self-control and self-sufficiency, must be read in the context of unlimited desiring of the body and, finally, the *cogito* itself. The second maxim contends that one ought to treat probable beliefs as if they were certain in order to avoid indecision. Superficially this maxim reads as a modest maxim of prudence; but as the goal of the maxim is to deliver us from 'repentance and remorse' (22*) we should be alerted to the possibility of larger issues being stake. In order to get an idea of what these larger issues might be we must turn to Descartes' *Passions of the Soul*, where, in Part III, in relating the passions to the will the central doctrines of this 'ethic' are enunciated. These doctrines lie just below the (opaque) surface of the provisional moral code of the *Discourse*. In *The Passions* Descartes specifies repentance and remorse as significant failures in 'generosity', the supreme Cartesian value. Generosity is self-esteem deriving from the autonomous operation of the will, from the sense we have of having made good use of our freedom for that alone is what 'truly pertains' to us. No mention is made of what are good and evil acts; on the contrary, Descartes insists 'that there is no reason why [a man] should be praised or blamed unless it is because he uses [his free will] well or ill.'[21] To use one's will well, then, is to have a 'constant resolution to use it well', and never to fail to 'undertake and execute all the things which [one] judges to be the best', *whatever* they are.

Generosity promotes a radical self-sufficiency whereby there is nothing essential to the self that depends upon any others. Thus the self-directedness recommended in the second maxim anticipates the stoic and passive sounding recommendations of the third maxim. The appearance of passivity in the motto 'always to try to conquer myself rather than fortune' is belied by the ethic of generosity and self-sufficiency which lies behind it. The maxim is not, as it first appears to be, suggesting that one conform to the ways of the world; rather, the philosopher 'must learn to contain his world in himself.'[22] The subject changes himself, but not in the direction of conformity with the world, which would promote dependency on others and so irresolution, vicious humility, weak-mindedness, and the like. Instead, he attempts to attain a state of self-sufficiency whereby all such dependencies on the world are dissolved. As has been rightly remarked about this maxim: 'What looks like an expression of humility and self-effacement is really an expression of cynicism about the possibility of direct discourse and public self-revelation.' In reality, the self-sufficiency which is the cornerstone of the new ethic is the ethical equivalent of the call to make ourselves 'masters and possessors of nature'; in both the liberated body of desire is harnessed to an unconstrained willing.

In narrative terms the provisional moral code provides only pieces of prudential wisdom for the traveller; its provisionality appearing to undermine the imperatives of form it enjoins. Thus, narratively, no resolution to the original question of identity is provided. Yet if all of us are all the time travellers, then the provisionality of the code becomes a statement of the contingency and dependency of all forms on the self and its comprehension of its circumstances; there will be no contentful resolution to the question of identity because the self-sufficiency of the self ensures that any possible form adequate to the self will be a product of the self accepted for reasons of expediency. The much overstated thesis that the novel has no forms proper to itself is just a misdirected statement of the thesis that all forms are ideologically bound to an ontology of self-invention; the 'openness' of the novel is just the openness, the autonomy of this new self. The problematic individual is the formal narrative equivalent of an ideological ontology which by liberating the self from the past and community makes all selves necessarily problematic. If, in the novel, the problematic individual is in representational terms an 'outsider', one who must travel and invent or find an identity for him- or herself, then the lateral

message of the form is that its stated premise contradicts the
represented world; selves are bound by the past and the reigning
social order, but in ways which not only contradict the forms of
the practice of novel writing, but equally provide no adequate
sense of identity or self. In other words, the 'figure' of the
problematic self joins together the (repressed) experience of
social alienation with its ideological recuperation in the
Cartesian ontology of self-invention. Hence the promise broken
and the liberated body of desire figure the practice of the novel
generally just as they condition Descartes' narrative programme. What distinguishes Descartes' novel from all that
followed is the claim that his resolution of the question of
identity is no fiction, that his novel is absolutely true, and is
hence an absolute novel.

4 THE ABSOLUTE NOVEL: FICTIONS AND
   PARALOGISMS

But when you say 'I' do you know yourself or not? You must know
yourself, undoubtedly, since otherwise you would not name yourself.
                                                        (P.Gassendi)

In the novel life is figured by form, narrated events are brought
under or figured by a conceptual system which transcends their
'natural' order of determination. Because the form is always
unnatural the narrative as a whole can only be a fiction, a figure
of desire. Descartes' autobiographical novel avoids the fictive
fate that awaits novels generally by divising a self-abolishing
narrative, a narrative whose very movement requires that it
become more than narrative, a movement which requires that
narrative become system. From the perspective of the practice of
novel writing this procedure sounds paradoxical since the
problematic of the novel is generated precisely by the diremption of system from representation, of concept from event. The
Cartesian programme can succeed only by producing a system
that lacks abstractness, by producing a moment of universality
from within the confines of an existential career. The *cogito*
pretends to this status.

The autobiographical narrative of the *Discourse* has pro-
ceeded to a moment where the hero must produce a philosophical system because, in part, the world expects it of him; in
part because philosophical truth, metaphysics, was thought

necessary in order to give dignity to other forms of discourse, in this case the method of truth for the sciences; and finally because neither the method nor the provisional moral code proved sufficient in answering the question of identity. Because the crisis of the hero is at one and the same time a crisis of reason and a crisis of identity then, while the latter evokes and validates the adoption of an autobiographical procedure, the former legitimates a transition to the level of pure reason as a plausible avenue for the overcoming of both crises. None the less, because reason and identity are not isolated or separable narrative problems the transition to the level of pure reason is not unconstrained by the autobiographical format; not only must the resolution of the problem of reason produce a resolution to the crisis of identity, that is, produce a moment of self-recognition, equally the movement of reason itself must be autobiographical, that is, the truth of reason must itself be an autobiographical truth, a truth about 'me'. But how can autobiography be absolutely truthful, for if an autobiography is to attain to absolute truth them must it not be itself absolutely truthful?

Certainly this demand, the demand for sincerity, has been thought from Rousseau to the present to be an essential feature of the autobiographical enterprise. And Descartes accedes, indeed institutes, this demand; he is sure that 'everyone will find [his] frankness to his taste' (6*). Frankness, or what will later be called first sincerity, and then authenticity, is the ethical form of self-relatedness appropriate to autobiographical discourse for a self for whom ethics has become a question of self-relatedness. Frankness, we might say, is the only possible ethic for autobiographical discourse once all allegiances to others have been reduced to expediency. Frankness is the form of generosity appropriate to autobiographical writing because, as Jean-Luc Nancy states it, a frank writing 'frees itself from the fabulatory condition of doctrinal and authoritative discourses',[23] which is to say, it frees itself from dependency on others. If autobiography is the genre appropriate for a writing that withdraws from a position of authority and renounces all teaching, then only frankness can serve as the ethic of that writing. Certainly, the constitutive belief governing Rousseau's *Confessions*, that telling all justifies all, is only comprehensible in an ethic in which generosity is the highest virtue. None the less, one might wonder

here whether this line of development does not press Descartes'
Discourse away from fable and into autobiography. While this
belief follows on naturally from the governance of the *Discourse*
by frankness, we have already noted Descartes' disclaimers of
frankness – disclaimers which confirm the image of the masked
philosopher (*lavartus pro deo*); and does not that image recur in
Rousseau, his desire to write and hide? Now we may be correct in
believing that fiction (hiding, masking) and autobiographical
truth (frankness) are contraries; after all they stand to one
another, nearly, in the relation of active production to passive
contemplation, or so the image of frankness suggests. Yet, the
injunctions of generosity cannot, I think, be flattened out intc
our quaint conceptions of sincerity. On the contrary, autobiographical generosity, frankness, the ancestor of sincerity, grounds
an ontological indifference to genre difference; and it is this
ontological indifference, however imaginary it may be, which
presses these different institutional practices towards one another. In order that we might see this as a historical result, it will
prove useful to scan briefly the operation of generosity in the
Confessions.

Whatever the implications of generosity generally as a
leading virtue, and the history of subjectivity will have to wait
for Nietzche for those implications to be finally elicited,
frankness appears at best a quixotic at worst an impossible
imperative to satisfy. Worried and unnerved by the im-
plausibility of his project, Rousseau offers us his fateful and
plaintive reformulation of the autobiographical gesture:

I may omit or transpose fact, or make mistakes in dates; but I cannot
go wrong about what I have felt, or about what my feelings have led
me to do; and these are the chief subjects of my story. The true object of
my confessions is to reveal my inner thoughts exactly in all the
situations of my life. It is the history of my soul that I have promised to
recount, and to write it faithfully I have need of no other memories; it
is enough if I enter again into my inner self...[24]

Appearance and reality are here governed by a crude
inner/outer dichotomy; by entering into his inner self Rousseau
believed he was freed from the possibility of error. But from what
sort of error has he been freed? It cannot be from factual error,
for while it is true to say that I cannot be wrong about the rose
appearing red to me, to say in retrospect that it appears now as if
I loved Marguerite does not entail that I did love her, and the

gap between appearance and reality here has more than epistemological consequences for the mis-identification of my former state is equally an act of self-deception. The inner/outer dichotomy leads to, but does not entail, an ethics of intention, exculpations grounded in the purity of the motives behind the apparent misdeeds. Generosity, which is equally governed by an inner/outer dichotomy, does not require categorically good intentions because the self-esteem occasioned by generosity is anterior to any classification of intentions.[25] To claim a lack of remorse, as Rousseau often does, does not therefore involve revealing appropriate intentions, but rather that the will's autonomy has not been abrogated by passions which would lead the will to esteem itself for reasons external to it. If this is correct then the autobiographical gesture becomes systematically ambiguous: what is represented becomes ethically subsumed under the generosity of the act of representation, thereby leaving the represented acts suspended between a present of virtue and a past of apparent vice.

Rousseau wished to reveal the generosity of his past self, or at least the generosity of his present self in relation to that past self, but past representations invoke an otherness which the will cannot fully internalise. Necessarily, then, all that can be praised or blamed is the generosity of the act of representation itself. This latter is the source of Rousseau's confidence in the impossibility of error: because generosity concerns the will's relation to itself it necessarily excludes the troubling otherness of past selves. The veracity of a representation of the past thus becomes the frankness of the present performance of re-presenting. What troubles this confidence is the content of those acts of representation. Inevitably, the epistemological distinctions between truth and falsity, and history and fiction become eroded under the pressure of a writing which must constantly provide representations whose otherness can never be fully negated, but whose ethical opacity provides the necessary condition for the present act of negation and self-affirmation. Rousseau cannot reveal or represent his generosity without representing himself; he would not need to represent his generosity without the rigid inner/outer dichotomy pre-supposed by generosity. Thus the confessional gesture is linked with the autobiographical form of representation. However, because of the radically atemporal structure of generosity the originally dualistically sustained inner/outer dichotomy comes to invade the relation between past and present self, thus infecting the representational programme with the otherness it was designed to overcome. The negating movement of generosity can be sustained within the autobiographical enterprise only by removing its focus from external acts onto the referential content of the representation of those acts. Such an alteration, however, would undermine the purpose of providing representations at all. Therefore, in order to avoid the atemporal structure of generosity coming into open conflict with the extension proper to narrative, generosity must be temporalised: self-possession, which is the essence of generosity, becomes the ecstatic goal of narrative-telling rather than the ethical presupposition of the telling itself. Autobiography cannot survive as history if the ethical imperatives of generosity are to be fulfilled; generosity cannot survive as an ethic if the narrative imperatives of autobiography are to be satisfied. As generosity transforms autobiography from history into fiction, autobiography transforms generosity from an ethic of self-possession into an epistemological quest for lost times and past selves.[26]

Cartesian frankness, from the outset, accepts the referential opacity of its representations; the precise suspension of his narrative between fable and autobiography brackets the historical and empirical significance of the narrative while asserting its existential grounding. Equally, self-possession is the *telos* of the Cartesian narrative, but not as an act of repossessing a past self; because Descartes accepts completely the negativity of generosity, he accepts the implication that self-possession entails the negation of the past, and hence the negation of narrativity itself. Narration will forever be a feint or fiction within capital because the ideological conditions for its reproduction will forever privilege a negativity whose first victim is a narratable past. If, with modernism, narration becomes a demonstrable casualty of capital, as Benjamin urges (against Lukács), this is only because the feint necessary for narration in capital could no longer be sustained. Not only is the self-abolishing character of Cartesian narrative essential to its frankness, but the system narratively generated can separate itself from its historical and narrative conditions of production only by grounding itself in a negation of those conditions. This is the real, historical meaning of Cartesian doubt.

The frankness of Cartesian autobiography is a product of its fidelity to the self against its past; its frankness is a negativity where by doubting everything it can show the self itself, the self as standing in the truth, truth as lit by the luminosity of self-possession. For such a self nothing is worthy of imitation because to ground one's sense of worth in actions external to the self is to make one's self-worth depend on others, on what is taken by others to be worthy and exemplary. Self-possession figures the self in a negativity which can tolerate no otherness; history, sociality (state and religion), even God are transformed from conditions for self-realisation and self-knowledge into externalities whose very existence serves as a threat and a temptation to the autonomy and productivity of subjectivity. In epistemology generosity is converted from an ethic of self-possession into a requirement that the true be self-evident, which is to say, immediately evident to the self. Thus:

> For we shall not, e.g. all turn out to be mathematicians though we know by heart all the proofs that others have elaborated, unless we have an intellectual talent that fits us to resolve difficulties of any kind. Neither, though we have mastered all the arguments of Plato and Aristotle, if yet we have not the capacity for passing a solid judgement on these matters, shall we become Philosophers; we should have acquired the knowledge not of a science, but of history.[27]

Epistemologically, the otherness of history is inadequate to the needs of self-possession demanded by the Cartesian conception of subjectivity. The typically modern separation of science and history, the suppression of history for the sake of science, is itself a product of a conception of the self in which all altereity, defined originally in terms of a mind/body dualism, is posed as a threat to individual autonomy and self-possession. Thus the ethical need for the transcendence of narrative by system as performed in the *Discourse* comes to be epistemologically formalised in the dualism of history and science.

If history represents a domain of altereity, then what of the natural world? In practical terms the call for a mastery of nature clearly represents an attempt to reduce nature's otherness with respect to human needs and desires. An analogous reduction is present epistemically in the institution of Cartesian science, for it too is marked by a movement of negation (doubt) and free invention 'I even resolved to leave this whole world to their [the learneds'] disputes, and to speak only of what would happen in a new world, if God were now to create somewhere, in imaginary space, enough matter to compose it, and ... He made of it a chaos as confused as the poets can imagine' (35*). On one level, the imaginary space Descartes creates for his new world is a feint designed to placate the Church and avoid offence. On another level, that very feint writes the new science in a space outside history, thus reducing scientific rationality to mathematical certainty. Cartesian science thus becomes the invention of the (a) world out of chaos; the world order is epistemically imaged in terms of the mathematical ordering of the world by a self which knows no antecedents. But this is as much to say that for a Cartesian self any representation of the world is finally a representation of its formative powers, a revelation of the act of production rather than what is produced.[28]

Like all novels Descartes' depends upon a feint or fiction, a negation for its institution. The novel must deny the world as it is in order formally to figure it in the image of desire and need; its ultimate fictionality is its formal figuration as the transgression and transcendence of its mimetic ambitions. Descartes' absolute novel differs only in its radicality; its negation of the world is absolute, a reduction of the world to chaos; the goal of the reduction, however, is not to free the self from the demands of mimesis in order to produce a perfect fiction; rather, the production of a *perfect* fiction, a new world, would reduce the meaning of mimesis to a representation wholly adequate to the self, to self-invention and self-possession. The absolute novel images the possibility of a utopian capitalism, capital as the freedom from history and the curse of Adam, the productivity of capital as the mastery of nature without end other than absolute self-possession, limitless self-invention in the name of the liberated body of desire. Because all the possible contents of the absolute novel are products of self-invention, however, its only true content is the self itself, the *cogito* as the perfect act of self-possesson. 'If the *cogito* is unshakeable,' says Jean-Luc Nancy, 'it is because it forms the point where I can no longer feign, the point of an impossible feint or fiction, or rather, the point of the feint's passage to its limit.'[29] The truth of the absolute novel is no fiction because it is fiction's resistance to all fabulation; fiction turns into truth with the impossibility of my doubting my existence, thus revealing the self as beyond history and fiction good and evil.

The *cogito* provides the moment of self-recognition within the absolute novel; it is, however, a troubled moment because the self recognised is discontinuous from the historical self of the narrative whose need for self-recognition, for an answer to the question 'Who am I?' launched the narrative in the first instance. This is overtly the case in the self-abolition of the 'historical' narrative for the sake of system; the negation of the narrative history is equivalent to the negation of the self whose history that narrative represented. Thus the conditions for the assertion of the *cogito, the* act of self-recognition and self-possession, prohibit it from being an answer to the question of which it is presumed to be the answer. That the *cogito* is no empirical, historical self is made equally clear as Descartes proceeds on the basis of the *cogito* to ask about his true nature: 'Then I examined closely what I was, and saw I could pretend that I had no body, and that there was no world nor any place where I existed . . .' (28*). The self that comes to self-recognition in the *cogito* is not, then, the self whose narrative we have been following; indeed, it is not the kind of self for whom self-knowledge and the questions of identity could ever be at issue for any empirical predicates, predicates which would give empirical specificity to this self, would necessarily modify and limit the negativity which conditions its self-possession. The universality of the *cogito* is guaranteed by its ubiquity and anonymity; but as ubiquitous and anonymous it fails to name the self, 'my' self.[30]

In the 'Paralogisms of Pure Reason' Kant examines the variety of fallacies attending the 'I think'. Central to his analysis there is the claim that although the 'I think' must indeed be capable of accompanying all our thoughts, otherwise there would be thoughts belonging to no one, the 'I' of the 'I think' is not a referring expression, and the 'I think' as a whole does not provide any knowledge of the subject. 'Certainly, the representation "I am", which expresses the consciousness that can accompany all thought, immediately, includes in itself the existence of a subject, but it does not so include any *knowledge* of that subject, and therefore also no empirical knowledge, that is, no experience of it' (B 277). In other for there to be knowledge of the subject there must be an intuition, an individual that is characterised by some empirical predicates; but the 'I' of the 'I think' does not pick out or refer to any individual. The negativity of thought and the self is precisely its freedom from all empirical determination. Kant calls the negativity of the self 'spontaneity'. The consciousness of myself in the representation "I" is not an intuition, but a merely intellectual representation of the spontaneity *(Selbsttätigkeit)* of a thinking subject' (B 277). Therefore, although the 'I think' is a necessary representation, it is not a source of self-knowledge; further, because the 'I' of the 'I think' does not refer, then although in thinking anything the 'I think' is unfailingly present, as a formal condition of thought it does not reveal 'my' self, my numerical identity through time (A 363).

If the novel is the discovery of the self, the self discovered cannot be simply the ordinary, empirical self, for the priority of this self depends upon the priority of the *cogito*, the transcendental self which is the condition for all thought. Descartes' absolute novel is absolute because the self-recognition it provides is not Descartes' recognition of who he is, but the self-recognition of The Self, of the priority of the transcendental self before all else. Kant's critique of the *cogito* is just the clarification of the distinction between the transcendental and empirical self, the demonstration that the statement of the *cogito* cannot be an historical act of self-possession for any particular self. For Kant the 'I' of the 'I think' is the *logical* and not the existential subject. How are we then to understand the 'I think'?

Heidegger provides the following concise summary of Kant's central thesis:

'I think' means 'I bind together'. All binding together is an '*I* bind together'. In any taking-together or relating, the 'I' always underlies.... The *subjectum* is therefore 'consciousness in itself', not a representation but rather the 'form' of representation. That is to say, the 'I think' is not something represented, but the formal structure of representing as such, and this formal structure alone makes it possible for anything to have been represented. When we speak of the 'form' of representation, we have in view neither a framework nor a universal concept, but that which, as εἶδος, makes every representing and everything represented be what it is.[31]

Now there is an equivocation in Kant's account of the 'I think' which is important to grasp, an equivocation that is in Kant and which Heidegger accurately characterises. There appears to be a lack of equivalence between the 'I think' as 'I bind together', and the 'I think' as a form of representation. The former characterisation of the 'I think' accords well with the negativity and self-invention which Descartes ascribes to the self; as such it propels us into reading the 'I' of the 'I think' existentially. After all, if the 'I think' is to be read positively as 'I bind together', then must not any *act* of binding together be the act of some particular person? Conversely, as a form of representation the 'I think' is anterior to any particular 'I', and is that which allows any 'I' to represent anything to itself at all. In the first case the transcendental comprehension of the subject takes itself to be characterising the selfhood of the 'I' *qua* self; in the latter case something more remote and complex is denominated, namely, that universality of whatever it is that bestows upon the self the possibility of being a subject for whom there are representations. About this latter conception of the self I shall have more to say in the next chapter.

To understand the problematic placement of the self in the novel is to understand both the (paradoxical) exemplarity of the Cartesian narrative and its failure; and further, to comprehend the Kantian restructuring of the *cogito* as both clarifying its meaning and compounding the paralogisms latent in it. As the absolute novel the *Discourse*'s narrative discovery of the self installs the self in a position of privilege; this privileged position and the narrative journey which led up to its discovery will henceforth appear as the form appropriate for any representation of the external world. Narratively, one can only represent the world by representing the self's journey through the world in search of self-recognition. However, this self is necessarily problematic both because the world is inadequate to the needs of the self, and because the very kind of subject bequeathed to us by the *cogito* is inherently and necessarily in a problematic relation to its social environment. The negativity of the new subject necessitates that any social identity it might find will fall short of the form of self-possession imaged by the *cogito*. Since any empirical form of self-recognition must be inadequate to the true nature of the self, then there can be no proper, formally adequate place for novels to end. The apparent apodicticity of the *cogito* makes its placement of the self exemplary and unsurpassable, while the transcendental negativity of the self places it forever beyond the possibility of self-recognition through narratives genesis.

Kant formally restructures the Cartesian transcendence of narrative by system and its consequent suppression of narrative history for the sake of subjectivity through his theoretical distinction between *transcendental* reflection and subjectivity, and *empirical* reflection and subjectivity. Henceforth, the 'empirical' narrative of the self's journey toward self-recognition will be only a reflection or figure (symbol, metaphor, allegory) of the authorial consciousness's 'I bind together'. The Cartesian movement from narrative to system comes to be expressed Kantianly in the novel in terms of a hierarchial or levelled structural relation between narrative and narration, mimetic or represented acts and authorial or representing acts, between, finally, mimesis and form-giving. In the novel autobiographical form recapitulates biographical form because the meaning of biographical form, its origin and validity, is located in the autobiographical ontology of the 'I think' as reformulated by Kant.

Now we have already seen that Descartes' paralogistic conflation of the empirical and transcendental infects even Kant's reformulation of the 'I think'. As the form of all representation the 'I think' is supposed to be the ground for the possibility of objectively valid representations; however, as an '*I* bind together' the spontaneity and negativity of transcendental subjectivity is reinstated. Thus authorial form-giving comes to occupy an ineliminably contradictory space, being the only possible source of objective forms whose every *act* of form-giving denies the objectivity of those forms. In the novel irony is the strategic and formal working through of the paralogism of transcendental subjectivity.

In his account of self-consciousness in the *Phenomenology of Spirit* Hegel traces the origin of the distinction between transcendental and empirical consciousness to the self-deceptive movements of scepticism. Sceptical consciousness, aware of the negativity of consciousness, engages in the pseudo-praxis of negating the world in *thought*. Because the world to be negated is made

accessible to consciousness through ordinary empirical awareness, sceptical consciousness must naturally be aware of itself
as a 'wholly contingent, single, and separate consciousness ... in
fact, [an] animal life, and a *lost* self-consciousness'; because its
sense of its essential freedom with respect to the natural world is
denied by the infinite givens of sense awareness it actively
negates the reality or essentiality of these givens for it in thought.
In so doing it affirms itself as 'universal and self-identical; for it is
the negativity of all singularity and all difference.'[32] Because,
however, reality is not really negated by thought, sceptical
consciousness must still *live* in the world it claims to have
transcended, forever unable to unite its different conceptions of
itself. For Hegel individual transcendental subjectivity is an
illusory expression of human freedom trapped in a world it is
powerless to transform and make adequate to itself.

The sceptical feint, the transgressive fiction of Cartesian
doubt is the illusory appearance of the discovery of human
negativity and freedom accomplished by the triumph of the new
science over theology, and the sociality of capital productive
relations over the collapsing feudal system. The twining of
protestant and sceptical inwardness with the new science of the
body produced the ideological figure of the new subject, a
transcendentally free subject whose infinite and unsatisfied
desiring imaged the restlessness and pointlessness of capital
production itself. Whether the ideology of capital could have
been written differently is a moot question. What is true is that
Descartes' narrative practice fused a variety of existing discursive practices into an ideological figure which remained
commensurable and fruitful throughout capital's period of
emergence into dominance. The autonomy of the economic
moment in capital is the negativity of capital with respect to all
'natural' boundaries. That negativity is positively valorised in
the image of transcendental subjectivity. Transcendental subjectivity is the ideological form of a subjectivity *lost* in a reified
social world. Thus each act of self-validation is necessarily also a
fiction. The 'institution' of that fiction hence becomes a
repository and focus for our individual attempts at self-
possession, a self-possession which is forever an unnarratable
fiction.

VI

Transcendental Dialectic:
Irony as Form

Lukács makes three substantial claims concerning the place of irony as a constitutive, form-giving structure within the novel. First, irony is 'the normative mentality of the novel' (84), where the notion of something being 'normative' means, in this instance, that a particular strategic practice of novel writing is necessarily enjoined in virtue of the general problematic and intentions of the practice as a whole, and further, that this strategy emblemises the problematic character of that practice as a whole. Irony, then, will be said to be a kind of master-practice, a practice which governs the meaning of the sub-practices of the novel which simultaneously 'corrects' and instantiates their deficiencies. The thesis that connects ironic structuring with novelistic form has become quite familiar since Lukács first put it forward, and I shall argue that it is the only one of his three theses that can be fully validated.

His second claim is that irony provides for 'the objectivity of the novel' (90). Sometimes Lukács means by this that irony provides the novel with all the 'objectivity' it is capable of possessing, without this entailing that irony provides the novel with an unequivocal objectivity. A version of this claim can be defended. Sometimes, however, he notes how ironic structuring may create an illusion of objectivity; now unless this illusion of objectivity is clearly demarcated from the kind of real, but weak, objectivity the novel can have the very idea of objectivity will come under threat. Lukács is not always clear in making this necessary separation. He concludes his account by stating that irony, or rather ironic consciousness, 'is the highest freedom that can be achieved in a world without God' (93). This claim joins his historical pessimism with a metaphysical trope of Romantic Irony. It is the least convincing of his theses.

All three claims are rooted in what Lukács regards as the central categorial problematic of the novel form: the antinomic relation between subject and structure, between form-giving subjectivity with its premised freedom and reified structural complexes which leave no room for freedom or (authentic) subjectivity. Irony thematises this fundamental problem and through the mediation of form attempts to overcome the dualism it initiates. The original Romantic theoreticians of irony thought that irony could truly overcome subject–object dualism, at least in so far as it could be overcome, and consequently believed literary practice to be of metaphysical significance, to define a fundamental mode of being in the world, an existential category. This exaggerated view of irony can be heard echoing in Lukács's third claim that irony provides for the highest freedom that can be achieved in a world without God. Because he tends to appropriate the language of Romantic Irony rather uncritically, a full evaluation and reconstruction of his affirmative theory of irony will require us to examine the ancestry of his doctrine.

Not surprisingly, what all the claims and problems about irony share is a concern for the problems of transcendental subjectivity as identified in the last chapter. Irony, we might say, is a formal expression of the division between and irreconcilability of empirical subjectivity with transcendental subjectivity; that division, however, is itself an expression, perhaps the fullest expression in the novel, of subject–object dualism. Because it is that dualism, as generated by categorial contemplation, which structures the inner world of the novel, then the delimitation of irony as the focal or focusing novelistic practice becomes the most complete inscription of the novel in society.

The obstacles confronting an adequate comprehension of novelistic irony are daunting. In order that these obstacles may be surmounted this chapter will take the following pedagogic course. In the first two sections I shall sketch Lukács's general argument about irony and track down the false leads instigated by his borrowings from Schlegel and Kierkegaard. In section 3 I shall provide irony with a conceptual structure which is directly dependent on the Kantian conception of a split or divided subjectivity. In the following section I shall attempt to provide a non-metaphysical account of the divided subject, and then apply my revised analysis of irony to the novel. I conclude the chapter with an attempt to 'identify' the transcendental subject.

1 NARRATIVE IRONY

In the opening paragraph of the chapter entitled 'The Historico-philosophical Conditioning of the Novel and its Significance', Lukács quickly specifies the novelistic problem which ironic structuring is to answer. He begins by stating that

the composition of the novel is the paradoxical fusion of heterogeneous and discrete components into an organic whole which is then abolished over and over again. The relationships which create cohesion between the abstract components are abstractly pure and formal, and the ultimate unifying principle therefore has to be the ethic of creative subjectivity, an ethic which the content reveals. (84)

The 'heterogeneous and discrete components' are those of the language of experience; through the force of form (of plot and thematic ordering) this experiential diversity can be unified. Because of the resistance of the discourse of experience to form, of the distance between abstract, conceptual form and the protocols governing the language of experience the order proffered collapses (74–5). What is revealed thereby is the activity of the self in giving form to experience. It is the revelation and celebration of the self as form-giver which is intended by Lukács's 'ethic of creative subjectivity', a celebration common to at least those portions of the Romantic tradition which argue for the dependency of the world on human imagination for its redemption or completion. Such an ethic, however, is alien to Lukács, who goes on to argue that this 'ethic must surmount itself [in order that] the author's normative objectivity may be realised' (84). Lukács's point here is simple: the thesis of creative subjectivity contends that all forms and norms are products of (conscious or unconscious) acts of individual subjects; but this thesis cannot be accepted as such, be made into an 'ethic', for this would deny the normativeness of the forms offered. Either a form is normative – defining right and wrong, say – or it is simply an expression of what 'I' desire, want or believe. In other words, either form is immanent within social experience and constitutive of it, or all norms are a reflection of individual choices and desires.[1]

But this latter alternative is self-defeating for the idea of something being normative entails that it transcends individual choice; therefore subjects cannot simply create forms of experience which truly possess normative force. Saying the world is ethically constituted in such and such a way does not make the world into something so constituted. The ethic of creative subjectivity, then, represents the negativity and spontaneity of transcendental subjectivity; while the mention of the 'author's normative objectivity' points emphatically to transcendental subjectivity as the form of representation, and thus the support of all objectivity. No individual act can give to a form normative force simply through its assertion; but individual transcendental subjectivity has no other avenue for realising its grounding normativity except assertion.[2] The normativity and productivity (spontaneity) of transcendental subjectivity thus appear to be incapable of being realised simultaneously; the negative movement which clears the way for subjectivity being the ground of all objectivity equally prohibits it from concretely realising its normative vocation. This is the paralogism (or antinomy) haunting transcendental subjectivity; it is the most acute expression of the antinomy problematising the dialectic of form-giving and mimesis, and thus the place within the practice of novel writing where its historical predicament reaches its most acute formal expression. Since irony is the strategic response to this problem it can be confidently denominated the normative mentality of the novel.

In purely textual terms we know that authors create formal patterns of experience which are intended to transcend their subjective origin and be constitutive of the experiences they inform. However, the immediate interaction of abstract, conceptual forms with experiential heterogeneity reveals, as often as not, more about the intentions and prejudices of the author than about the objects of his formative activity. All too often we are aware of an author manipulating plot, characters and events; our attention is distracted from fictional space and time, and we are made conscious of the process whereby that fictional world is generated. To produce successful realistic narrative an author must remove the disruptive traces of his activity from the text, that is, he must remove from the text all those elements in it which point more emphatically to his activity as producer than to the significance of the narrative itself. It follows from this that the ethic of creative subjectivity 'needs a new ethical self-correction, again determined by the work's content, in order to achieve the "tact" which will create a proper balance. This interaction of two ethical complexes, their duality as to form and their unity in being given form, is the content of irony, which is the normative mentality of the novel' (84). On the point at issue here Lukács makes confused if not contradictory assertions. On the one hand, he appears to claim that any compositional tact which allows an author to displace his subjective desire into novelistic form is an achievement of irony (74–5); on the other hand, he states explicitly that 'wisdom [i.e. the author's awareness of the complex relation between idea and reality] can be expressed through the act of form-giving; it can conceal itself behind the forms and does not necessarily have to surmount itself, as irony, in the work' (84). Lukács is quite consistent in his claim that in order to approximate epic totality the novelist must be 'tactful' in his ordering of experience if he is to achieve a wholeness that does not overtly implicate its creator in its existence. What is at issue here is whether every such ordering must employ ironic means to achieve this end. Since it is evident that many novels that do succeed do so without recourse to irony, it is more appropriate to ask why it is that Lukács seems, sometimes, to conflate form with irony. And the answer to this question is that he has simply uncritically accepted this conflation from the foremost theoretician of Romantic Irony, Friedrich Schlegel.

Schlegel's goal was to bring about a reconciliation between the Classical and the Romantic, where *das Klassiche* has finitude as a principle of simplicity, unity and form as its founding axiom, and *das Romantische* has infinitude as a principle of richness, complexity and variety as its founding axiom. Instead, however, of actually reconciling these contrasting perspectives, Schlegel argues that it is the contradiction between them which lies at the heart of reality, that they mutually require and depend on one another, and finally that any halt in the conditioning movement which holds these two aspects of reality and consciousness in being would involve the disappearance of consciousness and so reality. If we ignore the metaphysical setting (derived from Fichte) in which Schlegel places his thesis, it becomes apparent that he is providing nothing more than a (metaphysical) rewriting of the Kantian dictum that intuitions (experience) without concepts (form) are blind, and concepts without intuitions are empty. The difference between Kant and Schlegel is that Schlegel's Romantic infinite denotes not particular objects and intuitions (which are individuals in Kant's system), which for Kant are finite because particular, but rather the infinite striving of consciousness and the infinite which transcends ordinary experience : God and the cosmos as a whole. In a sense, then, Schlegel is using the Kantian model of cognition to solve (dissolve) the Kantian antinomy of finite and infinite.

For Schlegel the artistically-informed experience is ironic because the infinity suggested by the artwork is one which transcends direct conceptual representation; the art work is a visible representation of the invisible, a finite allegory of the infinite. The ironist, unlike the classical artist, is aware that the infinite is not directly representable and consequently attempts to insinuate the limits of representation in his formal present-ation. It is this need to indicate the essential incompleteness of particular works which explains the formal and material complexity of the ironically wrought work. What is important for us to notice here is that this irony, this self-limiting of the literary work, sounds like but is not in fact commensurable with the irony of a Lukácsian author. The Lukácsian novelist is not concerned with the cosmic infinite, but only with the relative 'infinite' complexity and diversity of ordinary experience. Compositional tact is required to correct the ethic of creative subjectivity, not to avoid the dangers of wilful classicism. Consequently, Lukács was right to say that authorial wisdom can be accomplished without the use of irony. Any refraction of individual desire into novelistic form can serve as a repression of the self-defeating creative ethic. Lukács goes astray, identifying irony with form, only when he uncritically borrows his materials directly from Schlegel. For example, Schlegel states that the complexly structured literary work, what he called 'the arabes-que', presents to the reader 'artfully ordered confusion, a charming symmetry of contradiction, this wonderfully perennial alteration of enthusiasm and irony which lives even in the smallest part of the whole ...' And here is Lukács:

> The irony of the novel is the self-correction of the world's fragility: inadequate relations can transform themselves into a fanciful yet well-ordered round of misunderstandings and cross-purposes, within which everything is seen as many-sided, within which things appear as isolated and yet connected, as full of value and yet totally devoid of it, as abstract fragments and as concrete autonomous life. (75)

Lukács's arabesque ignores the differences between his project and Schlegel's. Thus:

(i) for Lukács it is discrete experience and conceptual form which stand opposed to one another, not the finite and the infinite considered as metaphysical elements of the world;

(ii) conceptual form is unable to totalise social experience, not because the finite and the infinite are forever in contradiction with one another, but because the imagination cannot resolve by itself a contradiction that has been historically caused, i.e. ultimately, conceptual form and social reality can be brought into harmony only through social change;

(iii) technically, it is form not irony which corrects the world's fragility; irony corrects the wilfulness of form.

There are, of course, analogies to be drawn between the metaphysically problematic world which faces the Schlegelian author of the arabesque and the Lukácsian novelist who confronts a socially problematic world, but these analogies need theoretical delineation before the theory of the novel can appropriate for itself Schlegel's Romantic theory; Lukács nowhere provides the needed delineation and his appropriation runs contrary to the main lines of argument in his text. Whether these borrowings infect the rest of his account we shall see as we progress.

Despite Lukács's confusion on this issue, there exist independent reasons why one might consider at least some instances of compositional tact to be instances of ironic structuring. Remember the original compositional problem: the gathering of experiential diversity into systematic unity without making the experiential elements serve a merely pedagogic or illustrative function in relation to the thematic material. One can call the conceptual structures that provide a solution to this problem ironic structures if it is the case that they accommodate experiential diversity and discontinuity in a way which is impossible for symbolic and metaphorical structures, which, of their nature, tell fables of identity. It is, in the first instance, the non-reductive character of ironic structures which distinguishes them from symbolic and metaphorical structures. For example, with the conceptual schema provided by the proverb 'Pride goeth before a fall' we can have an elaborate plot replete with misunderstandings and eventualities whose sole purpose comes to light at the end of the story when the proud hero is brought low through his excesses. The task of composition here is to guarantee that this revelation occurs through the efficacy of the narrative events. Endings are not important because novels operate teleologically, rather one of the reasons that novels are teleological is that some types of narrative structure can save the appearances (experiential diversity and discontinuity) and provide for a conceptual unification that appears to be rooted in the nature of reality itself. The deep structure behind many of these ironic structures is the familiar one of the unintended consequences of intentional action. Discontinuity between intended goal and unexpected result is of the very nature of this structure. Poetic justice, the revealing of the evaluative truth behind the empirical appearances, fail to convince only when the hand of the author is too evident in the resolution. When formal structuring is successful our understanding of the work is derived from the whole of it and not from any of its parts in isolation from the whole. And this is the case with the unintended consequences pattern since with it we require the intentional actions of agents, their patterned interaction and development leading to the final reversal of expectation.

What justifies us in calling structures of this sort ironic is (a) their ability to comprehend discontinuity without reduction; and (b) that they instantiate the essential 'two standpoints' structure common to ironic statements. All ironic states must share (b), that is, for any statement or structure to be ironic there must be some appearance/reality contrast. For ordinary ironic statements the appearance level is the one in which the statement is construed in accordance with its usual sense (and where it must be conceivable for someone to so construe it), while the reality is the level in which the statement is construed as having the opposite meaning to the one usually assigned to it. In a novel the narrative prior to the resolution or regarded simply from the perspective of the intentions and goals of the characters provides the appearance, while the narrative as a whole with its reversal of expectations provides the reality. And this justifies, if anything can, Lukács in his contention that irony provides a semblance of organic unity, a 'self-correction of the world's fragility'.

2 OBJECTIVITY: 'A SURFACE RIDDLED WITH HOLES'

Still, the ironisation of the heroic plot can hardly be described as providing a direct confrontation with the ethic of creative subjectivity, not does it tie in directly with any of Lukács's three stated theses concerning the relation of irony to the novel. Moreover, narrative irony does not exhaust the possibilities of ironic structuring available to the novelist. Sometimes ironic structuring is an effect of narrational procedures (e.g. manipulation of point of view, manipulation of time structures, and so forth) whereby the fiction and its telling are consciously played off against one another, and where ironic disturbances on either the narrative or narrational level generates disturbances on the remaining level. Let us say that when this occurs the work as a whole is self-conscious in that it contains an internal, usually only implicit, meditation on its own principles of activity. Form *and* form-giving are both presented, and each is mediated through the other. It is this textual self-consciousness which Lukács primarily intends to capture by his concept of irony.

The obvious source of this view is Lukács's thesis that the novel, as opposed to the epic, is constituted by a double subjectivity: heroic subjectivity and authorial subjectivity. For Lukács every heroic plot insinuates or evokes an authorial plot: all narrative presupposes some narrational form, and every narrational form is implicated in some narrative. Now when the doubling of heroic and authorial plots takes place in a self-conscious mode we have an ironic structure.

The creative individual's reflexion, the novelist's ethic *vis à vis* the content, is a double one. His reflexion consists of giving form to what happens to the idea in real life, of describing the actual nature of this process and of evaluating and considering its reality. This reflexion, however, in turn becomes an object for reflexion; it is itself an ideal, only subjective and postulative; it, too, has a certain destiny in a reality which is alien to it; and this destiny, now purely reflexive and contained within the narrator himself, must also be given form. (85)

Any conceptual structure can be made the object of narrative reflection: love or death, utilitarianism or Christian belief, egoism, marriage, sexual identity, honesty or pride – there are no a priori limits on the thematic material a writer may consider. However, no matter how artfully rendered, any implementation of formal material in narrative terms may be considered to be only an imposition of the author, to reveal not the objective reality behind the appearances but, rather, the author's subjective prejudices: the proud *ought* to fall; love and death *ought* to beat together. Now this problem is unavoidably inscribed in the form of the novel as a dialectic of interpretation and representation. The epical desire for objectivity is always defeated by the interpretative, form-giving moment. Form provides all the objectivity we can possess, but it is always inadequate because it is but another human creation. Lukács's demand for a second level of reflection is the demand to reflect on this fact and give it form within the novel.

A recognition of this point will allow us to begin to appreciate the substance of the first claim concerning irony, namely, that it constitutes the normative mentality of the novel. As a historical permutation of the epic, the novel is constituted by the disappearance of 'formal a priori' (74) structures regulating human action and self-understanding, that is, by the disappearance of a 'marked convergence between ethic as an interior factor of life and its substratum of action in the social structure' (ibid). As a result of this form and experience no longer possess any necessary connections with one another, and consequently imaginative totalisations of experience may present us with 'only a subjective aspect of [the] totality ... obscuring or even destroying the creative intention of acceptance and objectivity which the great epic demands' (ibid.). Given the historical conditioning of the novel this problem cannot be circumvented; it must be overcome from within. Lukács states his point in what is for him pellucid terms:

'For such subjectivity is not eliminated if it remains unexpressed or is transformed into a will for objectivity: such a silence, such a will, is even more subjective than the overt manifestation of a clearly conscious subjectivity, and therefore, in the Hegelian sense, even more abstract' (ibid.). The novel only reaches full maturity as a genre when it becomes self-conscious; for the novel to be self-conscious it must thematise (give form to) the subjectivity of form. But it looks as if this can be done in a non-essayistic fashion only by letting the narrational and narrative levels of discourse mediate one another, which is to say, through ironic structuring. Since irony in its intentional mode is a form of self-consciousness (self-awareness and self-reflexiveness), the coupling of irony and novelistic self-consciousness appears justified.

What is involved in the idea of different levels of a text mediating one another, and hence what is involved in the ironic structuring of the authorial plot and hence in textual self-consciousness, will be discussed in more detail later. For the moment I want to focus on Lukács's second and third claims, which he sees as direct consequences of his plausibly argued first claim. His second claim, concerning irony and objectivity, has some credibility but not in the way he supposes; while his third claim, that irony represents the highest freedom we can attain, is a significant error. In fine, I shall argue that Lukács draws false conclusions from, or better misinterprets his own original thesis.

Lukács's argument for the second claim depends on an exaggerated and unjustified employment of his thesis that the epic proper appears as self-begotten, and that therefore the proper relation of writer to epic is one of passive reception on the writer's part. Lukács argues that the novelist surmounts the unaviodable excess of subjectivity involved in form-giving simply by letting it be. Maire Kurrick states Lukács's doctrine here as follows:

Irony is the novelist's '*docta ignorantia* toward meaning', whereby the novelist abdicates his intense search for meaning (90). He destroys his own authority as an author, but in that act his work comes into being as a totality. The work as a totality acquires transcendence in technique. In a world bereft of God, God can, paradoxically, but also truthfully, only be perceived in technical perfection, in 'material

authenticity' (92). The miracle of form is for Lukács . . . irony's likeness
to negative mysticism. The novelist's way to God can only be through
form. . . . [Irony represents] the novelist's inner sense that he neither
knows nor desires to know meaning, [and this] gives him a metasubjectivity that is not identical to the a-subjectivity that he may
crave, but an approximation.[4]

I find the thesis that somehow 'through technical immanence'
(92) together with a 'not-desiring to know and not-being-able-
to-know' a writer may 'encounter, glimpse, and grasp the
ultimate, true substance, the present, non-existent God' (90)
to be vague and unconvincing, even if God is being used
symbolically rather than literally, as Kurrick seems to suppose.
What is missing in this account is the establishment of a
theoretical connection between form or technical perfection
and God. A writer who provides such a connection is, again,
Schlegel, but Schlegel's metaphysics is remote indeed from
Lukács's concerns. Once more Lukács seems to be involved in
an uncritical and unjustified appropriation of Schlegelian
materials.

Schlegel rejected the Kantian limitation of knowledge to
experience, and argued for a return to intellectual (i.e.
unmediated) intuition, which he identified with aesthetic
experience. But aesthetic experience, as we saw earlier, is
equivalent to form-giving, where form is taken as being able
to afford us a glimpse of the infinite. The following two passages
from Lukács directly echo Schlegel's thesis that finite and
infinite are interdependent, and hence lead to the corollary
that form in art allows a glimpse of the infinite (God).

The self-recognition and, with it, self-abolition of subjectivity was
called irony by the first theoreticians of the novel, the aesthetic
philosophers of early Romanticism. As a formal constituent of the
novel form this signifies an interior diversion of the normatively
creative subject into a subjectivity as interiority, which opposes power
complexes that are alien to it and which strives to imprint the contents
of its longing upon the alien world, and a subjectivity which sees
through the abstract and, therefore, limited nature of the mutually
alien worlds of subject and object, understands these worlds by seeing
their limitations as necessary conditions of their existence and, by thus
seeing through them, allows the duality of the world to subsist. (74–5)

the objectivity of the novel is the mature man's knowledge that meaning can never quite penetrate reality, but that, without meaning, reality would disintegrate into the nothingness of inessentiality. (88)

In the first passage the 'alien worlds of subject and object' come to replace Schlegel's finite and infinite; the recognition of their interdependence being analogous to a Schlegelian intuition of the infinite. Since reification is a condition for the existence of the novel, it is right and proper that the hiatus between subject and object should be regarded as necessary for a work's existence; but this is a far cry from letting their duality subsist, for the justification for that would involve making reification into a metaphysical as opposed to socio-historical state of affairs. Lukács does seem to be doing here what Hegelians are often accused of doing generally: reifying an historical fact into a metaphysical fact. To see *through* subject – object dualism is to see it as a contingent and not as a necessary feature of experience. To hypostatise subject – object dualism is to deny the central premise of *The Theory of the Novel*, namely, that the dualisms which permeate the bourgeois world are the result of the reification and rationalisation of the social world caused by commodity production.

The second passage can be read in two ways. The first textually correct but invalid reading suggests the thesis that the infinite can only be grasped through the finite, but cannot be encapsulated by it – meaning is suggested or hinted at through form, but form never provides knowledge of meaning. A more useful reading has this passage marking the limits of imaginative form-giving by inscribing the novel in an antinomic conceptual space: fictional forms that order experience transcend experience, yet without the attempt to understand experience through form experience would disintegrate into inessentiality. In the misleading, Schlegelian reading emphasis is concentrated on the metaphysically necessary limits of knowledge; in the second reading stress is placed on the antinomic relation between the prescriptive, imaginative reconstitution of experience and described states of affairs which exclude the proposed meaning patterns.

In a sense, these two readings replay a central moment in Marx's critique of Hegel. In the *Philosophy of Right* Hegel both sees the ethical poverty of property relations and the market economy, dominated, as they are, by competitive individualism, but, unable to abstract from the present as a completion of all past history, he hypostatises these features of modern society into necessary and therefore ineliminable moments in the development of freedom. Consequently, the present, with all its contradictions, becomes frozen; freedom becomes the recognition and acceptance of the necessities imposed by civil society (market relations) and only a bogus common interest is achieved in the political institutions which are supposed to transcend the conflicting interests of competitors in the market place. Hegel thus reifies the difference between particular and common interests, making the former a necessary element in the existence of the latter; their limitations are seen through and hence their duality is allowed to subsist. Against this Marx argued that the abstract overcoming of the divisions of civil society in political union as presented by Hegel masks the central fact that without the *real* overcoming of commodity-based market relations the common interests of the state could be nothing more than the protection and preservation of economic conflict. Only by having the tendency towards equality represented by universal suffrage become truly essential through the dissolution of civil society, and so the state, can freedom be realised in fact as well as in idea. Now what I am suggesting is that Lukács's treatment of irony tends, like the Hegelian theory of the state, to reify difference in an abstract harmony: the difference between meaning and reified experience in the novel repeats the difference between the state (suggesting the possibility of freedom = meaning) and civil society. Irony and the Hegelian Idea function as synthesising operators, allowing the truly irreconcilable to find a moment of harmony in their relationship. The overall effect of this harmonisation is to repress perhaps the most distinctive characteristic of Lukács's understanding of the novel: its critical and therefore subversive relation to modern life. The simple glimpse of the possibility of meaning that irony allows makes it appear as if a *glimpse* is all we can ever achieve. A point which appears to be emphasised by the claim that irony provides the highest freedom in a world without God.

I have claimed that the Schlegelian origins of Lukács's locutions explain better than anything else his confidence in their meaningfulness. But the objectivity which ironic discourses achieve according to this theory is equivalent to an unjustifiable metaphysical intuition which itself depends on Schlegel's arcane metaphysics. The very arcaneness of this metaphysics, the fact that Lukács nowhere openly endorses it, and the fact that he had written on and was planning to write again on Soren Kierkegaard, has led one writer to hazard that it is the Kierkegaardian model which stands behind Lukács's affirmation of ironic writing and consciousness.[5] In his Preface Lukács himself hints at the idea that his conception of irony might be taken to be a secular equivalent to Kierkegaardian theory (18). What we must question, then, is whether Kierkegaard's conception of irony is, in fact, employable for Lukács's general purposes.

Kierkegaard was concerned, in a way Schlegel was not, with the relation of the writer to his text. Looking more to Solger than to Schlegel, Kierkegaard was fascinated with irony as a strategy of consciousness, as a negative power that allowed the writer to disengage himself from his words and from himself. The passive, spectatorial role assigned to the epic poet by Lukács also characterises the ironic consciousness as understood by Kierkegaard. 'The ironist is reserved and stands aloof; he lets mankind pass before him, as did Adam the animals, and finds no companionship for himself. By this he constantly comes into collision with the actuality to which he belongs.... Life is for him a drama, and what engrosses him is the ingenious unfolding of this drama. He is himself a spectator even when performing some act.'[6] So Kierkegaard ironised his own creations by producing narrators with a coherent set of attitudes and characteristics not attributable to Kierkegaard himself; and occasionally he even has his narrators produce a narrator whose perspective on things differs sharply from their own. And, as their names indicate – the hermit, the silent, the constant, the taciturn, and the watchful – these narrators are critics and spectators (novice ironists) who mime Kierkegaard's own detachment from ordinary affairs.

But why should a Kierkegaardian soul *desire* to remove himself from life, to negate and cancel each affirmation as it is put forward? In part the answer lies in the fact that *any* meaning complex *can* be denied; as consciousness attempts to articulate and bring forward an understanding adequate to itself and to the world it becomes even more evident that there are untold possibilities for understanding which are incompatible with what is being said. But if this is so, then each affirmation is erected on an Archimedean point of blindness to alternatives, to a something else that could be said from an elsewhere. The ironist who lives 'completely hypothetically and subjunctively' is only being true to the nature of consciousness in its inability to encompass reality. What the totality of mutually incompatible discourses demonstrates is the limits of consciousness, the necessary failure of all human projects entailed by man's essential finitude. Ordinary men, in their quotidian dealings with the world, forget this terrible fact. Kierkegaard felt it his task to remind them of the fragility, the unreality of the composed and secure world they inhabited.

This negative result cannot stand by itself, for by itself it yields only the nihilism of uncompromised metaphysical doubt. At the end of *The Concept of Irony*, in the section entitled 'Irony as a Mastered Moment', Kierkegaard demands that irony be overcome in order that reality might be actualised. In Shakespeare Kierkegaard thought he perceived such an overcoming, but the overcoming attributed to Shakespeare appears to be the kind of structural irony discussed above, where there is a dominance of form which allows the poet to distance himself from his work. 'Irony is not present at some particular point in the poem but omnipresent in it, so that the visible irony in the poem is in turn ironically mastered.'[7] The mastery of irony and the 'return to home of all things' (92) which Kierkegaard thought he saw in Shakespeare is not available to Kierkegaard himself. For Kierkegaard the call for the mastery of irony is never answered. All that Kierkegaard can do is attempt to draw out from the failure of all human projects a redeeming lesson, a lesson of faith. God is the Unknown. 'What then is the Unknown?' asks a Kierkegaard narrator. 'It is the different, the absolutely different.'[8] In this we hear an echo of Lukács's 'seeing where God is to be found in a world abandoned by God' (92); or, as Josiah Thompson has it: 'God is revealed to man only negatively as man's limit. Man encounters God only by encountering his own finitude and incapacity. God is *dues absconditus*, never present, always absent.'[9] And with this we return to Schlegel: the infinite manifesting itself in the spaces between the words, in what is not said, not done, in what cannot be said or achieved. If Kierkegaard's universe lacks the metaphysical security of Schlegel's universe, it none the less resolves itself into a set of structural relationships which parallel those postulated by Schlegel; if it is not the case that the Kierkegaardian infinite exists in a state of reciprocal dependence with the finite, it remains true that the infinite is captured only in the recurring dissolution of the finite and the finite's discovery of its own essential conditionedness.

Without the metaphysical assumptions of a Kierkegaard or a Schlegel, Lukács's claim for the objectivity provided by irony fails. Irony of itself is not a guarantor of objectivity; what irony can bring about is only one of the *characteristics* associated with epic objectivity, namely, the spectorial relation between the ironist, or reader, and the text. Thus we can posit an 'objectivity effect' which is to be likened to Barthes' 'reality effect'. In the same way in which certain details of a narrative (e.g. the fly in the bottle at the beginning of *Madame Bovary*) have as their sole function convincing the reader of the verisimilitude of the narrative, the precision and detail of description being evidently not symbolically motivated nor relevant to the plot, and hence only capable of serving to call attention to itself as a detailed and accurate description of the way things are – so irony can produce in the reader the sense that the narrative is objective, and he is being presented with what is more than a single person's view of how things are or ought to be. If nothing in a narrative *naturally* guides us into a perception of who has done the writing, that is, from what vantage point the narrative has been produced, then we sense that no one is *responsible* for what is being said. If no one is responsible for what is being said, then, like the true epic, there is no theoretical gain in assigning the work a place or space of origin. This 'negative irony', as I shall call it, on analogy with 'negative freedom', present in writers as different as Kierkegaard and Flaubert, allows for a systematic repression of the responsibilities of discourse, a denial that there is an ethics of writing which ties a man to what he says, and produces a pseudo-scientific objectivity (Flaubert's fascination with the methods of science should be remembered here), a disturbing illusion of objectivity. But an illusion of objectivity is all it is. If objectivity amounted to no more than a dissembling of the conceptual space from which a work is produced, then all ironically composed works would be equally objective. But to argue in this fashion is to reduce objectivity to one of its characteristic *effects*; a manoeuvre sanctioned by no set of conceivable assumptions. There is a great difference between the dissembling of the point of view from which a work is written and producing a work that is truly written from no point of view. Kurrick is wrong, then, in supposing that the achievement of a metasubjectivity, as she calls it, is an approximation to the a-subjectivity a writer craves; fool's gold may look like gold, but it is not gold of any sort, and hence not even an 'approximation' to the real thing.

Significantly, Lukács does not conflate the empty reduction of objectivity to one of the effects with objectivity itself.

The reality-creating transcendental form can only come into being when a true transcendence has become immanent within it. An empty immanence, which is anchored only in the writer's experience and not, at the same time, in his return to the home of all things, is merely the immanence of a surface that covers up the cracks but is incapable of retaining this immanence and must become a surface riddled with holes. (92)

The difficulty for Lukács here, as throughout his writings, is to explain how transcendence can become immanent, how what 'ought' to be is to be aligned with what 'is'. In *The Theory of the Novel* Lukács is forced to accede to the metaphysical posturing of Kierkegaard and Schlegel because he identifies his godless world with the very specific godlessness of the universe of Kierkegaard and Schlegel. For them there was a God whose relation to the world necessarily cancelled particular positive affirmations (Schlegel) or reduced to nothingness the totality of human projects (Kierkegaard). This is not the case for Lukács, for whom the term 'god' designates only the general idea of meaningfulness in an integrated social reality. Lukács never fully reworked the materials the tradition handed over to him, and therefore his position ends up affirming theses alien to it. What is more critical in this context is that we have as yet no conception of irony which could both bear the weight of Lukács's normative conception of it and simultaneously provide a satisfying answer as to what would be involved *in* the novel of surmounting its subjectivity. It is evident that any such account of irony must bring into play the imputed normativity of transcendental subjectivity, for if subjectivity did not carry that imputation then novel fictions would be indistinguishable from daydreams or wishes. A workable conception of irony, then, must invoke both the idea of a split subjectivity and the duality *within* transcendental subjectivity if it is to be a credible account of the normative mentality of the novel. If we return to the Kantian origins of the Schlegelian and Kierkegaardian conceptions of irony we can begin to bring the question of transcendental subjectivity back into focus.

3   IRONY AS FREEDOM AND SELF-CONSCIOUSNESS

The metaphysical antinomy in Kant's system which is at the root of nineteenth-century theorising about irony is that between freedom and causality. We remember from our earlier discussions that Kant argues that for any object to be known it must be locatable in a unified spatio-temporal system; what constitutes any object as an object, the concept of an object in general, are the categories of the understanding. Thus for any object to be known it must be somewhere and somewhen, and be subsumable under the categories of substance and causality. The only knowledge we can have beyond empirical (judgemental and scientific) knowledge of what is the case is of the formal structures (space, time and the categories) which make this knowledge possible. According to Kant what guarantees that the world is knowable is that we are ourselves responsible for the existence of the formal structures which constitute it as a (knowable) world. It is this imposition on reality of the formal structures making knowledge possible which is intended in denominating Kant's system 'idealistic'. As we shall see, Kant's idealism is irrelevant to the actual problems confronting us.

Now if all that can be known is restricted to objects and sequences of events in causal interaction with one another, then freedom must be banished from the knowable world altogether. This conclusion, however, is repugnant to Kant for in banishing freedom from the world, we banish all moral responsibility with it. A man cannot be held responsible for a deed if he could not have helped but do it. Indeed, our very conception of an action as opposed to a happening or an event assumes that men have reasons for what they do which are themselves uncaused, and that for any given action a man could have done otherwise. Kant reviews this problem in his 'Third Antinomy of Pure Reason'.

Understanding synthesises, orders and cognises experience item by item. All ordering of experience by the understanding is therefore only partial. Reason demands, however, that this partial synthesis of experience be made total; thus if some conditioned item is given in experience, it demands that the whole series of conditions conditioning that item be given till some absolutely unconditioned is reached, which is either the whole series of conditions or some member of it (e.g. a 'first' cause). Although reason demands the unconditioned, such an unconditioned could never be known since it would be an item which was not causally dependent on any other (earlier) item; but we have already learned that to know anything whatsoever is to know it as a member of a causal nexus, as conditioned and as conditioning. Thus, on the one hand, reason demands that the unconditioned be given – it being assumed that if a cause is uncaused then it is necessarily a 'free' cause: the initiator of a causal sequence – but, on the other hand, any uncaused event would, according to Kantian principles, be unknowable.

How is this contradiction to be resolved? Kant's answer is that the principle 'If the conditioned is given, then the unconditioned is given' is legitimate but only as a regulative principle which guides reason in its activities, not as a constitutive principle of experience. If the conditioned is given, then we are set the task of seeking after the unconditioned, but there is no reason to think that we can, as part of our experience, have knowledge of a free cause. The principle of causality – every event must have a cause – is true of phenomena in time, while the principle of the unconditioned must be true of things in themselves in relation to phenomena. The principle of causality and the principle of the unconditioned can be changed from contradictories into contraries only if we are willing to grant that space and time and all they contain do not comprise all there is, that there exists a realm of beings not in space and time and not constituted by the principle of causality. The world of experience is our empirical world of phenomena; the domain of freedom (and God) is the noumenal world of things in themselves.

As we have already seen, Schlegel and Kierkegaard in their different ways simply affirm the Kantian two-world schema.[10] Both accept the 'limits of knowledge' thesis on the ground of a dualistic metaphysic which firmly separates the conditioned and finite from the unconditioned and infinite. However, they both also share one crucial assumption which Kant does not possess, namely, that the world of the unconditioned *excludes* man in his totality, while the conditioned world of the finite includes man in his totality.[11] And it was on this theological basis that their respective theories of irony were erected. Irony for both is a way of indicating the essential finitude of the human, and thereby of giving us what access we can have to the infinite. The theory of Romantic Irony is, then, in its origins a highly theological doctrine. What is worse, even with its metaphysical excesses, it appears to lack the power to turn the negating power of irony into something positive. Kierkegaard's philosophy is open about this in that he believed that no theoretical construction – deductive, dialectical, ironic – could transcend human finitude. Neither he nor any of his pseudonyms have any positive doctrine to communicate. In thought only the limits of thought can be shown; what is beyond thought is revealed 'existentially' when the reader is forced to act without warrant, to realise the true extent of his freedom and in an act of radical inwardness to appropriate the divine. Whatever the validity of this theory, and I think it is minimal,[12] it is irrelevant for us since the insight achieved is not the direct result of irony.

In the play of finite and infinite, Schlegel's theory has a positive, progressive movement, but it is one which carries no conviction. Schlegel describes the play of finite and infinite in the following terms:

[It] is necessary to be able to abstract from every single thing (negate every specific affirmation of finitude), to grasp hoveringly the general (infinite becoming manifesting itself in finite being), to survey a mass, to seize the totality, to investigate even the most hidden and to combine the most remote things. We must raise ourselves above even our own love and to be able to annihilate in thought what we worship:

otherwise we lack, whatever other capabilities we might have, the faculty (sense) for the infinite, and with it the sense for the world.[13]

What makes tnis play progressive for Schlegel is that he thinks of the process of positing and negation as a spiralling movement whereby consciousness eternally approaches the infinite. Two considerations tend to vitiate this position:

(i) Nothing in Schlegel's theory justifies us in the belief that the becoming is progressive as opposed to being vacuously circular and repetitive.[14]
(ii) Even if the movement was to be confirmed as progressive, one might still contend that an *eternal* movement toward the infinite is indistinguishable from no movement, and consequently the progressiveness is vacuous.

Embedded as it is a metaphysics of the finite and infinite Schlegel's programme may appear to be a non-starter; yet, as we shall see in a moment, the activity of the ironic consciousness as he describes it, the abstracting 'from every single thing' in a progressive movement, tends to dominate less metaphysically-loaded accounts of irony. However, with or without its metaphysical burden, if ironic consciousness operates in the way Schlegel describes, then irony will only be able to serve a negative purpose. However, before we can evaluate the ethics if irony, we must first seek out a theoretical account of its proper domain.

What leads Schlegel and Kierkegaard into theological mystification is their belief that human finitude itself requires completion, vindication or redemption in the infinite. Without entering into the details of the dispute, it none the less appears more plausible to argue that if finitude, in whatever sense, demarcates the human as human, then any attempt to transcend finitude amounts to a cancellation of the human. As the theory of irony now stands, it looks to be seeking an answer to a problem most of us would regard as wrongly posed. By turning back to Kant I think we shall find that irony can be brought to bear on a problem that is both highly general and of immediate concern.

Schlegel and Kierkegaard err in making the essential antinomic relation exist between the finite (including man) and the infinite (excluding man). Kant's own two-world doctrine is not theological in this sense; his antinomy is between freedom and causality, and it was the incompatibility between these two this-wordly phenomena which forced him to propose two hetero-geneous domains: the knowable world of causally interacting phenomena and the thinkable, but unknowable, noumenal world of freedom. We need not have troubled ourselves with the conditions for moral action to see that free activity must be predicable of human beings. As we saw earlier, in the act of judgement itself we must distinguish between the *act* of judge-ment and what that judgement is of, even when we are making judgements about our own mental states. Thus we find Kant saying: 'I cannot determine (i.e. know categorially) my existence as that of a self-acting being; all that I can do is to represent to myself the spontaneity of my thought, that is, of the determination; and my existence is still determinable only sensibly, that is, as the existence of an appearance. But it is owing to this spontaneity that I entitle myself an intelligence' (B 157–8N). In Kantian terminology, the self as a spontaneous, non-causally conditioned judger and moral agent is called the transcendental self; while the self as categorially determinable, knowable, is called the empirical self. Kant's denial of in-tellectual intuition is the denial that the transcendental self can ever be determined, for to determine it would involve the use of concepts, but those concepts must be *used* in order to know anything, and therefore imply the existence, at any time, of a *user*. More accurately, for any time t, in any act of judgement, there is an asymmetrical, non-reversible relation between knower and what is known; the knower can only become known in another act of judgement at some later time $t + n$; but this act of judgement involves the existence of a knower non-reducible to its object, thus maintaining the original asymmetry. For the moment we can put off the question of how to characterise the transcendental self. What I want to argue now is that the self-conscious manipulation of this two-self construction gives us the essential structure of ironic consciousness as it has developed out of its original Romantic setting. The importance of this derivation cannot be overestimated for, as we saw in Chapter I, the antinomy between freedom and necessity is for Lukács the ideological expression of a free subjectivity finding itself ex-cluded from a world of its own making. The theory of transcendental subjectivity captures the affirmation of freedom together with an admission of its powerlessness, its inability to impress itself upon the world. If the irony which is the normative mentality of the novel is, literally, the figure or trope for this conception of subjectivity, then the novel's irony becomes the figure *par excellence* of the ideological boundaries of the present.

What makes irony, at least the Romantic Irony of the authorial plot (the novel's narration) the normative mentality of the novel is that it represents or perpetuates at the level of strategy what is enshrined metaphysically in the Kantian distinction between the creative self and the empirical self. The Kantian distinction is suggested by the need to separate the self which knows and creates from the self that is known. Lying behind Kant's thesis is the historical premise that where the productivity of spirit is affirmed but, because of the *naturlich* closure of the social world caused by the reifying processes of capital production, is unable to realise itself in the world, then the freedom that belongs to men in their collective activity will devolve into the individual. The *expression* of human freedom hence comes to be restricted to the individual self's capacity to deny or negate any particular empirical predicates which it or any other self may put forward in order to define it. In fine, in an age of alienation and reification, where men's labour power, their ability to create and produce, itself becomes a commodity, a thing, there exists a natural tendency to separate reflectively the self defined through commodity relations from one's real self. Romantic Irony is essentially constituted by this reflective movement from the empirical to the knowing or transcendental self. This reflective structure, this splitting of the self into a knowing and known self, is common to both traditional (Baudelaire) and contemporary (Culler) accounts of irony (what Baudelaire refers to as the 'comic'). Here is Baudelaire:[15]

The comic, the power of laughter, is in the laugher, not at all in the object of laughter. It is not the man who falls down that laughs at his own fall, unless he is a philosopher, a man who has acquired, by force of habit, the power of getting outside himself quickly and watching, as a disinterested spectator, the phenomenon of his ego.... [The comic is] a phenomenon that belongs to the class of all artistic phenomena that show the existence in the human being of a permanent dualism, the capacity of being both himself and someone else at one and the same time.

Similarly, we find Culler claiming that ironising the self as a whole

forces one to move through stages of self-consciousness, stepping back continually to judge one's prior judgements without finding firm ground on which to take one's stand and halt the process. The ironical self is divorced from the empirical self which it scrutinizes, and through the operation of scrutiny result in the new projection of a new and newly enlightened empirical self, a new ironical self must arise to judge it in turn. Irony is the desire of the subject never to let itself be defined as object by others but always to undertake a protective self-transcendence, which however, exposes more than it protects.

Baudelaire's formulation allows us to link irony explicitly with reification. For Baudelaire the reflective act, the stepping aside of one's self, which defines the movement of irony, functions to separate the self from the non-human world of which the self is a part. It is the revelation of the self as a *thing*, slipping on a banana peel and falling, which is the occasion and cause of laughter. The self that falls, the empirical self, is comic because prior to its fall it existed in a state of inauthenticity, blind to its true situation. The inauthenticity which provides the necessary condition for irony is in all cases equivalent to being in a state of 'reification' because the ignorance which causes inauthenticity creates a lack of freedom in the subject, and (creative) freedom is an essential characteristic of subjectivity. In so far as a subject is unfree he is an object, a thing, subject to the play of forces and laws over which he has no control.

The strength of Culler's statement lies in his recognition of the ability of ironic reflection actually to create by its movement a blindness in the empirical self, which is to say, the movement of the ironising consciousness transforms each ironic self into an empirical self, and hence transforms each subject-self into an object-self. The self becomes an object (thing) simply by being made the object of ironic scrutiny. According to this view the very nature of the ironising process prohibits it from having a natural terminus, a place of rest in which the self can achieve authenticity and become identical with itself. What is distinctive and troubling about this thesis is that it makes the negative power of freedom to cancel any standpoint of the self equivalent to inauthenticity, hence making inauthenticity an intrinsic feature of self-consciousness. It is here that the Kantian conception of the self and Romantic Irony reveal their inner identity; for both the alienation of the self from itself is a metaphysical component of self-consciousness and not a historical state of affairs. Employing the traditional vocabulary to which this hypothesis belongs, we can say that the philosophers of Romantic Irony identified objectification, which is the universal power of negation intrinsic to any consciousness which is also a self-consciousness, with alienation, which minimally, is any historically determinate state of affairs in which the objectifications created by human social practices systematically exclude or pervert expressions of subjectivity. To identify objectification with alienation is tantamount to claiming that all social mediations of the self, including the use of language, result in a diminishment, a restriction on human freedom.

Of course, merely to claim that a conflation of this sort is at work here falls short of a demonstration. Further, to have identified the theory of transcendental subjectivity with the theory of Romantic Irony says nothing about novelistic irony. What we need is, first, an account of ironic reflection that does not depend upon the metaphysical two-self construction, and then an account of novelistic irony which can both recognise and defuse the presuppositions of the two-self theory. To these two tasks we now turn.

4   THE IRONIC SELF AND LANGUAGE

Up till now we have treated the transcendental-self/empirical-self dualism, following Kant, in epistemic terms. But the point has been made, rightly, that the reflective disjunction between these selves only occurs by means of language. Through language subjectivity—the transcendental self—becomes possible; language gives us a mode of designation that is not referential as it is ordinarily understood, a way of distinguishing all that can be referred to and talked about from he who does the talking and referring. Benveniste, in his article 'Subjectivity in Language', proposes a linguistic account of the Kantian argument for the transcendental unity of apperception. Subjectivity, according to Benveniste, involves a psychic unity that transcends the totality of actual experiences and creates the permanence of consciousness. This consciousness of self is only possible, says Benveniste, if it is experienced as a contrast, a contrast which only language allows us to make, between *I* and *you*, between *I, here, now,* and *you (he, she, it) there, earlier than now or later than now*, and so forth. Moreover, the polarity of *I* and *you*, although formable only by contrast, and therefore complementary (according to an interior – exterior opposition), does not involve equality or symmetry: the 'self' or 'ego' always stands in a position of transcendence with regard to the *you*. At this juncture we might suppose that language institutes a transcendental – transcendent self as a necessary constituent of reality. But Benveniste denies that this is the case.[16]

Now these pronouns are distinguished from all other designations a language articulates in that they do not refer to a concept (are not universals) or to an individual (are not proper names).

There is no concept 'I' that incorporates all the *I*'s that are uttered at every moment in the mouths of all speakers, in the sense that there is a concept 'tree' to which all the individual uses of *tree* refer. The 'I', then does not denominate any lexical entity. Could it then be said that *I* refers to a particular individual? If that were the case, a permanent contradiction would be admitted into language . . . . How could the same term refer indifferently to any individual whatsoever and still at the same time identify him in his individuality? . . . What, then, does *I* refer to? To something very peculiar which is exclusively linguistic: *I* refers to the act of individual discourse in which it is pronounced, and by this it designates the speaker. It is a term that cannot be identified except in what we have called elsewhere an instance of discourse and that has only a momentary reference . . . . It is in the instance of discourse in which *I* designates the speaker that the speaker proclaims himself as the 'subject' . . . . Language is so organized that it permits each speaker to *appropriate to himself* an entire language by designating himself as *I*.

There is no self beyond the empirical self, the self that experiences and that has a determinate bodily and psychological history. It is the contrast made *within* language that establishes the reality of the ego as he who speaks and acts; but he who speaks and acts is designated not directly but only indirectly as the speaker of *this* discourse. Similarly linguistic space and linguistic time are self-referential: the time at which one is is the time at which one is speaking, and the space where one is is the where of one's speaking. It is because the various indicators of deixis have this ineliminable moment of self-referentiality that language as a whole is appropriable by each speaker; because the pronouns and the indicators of deixis are formed by contrast, the world of the self is a public world of objects in space and time where other persons who can appropriate language to themselves in the same way I can appropriate language to myself. The moment of transcendence, the sense that the self is not in a situation of absolute symmetry and equality with the non-self is not a metaphysical fact, it is a fact of language, the fact that the self is always interior to the speech act as speaker and that all 'others', place, spaces, times, persons, objects, are relativised to it. Because the speaker is designated by means of the moment of discourse and not objectively by means of his physical or psychological properties it may appear that these latter attributes are not part of the speaker, but this is to blur the central fact about the indicators of person and deixis, namely, that they are not ordinary referential expressions and consequently do not connect with their objects in the ordinary way (by means of properties).

As we saw, Kant proposed a similar line of argument in the 'Paralogisms of Pure Reason'. From the premise that the 'I think' (= the indicators of person and deixis = *I, here, now* and their contrasting correlates) must be capable of accompanying all of our representations (acts of judgement) none of the classical Cartesian these follows:

(a) that the 'I' is a referring expression taking an ego or self as its object;
(b) that the self so designated is simple and indivisible because the designation does not occur by means of attributes; because it is indivisible it must be immaterial; and
(c) that the self so designated – without properties – is the unchanging substratum of all changes that may occur to the self.

These three erroneous claims are all temptations which the peculiarities of the conditions for subjectivity, the peculiarities of the indicators of person and deixis, may lead one.

Now it would be strange indeed if the only place where the temptations of the language of subjectivity were to be manifested was in the technical writings of philosophers theorising about the nature of subjectivity and self-consciousness. And this is in fact not the case. Ironic discourse, especially ironisation of the self and its present predicament, continually attempts or is tempted to move from the fact that the ironising self can be designated without properties by means of the indicators of person and deixis to the conclusion that there is an ironic self that is different from the empirical self. In other words, the duality in means of designation of person, by pronouns and by empirical properties, is the pivot on which ironic discourse about the self swings. Without these two modes of designation ironic discourse about the self would be impossible. The possibilities of irony that the dual means of designation opens, however, also opens the ironic self to the temptations of reification summarised by the Cartesian theory of the ego – and worse. The confusion between the formal conditions for discourse and the transcendental self, the substitution of the latter for the former, is capable of generating a picture of the 'ironic self' as a deactualised, dematerialised self, a self whose every act cuts it off further from experience and the world. Thus Kierkegaard opposes the ironic self to the world, and shows the ironic self becoming 'worldless' and so unreal to itself.

If we return to the general designation of irony given above as infinite absolute negativity, this will sufficiently indicate that irony no longer directs itself against this or that particular thing, but that the whole of existence has become alien to the ironic subject, that he in turn has become estranged from existence, and that because actuality has lost its validity for him, so he, too, is to a certain extent no longer actual.[17]

The fact that the self can be designated non-empirically here takes on immense significance. Irony's bracketing of the given is here repeated so that it looks as if the empirical is done away with, that only the purity and emptiness of pronouns are 'true' to the self. Romantic Irony thus becomes the trope of the alienated man whose consciousness of his predicament deprives him of the ability to act. For him the historical world no longer contains possibilities worthy of realisation, and worthy goals are unattainable. 'What he calls irony is his attempt to bear up under his critical predicament, to change his situation by achieving distance toward it. In an ever-expanding act of reflection [the Schlegelian 'movement'] – he tries to establish a point of view beyond himself and to resolve the tension between himself and the world on the level of fiction.'[18] Because self-irony involves a refusal of the empirical, a refusal made possible by language, the only acts open to the ironic self are linguistic acts; but language of this kind can only regain the empirical world by making it different, i.e. by relativising the world to language. The projection by the ironic self of a fictive world adequate to itself is in fact only a reflection of the fact that irony is language bound, that it functions through its difference from the empirical world. *The world of the pure ironist is fictive because it is wholly linguistic.* Thus, that the only future adequate to the self is a fiction is a function of the language-bound character of ironic discourse; that the temporality of 'authentic' selfhood is defined by ironic discourse is a function of the reduction of authentic, free subjectivity to a purely linguistic existence. Irony defines a past of pure inauthenticity (because wholly empirical and causal) against the norms of a necessarily fictive future (a what 'ought' to be which if realised would be empirical and hence inauthentic);[19] this temporal movement, which Romantic Irony *is*, equally defines the relation between empirical and transcendental subjectivity. Thus authentic subjectivity has been reduced to a moment in a linguistic trope; the self has become no more than a figure of language.

Now if the reduction of selfhood to language in part defines the ideological domain of the novel, then novelistic irony cannot of itself transcend the ideality of its domain. Equally, however, it should not be assumed that the goal of all novelistic irony is either to prepetuate this reduction or project ideal but not realisable futures. On the contrary, the novel's irony might be precisely the means by which this reduction is most perspicuously revealed as a reduction. In order to see more clearly what is at issue here it will prove helpful to compare novelistic irony with experiential irony.

Experiential irony takes place in a multidimensional framework in which language is only one of many constituents. If the pronoun 'I', which makes self-consciousness and therefore ironic consciousness possible, signals the speaker as speaker or thinker as thinker, this does not imply the existence of a thinking or speaking self possessing no material or psychological predicates, or that we could even conceive of a self not possessing these ordinary properties. For an ordinary self, ironic reflection does not involve a removal of the self from the world, but only a bracketing of experiential *immediacy* in the name of objectivity and freedom. This bracketing is an intentional withdrawal from action which lasts only as long as the ironic reflection itself lasts. Whether this ironic reflection changes the self-understanding of the subject or not is here irrelevant; the central point is that ordinarily the pressures of the world force him to return to it. To maintain an ironic stance permanently, as Kierkegaard perhaps did, or tried to do, is not simply to refuse the call of society, politics and labour, but more, to deny that these are constitutive elements of the self. It is to flirt with madness. Irony cannot make an empirical self into a transcendental self; it can at most perpetuate a self's refusal of the world. Hence only the madman, the man who has stopped being a complete self, can fail in his attempt to return to the world.

The description of the ironic, alienated self provides us with a view of a man who has made ironic reflection his central and only mode of being, who continually projects himself into a fiction which in that mode of being can never be ·realised. Experiential irony begins, then, with a self with the capacity for free action but an inability to realise that freedom in the world, who in consequence resorts to fictions without end. Now this model neatly suggests that novelistic irony is only a repetition of experiential irony sustained by the purity of discourse which is the natural mode of existence of literary fiction. But the model is mistaken. *Novelistic irony begins with the fictiveness of its world, with the distance separating fiction (form-giving) and social reality, and ironically reflects on that fact.* For a person to reflect ironically on his situation he must bracket his given commitments, desires and beliefs. For a novel to come to self-consciousness is for it to call into question its own removal from or transcendence of experience. Novelistic irony begins with the madness of fiction. with the unreality of all that lies within its domain, with, finally, the reduction of the world to writing, and 'figures' through the instrumentality of form a return to the world. According to Lukács the novel is necessarily an interpretation as well as repetition of reality. This interpretative moment inevitably conflicts with the novel's mimetic ambitions, and more problematically, given the novel's mimetic ambitions the interpretative moment tends to masquerade behind the claims of mimesis. It is in virtue of this that the novel's so-called classical moment in the realist novel of Balzac and Zola becomes the novel's worst moment of bad faith and self-deception where interpretation is taken to be representation, and fictional totalisation is identified with theoretical totalisation. The novelist becomes a social scientist and the novel social theory. What requires ironic reflection and sublation, then, is this false self-understanding of realism, the novel's claim to objectivity.

To make this clearer it is helpful to distinguish between two different ironic strategies. These two strategies are related in terms of the negative – positive couplet. Negative irony employs the mystification of the self generated by the abstraction from the empirical which irony permits in order to promote a derealisation of the empirical, an ethics of fiction. Negative irony, in its pristine form, involves the author in treating his own in-formed products to scrutiny, thus denying the self's involvement with its products. To ironise the work in this way requires the continual deflation of suggested form. If Lukács's rhetoric is to be kept, we may say that God appears only as an absence. By scrutinising produced forms the ironising consciousness deprives them of their representational power, their power to be forms of experience. They become fictions. But if the fictions which anchor and organise reality lose their representational sense, then so does the discursive reality they in-form. With the loss of representational power we lose the sense of a subjectivity in-forming the discourses of experience, the self which appropriates language to himself and thus through language reality. To lose the sense of a subjectivity informing the discourses of experience is to lose the sense of a perspective from which a work is written because the language of experience appears always as quoted, as coming from elsewhere, rather than being a part of a homogeneous narration.

It is this kind of process Barthes has in mind when he says of Flaubert that 'he does not stop the play of codes (or stops them only partially), so that . . . one never knows if he is responsible for what he writes (if there is a subject behind his language) ; for the very being of writing (the meaning of the labour which constitutes it) is to keep the question "Who is speaking? from ever being answered.'[20] Without a speaker there is no 'saying';

we are forced, if we are to take the text on its own terms, to realise the text as fiction and as incommensurable with life. If we cannot answer the question of who speaks, then there is no place *in* the world from which the speech comes; if it comes from nowhere, then it is not part of the world; it is fiction. Fiction in this ideologically weighted sense does not mean that persons, places and referring expressions generally have no referents; it signifies rather the discontinuity in absolute terms between fiction and reality. In its most radical form this ideology makes all self-interpretation fictional for what else could self-interpretation be but self-reflection? But if the only form of self-reflection available is that defined by the two-self theory of self-consciousness; and that theory stipulates the projection of ideal and necessarily fictional futures as constitutive of the movement of self-consciousness, then self-consciously fictional works become authentic acts of self-reflection, and non-fictional self-interpretation becomes a form of inauthenticity. Ordinary self-interpretation thinks that its reflective acts are defining an *empirical* future; but this, the theory of self-consciousness tells us, is a logical impossibility, a transcendental illusion. If Lukács is right, this radical valorisation of the fictional over the empirical is a natural extension of the entrapment of form in fiction, and thus a natural extension of the traditional liberal defence of literature and the novel as housing our 'language of concern'.

To get beyond this stance we must turn to our second ironic strategy. It stands to the first ironic strategy as whole to part; if, as it transpires, the whole comes to appear as *nearly* indistinguishable from the movement of the part, this will be because the *pressures* which elicit irony as a textual strategy cannot be dissolved through irony. Only, however, by trying ironically to overcome the novel's irony can the boundaries, the limits of irony be ascertained. As we encroach on the limits of irony the limits of the novel come into view. The limits of the novel, finally, locating the novel in its world; the figure of the novel revealing itself and its world through its placement of itself in that world.

If the first ironic strategy ironises the forms produced, the second ironic strategy self-consciously scrutinises the very idea of producing forms; Flaubert treats particular representational modes ironically, while Mann, in *Doctor Faustus*, treats the very act of writing a fictional text ironically. The difference in emphasis allows for a difference in ethics. Mann, in allowing his work to be as a text *and* as a fiction, gives to his text an autonomy and substance which, while depending on the ethics of representation, realises that representation must be supplemented by interpretation. Hence the text takes on its significance as a transgression of the ethics of representation while none the less fully implicated in the demands of representation. This tension between the interpretative – transgressive character of the text and its representational ambitions is fully thematised within the novel. Zeitblom, the narrator of *Doctor Faustus*, is writing the biography of his friend Adrian Leverkuhn; Zeitblom recognises the art involved in his activity and explicitly queries it: 'Far be it from me to deny the seriousness of art; but when it becomes serious, then one rejects art and is not capable of it.'[21] None the less, it is only art which can do justice to the life of Leverkuhn.

Certainly the time in which I write has vastly greater historical momentum than the time of which I write, Adrian's time, which brought him only to the threshold of our incredible epoch. I feel as though one should call out to him, as to all those who are no longer with us and were not with us when it began: 'Lucky you!'....Adrian is safe from the days we dwell in. The thought is dear to me, I prize it, and in exchange for that certainty I accept the terrors of the time in which I myself continue to live. It is to me *as though I stood here and lived for him*, lived instead of him; as though I bore the burden his shoulders were spared, as though I showed my love by taking upon me living for him, living in his stead. The fancy, however illusory, however foolish, does me good, it flatters the always cherished desire to serve, to help, to protect him – this desire which during the lifetime of my friend found so very little satisfaction.

Zeitblom can protect his friend, live in his stead, only by writing the text.

But this is only half the story, for the text is allegorical: the life and fate of Leverkuhn paralleling and repeating the history of modern Germany. While this leads us to read the narrative allegorically, it also forces us to read the narration ironically: the novel as a whole intervenes self-consciously into German culture in the same way as Zeitblom's biography intervenes and attempts to recuperate the life of Leverkuhn. In fine, I wish to suggest that we can only read Mann's work *as an interpretation* of

German history. The ironising of the narration undermines the formal completeness of the work, and thereby the monadological, autotelic ambitions (and illusions) of the novel generally. Mann's genius was to grant the modernist critique of the tradition without falling prey to (the Devil's) modernism. 'The historical movement of the·musical material has turned against the self-contained work. It shrinks in time, it scorns extension in time, which is the dimension of a musical work, and lets it stand empty.... Only the non-fictional is still permissible, the unplayed, the undisguised and untransfigured expression of suffering in its actual moment.'[22]

Mann, in a work of sustained duration, was able to overcome 'the negation of narrative in German history'[23] through and by means of a humane narrative. He can remain within narrative and offer us a fiction, with all of fiction's traditional play and pretence, only by realising within the text both its fictionality and its essential interpretative function. *Doctor Faustus* is both an interpretation of history and self-consciously an interpretation *in history*. Writing is revealed as a moral act, authoritative where one least suspects it: in its interpretative function rather than in its mimetic function. Classically fiction authorised itself mimetically: its form was the fiction, the lie it added to experience. Thus the bourgeois interpretation of the novel claims it to be the off-spring of romance (fiction) and history (mimesis); while structuralist theories argue to a very similar conclusion. These are not only mistaken theories about the novel, but they are also mistaken self-interpretations which have influenced the novel's own history. Because the objectivity of transcendental subjectivity could not be directly realised, the negativity of subjectivity was deployed to create a transcendental illusion, the illusion of objectivity. This troubling illusion could itself be dissimulated in a further ironic reflection, emphasising thus the dissonance and absences haunting the only partially figured represented world. Hence, the realist novel was torn in its recognition of transcendental subjectivity between irony as a means of generating an illusion of objectivity, and irony as the affirmation of dissonance. In both cases, however, our contemplative relation to reality is affirmed and deepened, form remaining an ideality, an expression of what ought to be in the face of a recalcitrant reality. Mann's irony, and irony as the novel's normative mentality, its self-consciousness of the subject-ivity of form, reverses the classical thesis: mimesis lacks au-thority because compared to reality it presents us with an illusion; form in its self-conscious mode signals the interpretative movement of the text, and thereby the ethics of narration. That ethics locates the act of narration in history, thus returning the text to the circuit of social practices which its fictional and formal vocation appears to deny.

5   History and Transcendental Subjectivity

This unity of being-for-another or making onself a Thing, and of being-for-oneself, this universal substance, speaks its *universal language* in the customs and laws of its nation.

(G.W.F. Hegel)

Mann's text *figures* his text's return to history, but as an act of figuration that return itself becomes subject to a final irony: the affirmation of the historical and interpretative movement of the text it itself textualised, the denial of textual autonomy thus affirmed as it is stated; the figure of the text's historicality becomes, ironically, a statement of its negativity, of its dis-tance from its object and from its practice. Now, at least in part, the explanation of this eventuality must be that from *within* the confines of the practice of the novel the figure of the novel's return to the concrete historical world of social practices itself appears as form, can be nothing else but form, and thus inherits the ideality and abstractness that characterises all novelistic forms. Although, then, Mann's text is a historical and interpretative act, his text can represent that act only as form; but as form the reality and validity of that representation is undermined. Mann's text is an emblem of the novel as a pseudo-praxis, as an unhappy consciousness at home neither in the idealities of fiction nor in the realities of history. How is it possible, we may wonder, for the ironies of art to invade even the concreteness of its practices? How can the historical specificity of novelistic acts be turned into idealities by their very accomplishment?

In order to answer this question it will be helpful to ponder on a related problem we have as yet failed to analyse, namely, how can the irony which functions as the overcoming of the paralogism of transcendental subjectivity receive the very different forms given to it by the tradition of realist fiction and Mann? How can irony figure both the historicality of the text and the denial of history? Implied in the two different ironic strategies analysed are two different answers to the question 'Who is the transcendental subject?' This question, we can now see, is the inevitable heir to the thus far unanswered question with which our considerations of the self and the novel began, the question controlling the Cartesian narrative, namely, 'Who am I?' The conditioning of the novel ensured that the novel could be written only so long as this question remained unanswered and, indeed, unanswerable. Its unanswerability was guaranteed by the ahistorical and unnarratable character of the *cogito*. Thus the negativity and productivity of subjectivity made the dilemmas of subjectivity incapable of resolution. It is natural, then, to suppose that by identifying transcendental subjectivity insight into the paralogism to which it gives rise can be gained.

The practice of the novel consistently images the obvious Kantian answer as to the identity of the transcendental subject: it is each individual person in their capacity as a self-conscious being, capable of transcending the natural world through the spontaneity of their intellects. This answer, we have seen, is lacking because the normative universality of transcendental subjectivity does not naturally devolve onto the empirical individual; on the contrary, the negativity and spontaneity of individual transcendental subjectivity places his being as a self-consciousness in a relation of externality with every other self-conscious being. Irony is then used as a strategy of negation in order to suppress the negativity of subjectivity in favour of its purported objectivity and universality; but because irony as a negativity is itself a function of the distance between empirical and transcendental subjectivity its employment only deepens the separation between ideality and reality, universality and the existing historical world. Not only then is there an antagonism, a contradiction between the universality and negativity of subjectivity, but equally there is an unbridgeable gulf between transcendental and empirical subjectivity.

For Kant the universality of transcendental subjectivity is a product of the a priori necessity of the *categories* essential for the possibility of experience. Benveniste reads the Kantian categories in terms of the impersonal linguistic indicators of person and deixis which allow *each* speaker to appropriate to him- or herself an *entire* language. Thus where Kant interprets the 'I think' as the logical subject of a judgement, as the form of representation, Benveniste offers the 'I speak' as the linguistic function whereby the structures of language become appropriated by each individual speaker. For Benveniste the 'I speak' is *intersubjective* both because what is appropriated by each speaker is a language, and because the 'I' of the 'I speak' is in a relation of asymmetry but necessary reversibility with respect to 'you'. To be an 'I' is always an 'I' for some 'you' ('he', 'she', 'it', etc.) who is not here where 'I' am; and further, to be an 'I' is necessarily to be a possible 'you' for some other 'I' who appropriates the here and now to him- or herself. Finally, then, for Beneveniste the 'I bind together' is a necessary entailment from the fact that each speech act institutes a relation of assymetry between the speaker(s) and some other(s).

Mann adds one further element to this story; because he believes that the objectivity of his interpretation of history depends upon its being socially recognised, he thereby necessarily construes the concrete objectivity of forms in terms of their social and historical recognition. What such social and historical recognition means for Mann can be gathered from his recognition of the historical irony of ironic art with which we introduced this section. For Mann the historical irony which returns his work to the domain of fiction from history is equally the negativity of art generally, its power to preserve itself and its forms against 'the destructive power of the whole'. 'The whole', what Hegel calls the 'universal language' of a time's customs and laws, its social practices, is then the final or ultimate concrete subject.[24] Transcendental subjectivity is concrete social practices as the bearers of history, a 'we' 'which brings about the unity and separation of I's'.[25] The specificity of our time is that this unity appears not as *our* self-possession and negativity, but as an externality, a negativity against us, making our separation not a moment of individuation and self-realisation, but a moment of isolation and diremption from the totality we are. With this gesture the nature of Lukács's conception of totality begins to come into view. Clearly for Lukács the concept of totality is both methodological (descriptive) and normative. On the methodological level he conceives of totalisation as equivalent to discovering the meditations which structure, intentionally and causally, apparently isolated phenomena. In Hegelian terms, particular items are 'abstract' in the sense that in seeing them in isolation we ignore the manifold determinations which make them what they are. The result of the analysis of capital in these terms make it a decentred totality, that is, a whole which is irreducible to the directly intended actions of its member parts. For Lukács that capitalist social formations are decentred is a result of reification, a sign that the *dominant* mechanisms of social reproduction are working behind the backs of men. Now Lukács has often been criticised for normatively postulating a centred totality as the utopian resolution of present fragmentation. Lukács's own employment in *TN* of utopian language simply invites this criticism. None the less, this view is mistaken because for Lukács the relation betweeen centred and decentred is not analogous to the relation between redeemed history and fallen history; nor, as I suggested in Chapter II, is the converse of ideological illusion either scientific knowing or social transparency.[26] Reading Lukács in this way makes his theory contemplative, and his conception of the relation between man and world epistemic rather than praxial. In other words, utopian readings of Lukács overlook the fundamentally practical, historical and hermeneutical features of his thought. As I suggested earlier, *the converse of the ideological for Lukács is the cultural.* It is no accident that in both *TN* and *HCC* he designates the modern social world a 'second nature'.

This identification of normative totality with culture is all but explicit in Lukács's criticism of Tolstoy for seeking totality in nature; 'a totality of men and events,' Lukács says, 'is possible only on the basis of a culture' (146–7). From whence, we might ask, does this conception of culture or (true) totality come? In *TN* Lukács's answer is unequivocal: it comes from the *reading* of the novel, it is the *result* of that theoretical reading as guided by methodological totalisation. It is the formal features of the novel which tell us that the novel's 'ethical' form is abstract in a *double* sense: form is abstract descriptively when it is regarded as 'given', when literary works, or artistic works in general, are simply regarded as having an aesthetic form (as opposed to their 'content', say). Lukács claims that aesthetic or literary form as such is a product of form becoming *socially abstract*, isolated in an autonomous domain. Culturally understood, form would be concrete if it constituted the social world; hence abstract form becomes a negativity with respect to 'second nature' because it lacks the power of constitution. Transcendental subjectivity as an ideological figure is the remnant or preserve of a normative totality that has lost the power of constitution. As a reality transcendental subjectivity is the decentred totality of modern social formations which 'constitutes' a world without norms, a 'worldless' world. In the next Chapter I shall suggest a necessary condition, a narrative condition for there to be a normative totality, a culture, a world.

Irony, as the figure of transcendental subjectivity, is the normative mentality of the novel because in its negativity it registers the *becoming* abstract of form; irony sees through the negativity of the *cogito* by figuring its negativity as abstract, as a loss of constitutive power. Because Lukács locates the problem of the subjectivity of the novel at the level of transcendental subjectivity he is able to identify correctly irony as the normative mentality of the novel. Because he recognises that the ironic mastering of subjectivity creates only the illusion of objectivity, 'the surface riddled with holes' (92), he correctly identifies the negativity implicit in the novel's forms. Despite his reliance on the language of Schlegel, Lukács never really conflates irony with objectivity:

irony sees the lost, utopian home of the idea that has become an ideal, and yet at the same time it understands that the ideal is subjectively and psychologically conditioned, because that is its only possible form of existence... when it speaks of the adventures of errant souls in an inessential, empty reality, it intuitively speaks of past gods and gods that are to come; irony has to seek the only world that is adequate to it along the *via dolorosa* of interiority, but is doomed never to find it there. (92)

What Lukács could not fully understand in 1915 is *why* the path of interiority was doomed; because he could not separate the appearance of transcendental subjectivity from the reality he felt he could do no other than follow that doomed path. Lukács's failure is instructive for it informs the sceptical depreciation of irony by modernists like Culler and de Man. They, of course, do recognise the difference between empirical and transcendental subjectivity, but not the true nature of transcendental subjectivity. Like Lukács they, following Kant, identify the individual *appearance* of transcendental subjectivity as its reality; thus in their hands Lukács's agnostic historical pessimism becomes a general epistemological scepticism. 'Ironic language', de Man says, 'splits the subject into an empirical self that exists in a state of inauthenticity and a self that exists only in the form of a language that asserts the knowledge of this inauthenticity. This does not, however, make it into an authentic language, for to know inauthenticity is not the same as to be authentic.'[27] de Man locates the negativity of irony in language as opposed to asking why the negativity of self-consciousness has become language-bound; and he cannot really ask this question because he identifies transcendental subjectivity with its individual instance, thereby guaranteeing that, like the *cogito*, self-possession ('authenticity') remains unnarratable, a negativity without positive resolution. In de Man's hands, Descartes' negation of history becomes irony's 'discovery of a truly temporal predicament':

The act of irony...reveals the existence of a temporality that is definitely not organic, in that it relates to its source only in terms of distance and difference and allows for no end, no totality. Irony divides the flow of temporal experience into a past that is pure mystification and a future that remains harassed forever by a relapse within the inauthentic. It can know this inauthenticity but never overcome it...it remains endlessly caught in the impossibility of making this knowledge applicable to the empirical world.

de Man conflates the historically conditioned negative strategy of irony with some supposed universal structure of language and selfhood. He does not see that the non-resolutive force of ironic consciousness is a function of the dislocation of transcendental subjectivity into a negativity opposing individual consciousness, thus reducing the negativity of individual subjectivity to pure ideality. From the perspective of the individual subject the attempt to apply the glimpsed authenticity provided by the negativity of irony would be a relapse into inauthenticity, into acceptance of the reified world; but for us this is only to say that form has been exiled into fiction.

If we look closely at the temporal predicament de Man believes is revealed by irony we shall discover not an illumination of the temporality of selfhood, but the reduction of temporal experience into sheer externality with respect to the self. How can irony, we might ask, reduce the past to pure mystification, and further guarantee that the future will be *forever* harassed by the threat of a further fall into inauthenticity? The past can only be *pure* mystification if, by definition, the past is never 'my' past; but for this to be so 'I' must always be different from the past that was mine. So the past is never either a constraint upon the present nor a source of unrealised possibilities, possibilities whose future realisation depends upon them having once been possibilities. This entails that all possibilities are equally real, because equally ideal (fictions), from the perspective of the present. Thus the past is reduced to what was but is no longer, and the future reduced to what will be but is not now. Only the present is real; all change is reduced to repetition, and no distinction is or can be drawn between real possibilities (potentialities) and the idle possibilities of dreams and wishes. Ironic reflection, then, becomes the textual expression of the negativity of transcendental subjectivity (the *cogito*) and, what is worse, transcendental subjectivity itself, because it is incapable of empirical existence, is reduced to a linguistic trope. By carefully elucidating and thinking through the implications of irony in modernity de Man has discovered the exile of authentic selfhood into form and fiction. Only contemplative consciousness could mistake this loss of an authentic past and future, this harassment by capital, for a discovery of the human temporal predicament.

Because de Man's theory does articulate the modern predicament of literature, however unintentionally, it can be useful to us in trying to understand Mann's own predicament. de Man argues that the wisdom provided by irony remains demystified so long as it remains within the realm of language appropriate to it, namely, literary fiction; and that it is vulnerable to a renewal of blindness and inauthenticity as soon as it attempts to leave that domain for the empirical world.[28] Because fiction is the exile of form, it conditions and makes possible the negativity of form with respect to the empirical world; this negativity, the negativity of the self and its forms, is the wisdom of irony. The novel's power to illuminate the absences in reality, its fictional figuration of empirical discourse, must lack empirical applicability if it is to sustain itself. This too is part of irony's wisdom: but for de Man this is a mataphysical insight, while for Mann it is a historical fate. For Mann, because the novel is the preserve of form we naturally attempt to preserve it; yet, because the novel can speak only of the inapplicability of its forms to the world we can preserve it only by going beyond it, which is to say, beyond the language and practices that keep form fictional, a negativity in the face of reality. Mann's text is balanced precariously between these two modes of preservation: the negativity of (German) history has left only art, the novel, with its power of the negative; but that negativity is only meaningful in its relation to history. Mann's irony, then, explicitly thematises both the negativity and normativity of transcendental subjectivity by making his novel's negativity in the face of history, our decentred totality, a statement about both its and the world's lack of a normative substratum. The only possible normative substratum for a 'literary' work would have to lie outside the work, in social practices normatively constituted. Because our social practices are governed, for the most part, by the exigencies of a non-normatively constituted economy, the novel's form turns into a negativity against its only possible ground. In a very precise sense, Mann recognised the *limits* of the novel as the condition for its (specifically novelistic) meaningfulness; he thus saw, more clearly than the young Lukács, the doomed nature of the *via dolorosa* of interiority.

VII

Practical Reason:
Marxism and Modernism

As eminently constructed and produced objects, works of art, including literary ones, point to a practice from which they abstain: the creation of a just life.

(Theodor Adorno)

Mann's failure, the success of his failure, deepens our awareness of the autonomy of modern literature, an autonomy which is inescapably affirmed through its attempted negation. What distinguishes Mann from other modernists, from those who hypostatise the social alienation of literature into a metaphysical fact, is his recognition that it is history which produces the autonomy of literature, and thus history which extrudes literature from its internal dynamics. Because *TN* is premised on the historical autonomy of literature, the becoming 'literary' of the forms of epic writing, it would appear reasonable to regard Lukács's theory as a 'modernist' conceptualisation of the novel form. Yet, despite what one might naturally regard as a theoretical sympathy of *The Theory of the Novel* for literary modernism, Lukács, in fact, did not anticipate the modernist reworking of the novel form; on the contrary, he anticipated a quite different modern literary phenomenon, namely, 'an ever increasing similarity between the great novel and the entertainment novel' to the point where 'the final merging of the two could not be avoided' (105). Only in Dostoievsky did Lukács perceive a strategy of resistance to this eventual collapse of the distinction between the ethically intended work and the novel which merely imitates the forms of serious novel writing. This strategy, as Lukács realised, was doomed to failure precisely because it travelled the *via dolorosa* of interiority and subjectivity. Thus Lukács's blindness to the possibility of the modernist response to the changing circumstances of novel writing comes to presage his later strident rejection of modernism and championing of realism from 'Narrate or Describe' and 'The Intellectual Physiogonomy of Characterization' (1936) to *The Meaning of Contemporary Realism* (1956).

In suggesting, however tentatively, that modernist techniques in the novel may be regarded as strategies of preservation, as a rejection of mimesis and the world represented for the sake of form, I should not want to be construed as believing that modernism is a natural ally or expression of left-wing thought. Rather, modernism inherits all the fundamental antinomies of realism with those antinomies now exacerbated and deepened rather than diminished. Thus the strategic preservation of the ethic of form-giving against the reification of the represented world enacts an increasing distancing of form from representation, a further isolation of the totalising and social impulse of form from the world to be in-formed. If the negativity of modernism performs an act of epic remembrance, performs, that is, an act of remembering the epic past against the forgetfulness, the social amnesia represented by the collapse of the 'great novel' into the 'entertainment novel', it is equally true to say that those strategies of preservation threaten a different form of amnesia which parallels the original doubling of the serious novel by the entertainment novel. A convenient shorthand for the ethically voided double of the modernist text might be the novel of pure fabulation, the novel whose delight in fiction-making empties form-giving of its ethical intent leaving only the endless play of the 'surface'.[1] Because some modernist texts do maintain the ethical negativity dialectically implicit in form-giving against the encroachment of the social amnesia represented by both the entertainment novel and the novel of fabulation it is easy to understand why they have been championed by the left; none the less, as *novels*, as texts which recognisably remain within the *tradition* of the novel, that is, as texts whose practices are strategic continuations (deformations) of the practice of novel writing, these texts are implicated in the fundamentally pseudo-praxis of the novel. Adorno was correct in his formulation except for its modality; modernist novels point to a practice from which they *must* abstain: the creation of a just life.

The modernist novel involves a series of categorial alterations in the practice of the novel; its forms are answers to the question 'How do I go on writing novels in these circumstances?' The categorial way of 'going on' with novel writing enjoined by the modernist practice of the novel is conditioned by the constitutive rules of the novel practice of writing together with the need and necessity to make that practice conform with, be commensurable with the changed circumstances that practice finds itself in in this century. Now this way of theorising literary modernism stands exposed before two competing theoretical approaches corresponding roughly to the two forms of amnesia which threaten the novel itself: on the one hand, theoretical modernism (or post-modernism), the ideology of modernism, perceives in the modernist text a realisation of the metaphysical *telos* which it contends is intrinsic to the very nature of literature, of writing fictions; on the other hand, the ideology of realism, of which the later Lukács was an exponent, regards the formalism of modernism as a perversion of the 'naturally' mimetic impulse behind the novel. Theoretical modernism ignores, or fails to pay sufficient attention to, the larger social context which conditions (without determining) literary practices, and thus ends up reifying, making into a metaphysics, the historically inscribed practices of modernism; while the ideology of realism ignores, or fails to pay sufficient attention to, the specificity of literary practices, and thus the formal dimensions of the practice of novel writing, hence reducing the novel to an unproblematic empirical phenomenon. These twin errors, metaphysical reification and empirical reductionism, correspond to the two sides of classical Cartesian dualism of mind and body, subject and object. Whatever remnants of idealism *The Theory of the Novel* contains, and there are some, its essential strategy is anti-Cartesian and anti-dualistic; its dialectical history relating changes in the development of narrative, in epic production and consumption, to changes elsewhere in the social totality. The forms constitutive of epic narrative, forms specific to narrative practices, are shown both to carry social and historical content, and to vary in response to the changing social reality in which they exist. Before sketching the trajectory of this dialectic in this century I want first to examine, however briefly, the antinomy of literary modernism.

1 Metaphysical Reification or Empirical Reduction?

Proponents of literary modernism typically defend it on the basis of the claim that modernistic practices in the novel reveal and conform to the true metaphysical dimensions constitutive of fiction generally. With this comes the corollary that earlier novelistic practices, namely those of classical realism, are aberrations within the history of literature which tended to hide, obfuscate or repress fiction's true vocation. The true vocation which is fiction's on this account is fictionality itself: writing is an autonomous activity whose goal is the creation of verbal patterns neither constrained by nor responsible to the restrictive conventions (fictions) of communication and representation. A typical statement of this thesis comes from Roland Barthes. He claims that

modern literature is trying, through various experiments, to establish a new status in writing for the agent of writing. The meaning or goal of this effort is to substitute the instance of discourse for the instance of reality (or of the referent), which has been, and still is, a mythical 'alibi' dominating the idea of literature. The field of the writer is nothing but writing itself, not as the pure 'form' conceived by an aesthetic of art for art's sake, but, much more radically, as the only area [*espace*] for the one who writes?

However theoretical modernists differ, they all agree in claiming that the modernist novel represents a break away from the tradition of classical realism; that this break with the tradition is predicated upon a metaphysics of literary autonomy whereby the relations of mimesis and representation are displaced into the fiction itself; and finally that this displacement represents the true metaphysical vocation of fiction. Perspicuous examples of these theses can be found in Stephen Heath's *The Nouveau Roman*, Gabriel Josipovici's *The World and The Book*, and Edward Said's *Beginnings*.[3]

The claim that writing is an autonomous activity which creates formal patterns not reducible to the protocols of representation, and that consequently novelistic modernism represents a metaphysical break with the tradition, suffers from two interrelated errors. The first, and most important for our purposes, is its metaphysical reification of writing itself. According to theoretical modernists realistic prose narratives presuppose that there exists a transparent representational space which is fiction's access to reality: names designate fictional persons who are just like real persons; verbs designate the actions of those fictional persons which are just like the acts you or I commit; nouns refer to fictional objects which are just like the real objects we refer to when we use nouns, and so forth. The writing of realism re-presents the world to us; it covers the world with its discourse. Because fictional it is not responsible to the rules of empirical evidence employed by modern historians; but it is constrained by empirical plausibility and probability: things in fiction must be similar in kind to things that happen in reality; perhaps exaggerated, perhaps intensified, always more orderly, patterned and neat, but nonetheless similar in kind. Against this theoretical modernists contend, rightly, that reality cannot be had so easily. What we call reality is a 'complex formation of montages of notions, representations, images and of modes of action, gestures, attitudes; the whole ensemble functioning as practical norms which govern the concrete stance of men in relation to the objects and problems of their social and individual existence.'[4] Marxists may call this the world of practical ideology; Proust, and with him Josipovici, denominate it the domain of habit. Whatever it is called, it is not reality in itself. Realism, then, does not represent reality, but only repeats the received forms in which a society presents the world to itself and itself to the world. Instead of alerting us to the fiction we call reality, realism dulls our awareness of the problematic status of our representations and auto-representations, immuring us more deeply in the repetitions of social existence precisely by treating them as representations of reality. Modernism decisively breaks with realism by refusing to repeat the forms by which society (including the realist novel) stabilises and naturalises itself. What modernists do may be variously described: they de-naturalise the accepted forms of representation by reactivating them as *producers* of intelligibility as opposed to treating them as reality's givens; they loosen the ties of habit by showing the endless and inevitable gap which exists between fiction and reality, and this they accomplish by calling attention to their texts as texts – as made or contrived things. Texts do not stand in the relation of resemblance or similarity to reality, rather they are *in* reality, autonomous and self-validating constructs. In fine, texts do not repeat but rather produce meaning; they are not mimetically contrived, but rather composed or constructed.

Language, here, is not taken as a transparent medium allowing us direct access to the world; it is experienced, in its materiality, as an opaque reality, with a density and probity unique to itself. Language, the theoretical modernists tell us, is constructed of difference; the relation between signifier and signified is mediated and constituted by the diacritical relations holding between signifier and signifier. Language can only signify as a system or totality of relations between the continuum of sound and the continuum of thought; everything is defined by what it is not, by its relations to everything else. Thus every apparent signified is in fact only another signifier in the endless chain of signification. Representation is always second-hand, a halted moment in the play of language.

Theoretical modernism, then, is premised on a double critique of the relation between realism and representation: everyday discourse is discovered to be a product of a heterogeneous set of practices which solidify and congeal into the 'ordinary' and the 'natural', and thus is shown not to be the bearer of reality in itself; and language is discovered to be a complex synchronic structure which has representation as only a moment in the working of the system. Representation is neither innocent (the practical ideology thesis) nor naively attainable (the linguistic thesis). The modernistic text works against our practical ideology by self-consciously repressing the representational moment in the play of its language. Literary modernism, with its insistent auto-referentiality, shows the gap between language and reality to be unbridgeable. Only the text now remains.

But is the literary text *so* autonomous? Can the constraints of representation and mimesis be reduced to *pure* textual productivity? Evidently not, for the domain of practical ideology and habit is not itself an unsullied semiotic effect; behind the complex formation of representations and images stands, according to Marxism, the structured reality of capitalism itself, which includes *as part* of its own internal workings the distorted representations we call reality. This entails that the discourses of experience are already constrained and moulded, not artificially or arbitrarily (like the arbitrariness of the sign in Saussure), but consistently by the complex *material* and semiotic processes by which society continually produces and reproduces itself. No matter how far distant they may be from one another, the material processes of society condition and regulate, in harmony, contradiction or discontinuous distortion, society's doxic relation to itself. It is this systematic relation between material processes and their representation which allows those representations to be effective in social reproduction. If this were not the case then the domain of ideology could not even be superstructural; it would be superfluous. To put this same point another way: we cannot produce another reality for ourselves simply by producing different fictions; to alter our practical ideology in a radical manner requires that we alter the material relations of production and consumption which condition and constrain that ideology in the first instance.

Once we recognise this, however, we can immediately grasp, with terrible irony, the Cartesian basis behind theoretical modernism. In place of the Cartesian subject, a subject notoriously *defined* by its independence from reality and the constraints of causality, whose whole being is to think, we now have the writing subject whose whole being is to write, to produce meanings in language. The central error of theoretical modernism (put the blame on Saussure, Heidegger, Derrida, whomsoever) was to suppose that the lynchpin and constituting feature of the tradition of modernity was its conception of representation; but representation has never been innocent or primary within the tradition. Descartes, our abiding witness, first establishes the autonomy of the thinking self from nature and society (= tradition and authority) and then is left with the problem of representation, of the truthfulness of his thought. This problem he solves, if at all, by the proof of God's existence and the assumption of His epistemic benevolence. This solution is dissolved by later philosophers, but nothing substantial is put in its place. Nor was the Cartesian *ego* a stable element in the tradition; no sooner had Descartes proffered the self, then Hume undermined it. If the whole essence of the self is to think, then all there is and can be of the self, Hume reminds us, is congeries of thoughts. Theoretical modernism gains nothing by its turn to language: the dissolution of thought into language and of the self whose whole being is to think into the self whose whole being is to produce meanings in language should not hide from us the deep metaphysical structure underlying the modernist programme.

It was the enunciation of the autonomy and independence of man from nature and society which marked the break with the pre-capitalist past; a fact classical Marxism knew well and polemicised in its vigilant attacks on possessive individualism. Immediate access to the real always formed a bourgeois alibi against the more pressing ambiguity of bourgeois individualism: if reality was immediately accessible then the isolation and priority of the individual could be ignored: with a secure representational space explanations of sociality could go forward without recourse to social structures transcending individual cognition and action. By attacking the representational myth theoretical modernism tacitly colludes with the underlying myth of autonomy. By the time theoretical modernists decentre the self it is already too late for it is just the account of the real (history) which is not the self which differentiates Marxism from what precedes it and not a view in which the real is a priori inaccessible, a thing in itself, a fiction. Of course, the self of or in language is not a Cartesian 'writing', constituting self; the self is inscribed, written; it is the text that 'writes', for theoretical modernists, not the subject. But then the Humean self is no thinking self; it is impressions and ideas; it is constructed by the operations which connect impressions and ideas generally.[5] The shift, the slippage, here is not into another version of constituting subjectivity; rather, constituting subjectivity gives way to the play of language, to the tropes and figures which produce the illusions of referential transparency. The ideality of transcendental subjectivity is thus displaced by the ideality of linguistic effectivity. As we saw in our discussion of irony, because theoretical modernism fails to interrogate the ideality of transcendental subjectivity its transposition of the problematic of subjectivity into a linguistic register blindly preserves the ideality of authentic subjectivity. Cartesianism is not just subject – object dualism; it is that dualism because the autonomy of subjectivity is the dislocation of the subject out of its historical predicament. Theoretical modernism eludes the ineluctable pre-sociality of the bourgeois subject, but at a price: idealism.

The status of truth and representation in Marxist theory is of course different from that offered by bourgeois accounts; the overcoming of the contemplative character of those accounts requires that those concepts be redefined praxially. To make the real unavailable in principle would be, clearly, to make the claim that Marxism is a materialism a contradiction in terms. Against the background of bourgeois metaphysics it becomes evident, then, that the reification of writing and of the literary text is consubstantial with the traditional reification of thinking and the thinking self. Theoretical modernism's proclaimed antagonism to the tradition and its real continuity with that tradition generates a present more stubborn and paralysing in its resistance, all the more so because we think we have escaped from it. Later we shall see just how complex and fraught the modern autonomy of literature truly is.

The second error of theoretical modernism is more overt, if more difficult to characterise. It involves the claim that the transition from realism to modernism is necessarily progressive given the correct analysis of literary activity generally. The dual claim that the shift from realism to modernism is a *radical* transformation in the history of fiction and essentially progressive is nicely captured in this passage from Said.

The net result is to understand language as an intentional structure signifying a series of displacements. Words are the beginning sign of a method that replaces another method. The series being replaced is the set of relationships linked together by familial analogy: father and son, the image, the process of genesis, a story. In their place stands: the brother, discontinuous concepts, paragenesis, construction. The first of these series is dynastic, bound to sources and origins, mimetic. The relationships holding in the second series are complementarity and adjacency; instead of a source we have the intentional beginning instead of a story a construction. I take this shift to be of great importance in twentieth-century writing. Indeed, a principal argument of this book is that a strong rationalist tradition in modern writing has for too long been hidden behind a façade of gloomy, irrational nihilism linked to a dynastic ideology. The progressive advance of knowledge, to which this shift belongs, displaces the burden of responsibility from origin to beginning.[6]

The difficulty here, and the difficulty facing all analogous accounts, is that the terms designating the two modes of writing are not equivalent; realism is specified in accordance with concepts elaborating its ideological assumptions (or hopes), while modernism appears in terms of the concepts which accurately define the essence of textual productivity. Thus the very manner of identifying the two movements generates an appearance – reality contrast which slips between, while attempting to join, metaphysical and ethical analysis. The metaphysical (or methodological, or phenomenological) description of modernism hides the fact that in reality the method of realism, if the claims of theoretical modernism are true, must be the same as the methods of modernism for there is no other way to produce a text. Realism's 'façade', its self-deception or bad faith, is thus anchored in a descriptive analysis which begs the question at issue. By aligning the history of fiction with the history of philosophy modernism is provided with a bogus metaphysical validation; a gesture which simply blurs the question as to what history is here being recorded. If modernism does involve a shift in the history of the novel, then the discourse in which that shift is recorded must be sufficiently neutral to allow that shift to appear as an alteration in an on-going project; Lukács's language of practice permits precisely this kind of analysis.

In contraposition to the modernist case is the conservative case where mimesis holds way. Here a variety of options is available. Either it is claimed that modernism is continuous with realism, in which case the shift from the latter to the former is said to correspond to a shift from sociological realism to psychological realism, with corresponding emphasis given to the interior monologue and stream of consciousness techniques as hallmarks of modernism; or modernism is called into question for its overemphasis on form and pattern-making at the expense of mimesis; or these two in combination, as is the case in the later Lukács who sees naturalism as a degenerate form of realism, and modernism as both a degenerated naturalism and overly formalistic.

Naive attachment to mimesis and realism tokens a tacit embrace of the object pole of Cartesian subject – object dualism. Mimesis functions in literary aesthetics as the equivalent of causality and regularity in general metaphysics. Hence it is not surprising that we find mimetic theorists arguing either that modernism is mimetic, corresponding to the metaphysical claim that art is necessarily mimetic, or that modernism fails in not being properly mimetic, which corresponds to a normative claim about the status of mimesis. In either case the theoretical consequences are the same. First, the nature of literary representation is naturalised and the conventional components of representation ignored. So we find Lukács claiming that 'realism is not one style among others, it is the basis of literature; all styles originate in it or are significantly related to it.' After comparing the consistent anti-realist to Schopenhauer's consistent solipsist who could be found only in a lunatic asylum, Lukács continues by stating that 'the inevitability of realism is most obvious ... where descriptive detail is concerned.'[7] The assumption here is that the employment of a descriptive vocabulary, nouns and adjectives, is unaffected by the formal features of literary discourse: genre conventions, rhetorical conventions, distinctions of high and low style, degree of figuration in description, and the restriction on the modes of figuration (symbolic, allegorical, metaphorical) which different descriptive practices allow. But all these features do make a difference to description and that difference is in part to be gauged by what *conditions* (produces) the presence or absence of these controlling elements of descriptive discourses. Consequently, the presence or absence of descriptive detail does not in itself token the presence or absence of realism in any text. There is no natural or neutral way to define realism because there exist no natural or neutral markers against which the degree of realism in a text may be measured.[8]

The bracketing or ignoring of the formal (autonomous) features of novelistic discourse immediately generates the second and third consequences of naive realism. Secondly, because those forms which are specific to the novelistic enterprise are ignored novels have to be assimilated to other forms of knowledge (e.g. sociology or psychology), since by definition they have none which are specific to them. For anti-modernists this usually leads them to claim that modernism fails because it leaves society out of account; the job of the writer, it is claimed, is to grasp his 'epoch and its major issues'[9] and render them in artistic form, where 'artistic form' signifies nothing more than decorative embellishment, style, whatever it is that transforms a case history or sociological study into 'literature'. But whatever artistic form is, it is not regarded as a system of signification. Thus, some anti-modernists are led to embrace precisely what the theoretical modernists informed us was the ideological underpinning of realism, namely the world of practical ideology and habit, so aligning aesthetic cognition with everyday experience. Thus John Bayley:

A writer like Tolstoy whose intention is solely to communicate, to infect us with what he thinks and feels, will be indifferent to any notion of autonomy; all his work will strike us as connected together like our own experience of life, and present us with a complex perspective into which we move as if it were life.[10]

In sum, naive realists demand that fiction be truthful, an 'accurate account of reality',[11] as if the novel had no vocation of its own independently of the sciences whose job it is through inquiry and theorising to provide just that.

Finally, then, because the formal features of the novel have been removed from consideration the anti-modernist is forced to shift his attack from the aesthetic to the purely ideological level. What is wrong with modernism is that it affirms the ideology of existentialism which portrays man as an isolated, historically unchanging consciousness suffering from *Angst*.[12] Ultimately, modernism is guilty of departing from the liberal view of man and society which dominated the nineteenth-century novel.

Autonomy versus mimesis; metaphysical reification versus empirical reductionism; these are the twin poles which structure the realism – modernism debate and consequently prevent us from understanding either. If, as I have been arguing, these poles are indeed structured by the classical Cartesian dualism of subject and object, then it follows that we shall not be able to avoid the fallacies of both parties to this debate until we leave behind the presuppositions which generated it. This was precisely Lukács's great achievement in *The Theory of the Novel*.

2 MODERNISM AND DIALECTIC

It is only because the novel has a form that it can change in ways more specific and precise than that supposed by the crudely

Hegelian view that modernism represents a movement to the level of self-consciousness of the novel's fictional (formal) vocation. Textual self-consciousness is, at any rate, not the prerogative of modernism. *Don Quixote* and *Tristram Shandy* are self-conscious texts; but in a different way so are *Madame Bovary* and *Wuthering Heights*, neither of which possesses the kind of textual unconsciousness which traditional (pro or con) accounts of realism would lead us to expect them to have. For Lukács the novel is a pre-eminently self-conscious genre. The transgressive movement whereby a writer attempts to authorise his fictive reconciliation of experential discontinuity through the creation of a pretence of mimesis (form masquerading as representation) necessarily involves a tacit or implicit textual self-consciousness in all novels, a self-consciousness which becomes itself textually self-conscious in modernism.[13] It is not the self-consciousness of the text which is new to modernism, it is the consistent denial that the text is authorised by experience which, at this level of generality, appears as a departure from tradition; but since no novelistic text has ever been validated by experience, it follows that this is not as decisive a break as some writers would have us believe.

What is perhaps most distinctive about the narratives of crisis – metaphysical break, or descent into nihilistic, self-aggrandising play, depending on your point of view – is their dismissal of history as being an internal constituent of literary discourse. Literary form, I have been arguing, is reducible to neither representational substantiality non *sui generis* imaginative autonomy. Literary modernism can only be understood as a set of more or less coherent deformations[14] of the formal a priori of realism. Moreover, these deformations of the realistic text generate all the typical *responses* to modernism as their natural effects:

(a) Because modernism works against the formally embedded *ideological* assumptions of realism, against assumptions about time, causality and the self, we may consider modernism a new kind of realism; a demystifying of realistic categories in favour of more realistic, humane categories. So Virginia Woolf, in her 1919 protest against Bennett, Wells et al.: 'Life is not a series of gig-lamps symmetrically arranged: life is a luminous halo, a semi-transparent envelope surrounding us from the beginning of consciousness to the end.'[15] 'Life' comes to replace 'reality' in Mrs Woolf's vocabulary, but the appeal to the standard of 'reality' remains unchanged.

(b) Because the categories structuring the realistic text are those consecrated by the practical ideology of modernity, and modernism is a reaction against the ideology of realism, it follows that the modernist text can no longer employ to the same degree that realism had the discourse of our practical ideology. It is this which lies behind the oft repeated charge that writers like Woolf and Joyce are no longer concerned with life as 'we' ordinarily live it and experience it.

(c) Finally, because modernists no longer feel constrained by the protocols of our practical ideology they (the very opposite of (a) now), as writers or critics, no longer appeal to reality as the standard against which modernist fictions are to be measured. Once we recognise the social and ideological character of realism, including both its demythologising, critical relation to earlier allegorical forms and its own sublated interpretative dealing with its demythologised materials, it is not surprising to find modernism regarded as either a new realism or as the denial of all realisms.

Now while we have seen that there is no reason to accept the theoretical modernists' claim for the metaphysical autonomy of their texts, I think a case can be made for the claim that the realignment of the interpretative and representational elements which modernism achieves is indicative of a problematic and unprecedented achievement of *social autonomy* by literature as a social institution.[16]

Realism involves a sustained employment of experiential discourse, a subservience to the protocols of that discourse's practical ideology, together with a masking of its own formal dimensions. These formal and interpretative dimensions must be masked for it is precisely they which our practical ideology prohibits. Crudely, the demythologising tactics of realist fictions go hand-in-hand with the growing dominance of 'rationalisation' and 'reification' within capitalism: the replacement of teleology by linear causality; the shift from qualitative to quantitative modes of classification and categorisation; action's loss of its consensual, social parameters and its dissolution into motive and intention, and so forth. These alterations receive a specific shape and significance when placed into the context of literary production. To cite the most obvious changes conditioning the growth of the novel: the breakdown of the oral tradition and the cultic foundations of traditional art; the growth of printing and the development of a privatised reading public; the growth of magazines, lending libraries and large publishing firms; and finally the growth of public education and university systems which encourage 'literacy'. These changes in the social situation of literature, changes, roughly speaking, in the conditions of production, distribution and consumption of literature, bring about a series of corollary mutations in the ideological appropriation of literature: on the one hand, literature comes to be associated with non-practicality, uselessness, amusement, pleasure, bohemianism, even madness; while on the other hand, literature is said to be the conveyor of humane values, worldliness, ethical awareness, and a source of self-realisation.[17] If we follow how it is that the first set of social changes generates the set of ideological assumptions about the nature of literature, then we have, in broad outline, the sense in which literature became a relatively autonomous institution in the course of the nineteenth century. As in every other part of capitalism we find a privatisation of production and consumption linked with extended and intensified modes of distribution. Only the place of literature in education halted (halts) the extremes of privatised production (the mad artist) and consumption (the solitary, amused reader) from becoming ultimate.

Yet nothing spoke so firmly against the marginality and autonomy of literary *discourse* as realism and its ideology. Thus the breakdown of realism makes overt in literary discourse the autonomy that literature had already begun to achieve as a social institution. The causes for the breakdown in the realist system are manifold:

(i) With the fading memory feudalism and the *ancien régime* realism loses its target as a critical, demythologising force; the very success of the nineteenth century in secularising the world denies later writers sacred forms to oppose.[18]

(ii) With the growth of monopoly capitalism and the consequent blurring of class lines within the West, literature lost class situation as a self-evident mediating factor between individual experience and social reality (class being the real basis of the so-called unity of individual and universal in realist fiction[19]).

(iii) Hence as naturalism attempts to act on the ideology of realism in its changed circumstances the aesthetic poverty of the realist ethic begins to show through, a fact registered, as through a glass darkly, in Lukács's 'Narrate or Describe?'

(iv) These facts generate towards the end of the nineteenth century a new aesthetic self-consciousness (Flaubert, James), together with and reflected by the development of the art for art's sake movement, and the like.

(v) Finally, with the social disruptions of the early part of this century and the first world war we find even the popular imagination becoming suspicious of the proclaimed values or anti-values of modernity.

A combination, then, of fatigue, scepticism, self-consciousness and a 'sensed' breakdown of cultural and social norms serve as the preconditions for modernism which throw the realist paradigm into question.

The modernist response to all this is fore-ordained by the formal dimensions and practical ideology of realism which is its (modernism's) aim to negate. If we note carefully what modernism does negate then we shall be able to understand how modernism makes literature problematic – problematic because socially autonomous – in a new way. First, modernism must negate the formal categories of realism: causality and time (thus narrative in its realist sense), self and biographical form. Secondly, since these categories are conditioned by the protocols of our practical ideology, both that ideology and its carrier, experiential discourse, must be negated. Thirdly, since part of our practical ideology is a series of claims about what is mimetic, then the ethos of mimesis must be negated, which is to say, there can no longer be any mimetic claims for the novelist to hide his aesthetic form behind. The immediate consequences of these negations are twofold: the discourse of experience must be fractured; each verbal moment that looks to be representational must be twisted, turned, negated so as to produce a 'literary' moment no longer under the call of the 'given'. It is here, if anywhere, that the dialectical interaction between realism and modernism is most evident. Just as realism thrives, word by word, sentence by sentence, in its desacralisation of earlier discourses,[20] so modernism is energised by the reverse process, in its derepresentationalisation of realist discourse. In Virginia Woolf and certain later writers this is accomplished through the pressure of writing itself, by the subordination of accuracy or verisimilitude to the needs of rhythm and tempo; or by the piling on of descriptive vocabulary, adjective upon adjective, until the representational emphasis of the discourse is exploded, only 'sense' remaining. Of course, realist discourse did not provide accurate descriptions but rather the aura of descriptive accuracy. Over-writing, as in Virginia Woolf, explodes this pretence of accuracy. In post-modernists like Robbe-Grillet and Butor this technique is reversed: an extreme, even perverse precision is used to shatter illusionism. In Joyce's *Ulysses* the illusionist pretence is undermined by the regimentation of each bit of descriptive or narrative discourse to some *other* discourse: mythic, literary, rhetorical, sacramental, and so forth.

It is this mode of writing which generates the second consequence of the modernist negation of realism: pattern making, form, come to exist for their own sake, as, literally, the opposite or other of representation. The point here is not that modernist texts have an excess of form, but rather that form is problematic in modernism because its *raison d'être* is to be the denial of the representational illusion. Excessive figuration, the saturation of the text with figural ordering, creates the sense of the text as excess, as outside the domain of practical ideology. Modernist texts, at their most extreme, tend to deny any appeal to experience, 'what we all know', the norms embedded in experiential discourse and its ideology as a source of authority, and in consequence they can speak overtly in the name of values, archaic or visionary, prohibited by the governing discursive practices. But what values are these? It is a radical over-simplification to suggest, as Julia Kristeva does, that the other signified by modernism are the pleasure elements of experience, the body, woman, which are always repressed by the relations of production and reproduction.[21] These, of course, might be repressed elements in our practical ideology, but they are not the only ones. And which ones are signified is not of the moment, for it is the critical thrust of modernism, especially early modernism, which is the source of its energy, not, or not necessarily, the values it attempts to promote. As Adorno has stated: 'Art is the negative knowledge of the actual world.'[22] In Virginia Woolf, then, we find the world without a self, the world her heroines yearn for, associated not just with watery, emotional, erotic states, but as well with death and sleep.[23] The other of this (our) reality represents the repressed, but what is repressed is so enormous from within the horizons of our experience that it is the other of life *tout court*: death. Similar sorts of things could be said about Doris Lessing's critique of modernity in *The Golden Notebook* and *Briefing for a Descent into Hell*, where hallucinatory, mystic visions and madness are all that can be glimpsed of the real. In writings of this sort, although not in all modernist writings, the attempt to retotalise experience outside the reified totality we live can only be at the expense of all we usually know as reality.

The theoretical modernists mistake this enforced social autonomy of modernism with a metaphysics of autonomy and anti-representationalism. Meaning, theme, form as ethic and ethos have always, however, stood in an equivocal relation to representation in modernity: only the double (realist and modernist) misreading of realism blinded us from seeing this. Modernism breaks the uneasy tension and qualified truce which supported the ideology of realism; the denial of the denial of form as ethic and ethos leaves the modernist with *only* the resources of form which is not and has not been socially underwritten to support his or her endeavour. Once this autonomisation has *happened to* literature, it is but a brief step to where criticism follows suit. Thus in his *Anatomy of Criticism* Northrop Frye organises and structures the *now* autonomous forms of literary discourse and claims that just these *are* literature's resources; if we learn to read these forms, we learn what literature is. But to talk of literature in this way is to drop all the mediations which have created literature as a relatively autonomous institution in our time, one which can be guided by only its own formal laws. Frye's Herculean systematisation simply mirrors and solidifies the social process which has created literature as a self-enclosed system. The same point is clearer from the side of history. Monopoly and consumer capitalism no longer seek legitimation from without; their draining of sense from the world makes form into excess; since the life blood of literature is form, literature becomes the excess which society no longer needs. Its autonomy bespeaks both its power as the negation of reality and its isolation from reality. Thus the real double-bind of modern writing: to engage the world 'directly' is to once again feel the constraints of the practical ideology that denies form a place; to lose the negative distance that is literature's power over (against) reality, to affirm the ethos of form, is to accept the debt of distance from what comprises the social dynamics governing all literature is not.[24]

Theoretical modernism short-circuits the problematic situation of modernism by embracing literature's new-found autonomy; its metaphysic of writing teases us from the hard equivocality of our situation. By failing to worry the loss of representation, it fails to worry the knot which still ties literature to the world. Dialectical criticism cannot return literature to the plenitude of representation; but it can show that what has driven us beyond mimesis is a *force*, driving us; that we have not suddenly been released into a world of form in which we can play at our leisure, but that literature's negative power stands opposed to a world which encloses literature in itself. Perhaps this can best be shown by examining the fate, however briefly here, of just one literary category, the self.

3   MODERNISM AND THE SELF

One way of putting Lukács's claim about the role of the self in the novel is to say that in the same way as modern philosophy discovers the self as the ground of knowledge and right action, so the novel discovers the self as the primordial bearer of intelligibility in our understanding of experience. Since within the world of the novel the self acts as a formal principle of intelligibility, the claim that the novel is a representation of the world or reality immediately becomes ambiguous, or rather is immediately exposed to a shift in intention, a shift as evident in Descartes' autobiographical discourse as it is in Rousseau's. The prior intention to name (know) the world is transferred to a need to name (know) oneself. This paradigm is capable of indefinite variations: searches for identity and self-fulfilment; the privileging of sincerity and authenticity over truth; always a search for the stabilisation of the self through recognition, recognition which can never be attained because the primacy of the self creates a situation of asymmetry between self and other, so the other – society in its most general sense – always transcends what is internal to the self. In *Robinson Crusoe* this charade is given its exemplary characterisation: the self achieves recognition in a society of one; the society of one being the model for society in its totality. Friday is both property and another self; as another self he can offer recognition, but as property his role as a true other is displaced, repressed. This dialectic of master and slave, autogenesis and social production, alters in accordance with the various situations in which fictional characters find themselves. Thus, as soon as a society of other persons is evidenced, their position as true other must be similarly displaced if the primacy of the self as ground of intelligibility is to be maintained. 'In a novel such as *Tom Jones* ... the foundling is discovered immediately after birth, only to be rediscovered – and this is the function of the narrative – through a series of adventures that clarify the circumstances of that birth: he is given paternity.'[25] Tom's identity, for it is that which he seeks, is not autogenetic like Robinson Crusoe's, but is, finally, biological in character. Biological order thus masks the formality of the self as the condition for experiential and textual intelligibility. Indeed the family and all its surrogates – love, marriage, inheritance – provide an other who is neither fully social nor fully natural and which, like Friday, can offer recognition without fully challenging the social autonomy of the self and its privileged role.

Throughout the nineteenth century the domain of the family increasingly comes to be questioned as a 'natural' resting place from the pressures of society, and novelistic heroes begin to move out into the world of society itself. Lacking the natural contours of the family, this new setting offers novelistic heroes more possibilities for recognition and less opportunity for actually realising those possibilities. Thus we are returned to the pattern of autogenesis but in a less optimistic light. It is here we find the novels of education and failure – with the two inevitably intertwined. What novelistic heroes learn in their discovery of the world is the impossibility of self-realisation (= recognition plus self-possession) in the world. None the less, the pattern of autogenesis contains one of the most progressive features of the novel: its break with the reductive, static naturalism of pre-capitalist society which denies to the world the possibility of radical change. If the hero always fails in his quest this is not only because he runs up against a reified social world which has no room in it for radical alteration (the reflectionist claim) but also because the hero is pitted against society and history, while in fact it is society and history and not the isolated individual which is the true subject of autogenesis (the formalist claim). The novel, then, formally repeats and colludes with the practical ideology which is the source of its own frustrated movements. Stendhal, Balzac, Flaubert, each in their different way, trace the increasing isolation of the self and the increasing impossibility of recognition in society.[26]

If modernism is to succeed in its coherent deformation of the realist tradition then it must deform realism's employment of the self as principle of intelligibility. A classical instance of a deformation of this principle is to be found in the writings of Kafka. Traditionally Marxists have treated Kafka in terms of a homology between the Kafkaesque hero, powerless in a world of institutions which he can neither comprehend nor find a way of affecting, and the fate of the individual under the reified institutions of monopoly capitalism.[27] While it would be foolish flatly to deny the existence of this reflectionist (mimetic) moment, it fails to uncover the formal dimensions of Kafka's practice. Kafka interrogates the self as form by *keeping* the self as the bearer of narrative continuity, by obliging us with biographical form, but at the same time denying the self as a principle of intelligibility. Intelligibility is lodged, if anywhere, elsewhere: in the castle or the law. But the castle or the law cannot be principles of intelligibility if their significance, their role as providers of meaning and order must be tied to the experience of the self. Thus meaning always lies beyond the individual's grasp in Kafka. From the point of view of the protagonist the other is inaccessible, mysterious in its working; while from the point of view of the other (or, more properly, the other's representatives, its voices) the self seems wilful, unbending. This restless tension between the classical self and the other is the unrelenting source of movement in Kafka's texts. Allegorical readings – theological, psychoanalytic, sociological – short-circuit the lines of force which organise the Kafkaesque text: meaning is what is *lost* in the distance separating self and other. Only through the self can meaning be had; but with the self meaning can never be had. Kafka also probes the classical self's ability to render experience intelligible at a different level of formality. What is the self? Is it a grammatical function, a name or initial, say? Is it an experiencing consciousness? But if that is all that is required then perhaps the consciousness of an insect will do? The shock incurred in reading Kafka is supplied, then, by his habit of giving us the usual grammatical and formal props for narrative sense, above all a first person to identify with, and then showing how empty and/or ill-defined that prop really is, how little of experience it renders intelligible and how little about ourselves it presupposes.

Despite its poetic flow and erotic, lulling rhythms, Virginia Woolf's fiction is more formally violent than Kafka's. For her the hero, he/she who can render life whole is dead; not dead in a way which leads to a new life and new possibilities, but dead prematurely, dead as a missing centre. Mrs Ramsay's 'uncaused' (because narratively anomalous) death in the middle of *To the Lighthouse* is, because wholly formal in its resonances, one of the most disturbing deaths in all literature. All that had seemed to hold the work together heretofore, all that had seemed to unite and balance husband, children, friends and narrative, is, in parenthesis, suddenly found missing. Not that the fictional narrative with Mrs Ramsay at its centre had been the source of fictional order,[28] but it had seemed so, and her death launches us as well as her characters into a search for another source of order. The missing centre, the world without a self, is given its fullest rendering in *The Waves* which is constructed on the basis of the disruptive non-presence of the hero Percival. However, unlike her earlier fiction where authorial narration, with its dense figural patterning saturating the narrative events, took up the burden of fictional incompleteness, with *The Waves* we have six ghostly voices, hardly decipherable from one another, intermingling, commenting, describing, recording the experience of the six characters which seem to emanate from them. It is the voices of the waves which replace traditional novelistic character. 'These voices', Naremore comments, 'seem to inhabit a kind of spirit realm from which . . . they comment on their timebound selves below. Even while their voices assert their personalities, they imply knowledge of a life without personality, an undifferentiated world like the one described by the interchapters.'[29] This is Schopenhauerian fiction with a vengeance; only the striving of ego and will individuating us. With its cessation we return to the rhythms of nature, of time passing and, precisely, the voices of the waves. That it is nature and not community which Virginia Woolf complements to the self, forms the self's other, helps explain the formal constraints under which she placed himself, and thus the formal dilemma which conditions her fiction. If the self is no longer able independently to order the universe, and if only nature (sex and death included) is left, how is fiction to continue? Each of her novels is an aesthetic response to an aesthetic problem: how to write novels without characters. And each of her novels goes further along the road of denuding fiction of character, of a counterweight to the flow of language, something which might return us to this world. Finally, this world becomes the fiction (the Schopenhauerian conceit) with the real world lying behind and beyond it.

The tension, pathos and perhaps failure of *The Waves* derives from its being haunted by the absent self, by Woolf's inability to let the self go. The self functions both as absence and as a disruption (especially in the middle sections) in her text. A final deformation of the realist category of the self occurs in Joyce's *Finnegans Wake*. Unlike *The Castle* or *To the Lighthouse*, or even *Ulysses*, where the controlling effort is to displace or dislodge the narrative self, *Finnegans Wake* is premised on a discourse that prohibits the stable self from ever entering into account. Joyce's 'nightynovel' is only comprehensible if regarded as no novel at all, but as dream-work and dream-language urging a finite number of elements into an indefinite number of permutations and repetitions. Dream as the premise of Joyce's work is also the solution to the aesthetic impasse his generation faced, namely, how to avoid the kinds of patterns of meaningfulness demanded by realism and still satisfy some canons of order. If dream-work provides such canons of order, then *Finnegans Wake* is an orderly text. In it we do not have to ask who is dreaming or who in the text represents the dreamer, for in a dream any and every character may represent the dreamer; moreover, it is the problem of the dreamer to discover who he is, since dreams arise against our naive assumptions about identity.[30]

Finnegans Wake completes the modernist project of decentring the realist self. In Joyce the self becomes a position in a set of fluctuating relations: Oedipal, social (master and slave) and ethical (victimiser or victim; scapegoat or innocent). But these categories, not surprisingly, are simply the natural and essentially familial ones behind which the classical text masked its contrivance, and so displaced the central self. The movement out of history and society in their artificiality and into nature and history in their eternal, repeating cycles is both a loss and a gain. In the classical novel the other life which fiction provides outside of practical ideology is registered in its formal ordering. The repetition of society and the transcendence of form became reversed when mimesis suddenly appeared as the lie behind which the truth of form flickered dimly. Form, however, is not self-maintaining; hence the paradigmatic modernist text can only repeat its *own* forms of intelligibility, which are either past forms (the parodic, satiric text) or 'natural' forms (the psychoanalytic, anthropological text). Joyce's dream-work is a response to a precise historical situation, but not history in its political or economic sense, but to the history of literature in its mediated relation to that other history. For the Joycean text that other history is either wholly outside it or wholly inside it. History is what we cannot escape but also what we seem unable to create.

And this mirrors the problematic situation which literature has become for us. Autonomous literature is like Frye's anagogic phase in which nature is no longer the container but the thing contained, and the human mind, like the mind of a dreamer, is at the circumference and not the centre of the universe. It represents the culmination of a social process by which realism's ambivalent critical and collusive relation to our practical ideology was broken in two, one half of which, which we have been examining, preserves its critical impetus by creating a world apart, while the other half, the world of popular fiction, which inundates itself in the raw facts of power, money, success, middle-class sexual fantasies, airports, and automobiles, has lost all ability to write against our time. These two represent, as Adorno stated, 'torn halves of an integral freedom, to which however they do not add up.'

4 NARRATIVE AND ANTI-NARRATIVE

The historical materialist must abandon the epic element in history. For him history becomes the object of a construct which is not located in empty time but is constituted in a specific epoch, in a specific life, in a specific work.

(Walter Benjamin)

Universal history must be construed and denied.

(Theodor Adorno)

The story is told, the story, the history of a certain storytelling. But whose story is it? From whence does it come, and what is its source of authority? Is Lukács's (and our) history of the epic in reality an epic itself, pretending to the objectivity of the true-born epic? But the age of the epic is past, and with it the conditions for epic history have departed as well. Epic history is contemplative, a naive recording of the passage of things; for us to even mimic such a history would be to engage in a form of contemplation that produces only illusions of objectivity, only a simulacrum of epic unfolding. If the space and conditions for epic history no longer exist, then an epic history cannot be written. None the less, it is possible to conceive of *The Theory of the Novel* as having epic ambitions; it is possible, that is, to conceive of Lukács applying his own false analysis of the organic continuum of time (128) to his own history, conflating the illusion of objectivity with the real thing. Paul de Man makes precisely this charge against the historiographical scheme of Lukács's essay.

It seems that the organicism which Lukács had eliminated from the novel when he made irony its guiding structural principle, has reentered the picture in the guise of time. Time in this essay acts as a substitute for the organic continuity which Lukács seems unable to do without. Such a linear conception of time had in fact been present thoughout the essay. Hence the necessity of narrating the development of the novel as a continuous event, as the fallen form of the archetypal

Greek epic which is treated as an ideal concept but given actual historical existence.[31]

The implications of de Man's complaint are equivocal: his point might be that Lukács's text simply contradicts itself; but that would leave the validity of all Lukács's claims in abeyance. More likely, then, de Man believes that Lukács's ironic conception of the novel is true but his organisational scheme false. But this raises the issue of the relationship between the historical scheme and the point about irony. If the conception of *irony* depends upon the historical analysis for its validity, and we, with Lukács, have argued that it does, then in what sense is the historical scheme false or illusory? de Man cannot accept that the historical form of Lukács's essay and his conception of irony are necessarily joined; he must believe that the comprehension of the irony of the novel is itself available through some form of non-historical awareness. And this would be plausible if he believed that *all* narrative schemes, all accounts of continuous development, were fictions covering over, smoothing out, the non-linear discontinuities of experience. This would make of the novel a vehicle for the metaphysical discovery or illumination of the human temporal predicament, a predicament which traditional narrative schemes mask or occlude. But is this not a metaphysical hypostatisation of the narrative predicament of modernity into a universal truth concerning the boundaries of narrative?

The revenge of theoretical modernism would be a demonstration revealing that the historical scheme supporting the dialectical critique of modernism is itself a victim of the illusions which the experience of the modern has allowed us to escape. To avoid this reversal of fortunes it will be sufficient to indicate how the very specific historical phenomena which have now made narrative problematic infect the theoretical unravelling of narrative.

In his well-known essay 'Boundaries of Narrative', Gérard Genette contends that modernism's suppression or inclusion of narrative into the discourse of the narrative is, perhaps, only the result of 'a particularly acute sensitivity to certain incompatibilities of language'.[31] For Genette the comprehension of the strategies of literary modernism is not to be found in the social and historical circumstances inscribing a particular practice, but rather in a form of awareness that is identical to that of the theorist. It is these 'incompatibilities of language' which, perhaps, best explain the strategies of modernism, and which make of narrative, in the negative singularity at issue, 'already for us a thing of the past which we must hasten to consider as it passes away, before it has completely deserted our horizon.' What is the negative singularity of narrative here, and what are the incompatibilities of language which make of narrative already a thing of the past?

Genette's aim is to isolate the specifically narrative features of language through a consideration of the theoretical oppositions in accordance with which narrative is defined and constituted in the face of non-narrative forms. A premise of his analysis, then, is that narrative, pure or impure, is a semiotic universal which is what it is through the structures of language that make it possible; since the structures of language that make narrative possible are themselves universal, then changes in narrative practice are best understood as occasioned by alterations in the understanding of the theoretical inscription of narrative. Neither narrative practices themselves nor their theoretical comprehension are considered to possess any historical specificity. Thus in interrogating the Aristotelian and Platonic distinction between diegesis and mimesis Genette correctly notes that, ultimately, the theory makes no distinction between representation and fiction, between historical narrative and epic (fictive) narrative. For Genette the Platonic account of narrative is simply false; yet in the light of our previous analysis of the epic we can recognise in it the recording of a complex historical experience: Plato's theory registers both the experience of epic societies where the distinction between representation and fiction was not drawn, and the recuperation of the objectivity permitted by the oral tradition in Plato's own theory of forms where, given the Platonic account of degrees of reality, all non-forms are imitations which are less real (and hence 'fictions') than the forms they instantiate. Analogously, if more problematically, the neo-classical distinction between narration and description, which Genette claims lacks a semiological existence, records the radical diremption between spatial and temporal existence as it emerged, for example, in the new science. It would doubtless be a complex matter to trace the historical connections between rhetorical theory, science and other forms of discourse; nonetheless, it is clear that a full comprehension of rhetorical theory would require an elucidation of just those connections.

Genette's final oppositional pairing, and the one he believes does capture the negative singularity of narrative, is between narrative and discourse. Discourse always invokes a speaker speaking from some particular time and space; discourse always refers, implicitly or explicitly, to an 'I' defined only 'as the person who maintains the discourse', and thus relativises space and time to the instance of the discourse. In opposition to the 'subjectivity' of discourse there exists the objectivity of narrative, an objectivity defined by the absence of all reference to a narrator. In a pure narrative all that appears are events 'chronologically recorded as they appear on the horizon of the story. Here no one speaks. The events tell themselves.'[33] A pure narrative would expunge all references to the instance of discourse; it would not appear to be uttered by anyone, and thus none of the information it contained would demand to be referred to its source or to be evaluated 'in terms of its distance to the speaker and to the act of speaking'.

It is in the opposition between the objectivity of narrative and the subjectivity of discourse that Genette finds the 'incompatibilities of language' which license his scepticism about the future of narrative. Every intrusion into a narrative of a moment of discourse distorts the purity and objectivity of the narrative; discourse disrupts the purity of narrative while remaining external to it. Conversely, a moment of narration within a discourse is absorbed 'without effort or distortion' into the discourse; thus discourse remains discourse even when it contains narrative elements. In comparison with discourse, then, narrative possesses a purity recognisable through its inability to absorb other forms into itself without distortion. But this purity of narrative is equally its artificiality; in contrast to narrative 'discourse has no purity to preserve since it is the natural mode of language, the broadest and most universal mode, by definition open to all forms.' Narrative's artificial purity is the sign of its mortality; if narrative abstains from discourse it necessarily succumbs to 'dryness and sterility', but since discourse can only function as an external intrusion into narrative, then there is no mode of representation in which the purity of narrative can be sustained without betraying itself.

Now if we supposed that Genette's analysis and diagnosis of the boundaries and end of narrative had the universal applicability its linguistic and theoretical presentation insinuates we would be wrong, for the only literacy evidence he evinces for his theory is the novel. It is then the novel, its history and problems, which tells the story of the dilemma posed by the relationships between narrative and discourse. Why the novel, and the novel alone, evidences the problematic duality of narrative and discourse Genette does not explain; nor is any reason given for why the writers of the classical period were unworried by the direct intrusion of authorial discourses into their narratives, or why it was in the classic age of objective narrative, in Balzac and Tolstoy, that an equilibrium between narrative and discourse could be achieved. What Genette's mini-history of the novel seems to suggest is that for the novel (by definition?) the duality of narrative and discourse is a problem; some writers were unworried by this problem, others were worried by it and developed narrative techniques to deal with it; and finally, in the modern period 'certain aware and exacting writers' were (have been) so struck by the incompatibilities between narrative and discourse that 'certain manners of expression' became almost 'physically impossible' for them.

For us the reasons and causes controlling this narrative are now familiar. We can read Genette's discourse as form and his narrative as mimesis, and explain why form intrudes as a privative subjectivity into the objectivity of mimesis; we can detect in the singularity of narrative chronological movement the reduction of human, existential temporality to causal chains; we can explain the modernist retreat to discourse, its falling back 'on the vague murmur of its own discourse' by reference to the attempt to preserve the moment of form in the face of the deepening reification of the social world; and behind it all we can detect in the duality of narrative and discourse the fateful dualism of subject and object.

Yet, in showing the historical specificity of Genette's putatively theoretical and universal analysis we have not shown that analysis to be false; we have not shown that his diagnosis of the fate of narrative is other than he suggests it must be. On one level, in fact, we would not want to disagree with Genette, for the singularity of narrative he analyses is the entrapment of narrative reason in categorial contemplation. On another level, however, his diagnosis urges a conclusion we wish to resist: by casting the history of the novel in the light of the theoretical dualism between narrative and discourse Genette provides a *logical* guarantee that the future will demonstrate a victory for the subjectivity of discourse over the objectivity of narrative. Must we resign ourselves to this logical victory for privative subjectivity? Are the possibilities of narrative restricted to the structural possibilities implied by the dualism of discourse and narrative?

Genette assumes that a rigid and unsurpassable either/or exists between the 'I speak' of discourse and the objective flow of a narrative without narrator or speaker, and further that the subjectivity of discourse is always and necessarily privative with respect to the absolute objectivity of narrative. He contends that the 'slightest general observation, the least adjective a little more than descriptive, the most discreet comparison, the most humble "perhaps", the most inoffensive of logical articulations introduces into the fabric of narrative a type of utterance which is foreign and somehow resistant to it.'[34] For Genette, then, between the objectivity of scientistic and positivistic description and the faintest velleity of subjectivity there stands an unbridgeable chasm. Yet, we know that the objectivity of the ancient epic was not erected on the absence of a narrator, but rather on an indifference as to who the narrator was. What Genette cannot imagine is a subjectivity that is not privative and exclusive, a 'we speak' which neither collapses into many exclusive subjectivities nor pretends to the elimination of all subjectivity from narrative; what Genette's theoretical grammar does not envisage is a collective subject for whom the either/or of discourse or narration does not exist.

As we have seen before, at the horizon of the history of the novel, just as it was at the horizon of the history of modern philosophy, there stands the question of the 'we', the we who shall speak and make history. The idea of a collective narrative stands poised at the intersection of three distinct problem domains we have examined. First, in our discussion of praxis and class consciousness we noted the difficulty in the idea of a collective self-understanding which was not explained by structural categories but evolved in the course of political action. Second, in our discussion of narrative repetition, that is, the kind of narrative movement wherein the appropriation of past possibilities is the condition for the narrative itself coming into being, we noted the modern restriction of this form of narrative to that limit case where the art of living is inverted in the life dedicated to art. As a hint as to why narrative repetition should not be so restricted we instanced Hannah Arendt's claim that only through the narrative of a life could the identity of a person be revealed; 'who' someone is, uniquely and distinctly, is made manifest through the narrative accounting of their speech and action. Finally, throughout there has been the problem of the novel itself, the restriction of form to fiction, and conversely the exclusion of in-formed narrative from non-literary domains.

Let us begin tying the threads which connect these items by considering Arendt's linking of identity and narrative. She believes that the story of a life which reveals the identity of its hero can be told only after the fact because we do not make the story of our life but live it; a life is not a story while a person is alive because a life is not a thing made. A person's death, then, closes the sequence of events constituting a life and thereby allows the work of memory to begin, the ordering of the parts of a life into a whole; that order and that whole reveal who that person was. Thus only through death does a person's life become an object of contemplation, does the open-ended expanse of a life become an individual fate. The determination or co-ordination between individual fate and narrative telling is reciprocal: if an individual fate can only be revealed through narrative, it is equally the case that the narrative work of tying together beginnings and ends acquires its significance and intelligibility through the fact that human life is an extension between birth and death. As we suggested earlier, the point, and hence the intelligibility, of narrativity is, in part at least, conditioned by the temporal structures and temporal parameters of the human form of life. The uniqueness of a human life of the kind revealed in narrative is then both a product of narrativity and a condition for it. A world without the *human* experience of birth and death would be one, Arendt speculates, in which the practice of narrative would lack purpose and existential support.

The birth and death of human beings are not simple natural occurrences, but are related to a *world* into which single individuals, unique, unexchangeable, and unrepeatable entities, appear and from which they depart.... Without a *world* into which men are born and from which they die, there would be nothing but changeless eternal recurrence, the deathless everlastingness of the human as of all other animal species.[35]

For Arendt narrativity is not directly supported by the existential structures of human temporality for those latter are themselves components of a world, of the worldliness of the world. Now we have seen this concept of world before in our discussion of intervention in narratives: an agent's act of intervention in a state of affairs for which he is not responsible reveals the relationship between the intentional life of the agent and the world order out of which that life arises. The world is the place in which and out of which the intentional life of agents developes. The world is what one shares with others (as in 'sharing an outlook'), and it is the condition of that sharing. To have a world, in this philosophical lexicon, is to have a language in which the world is represented.[36] For Marxists, the concept of world is like that of a social formation, it is the complex structure of social practices constituting the life of an historical people. Normally, and for the most part, narratives are written in and against the background of a world; an individual life is narratively comprehended in accordance with the language of a world. Thus, as the phenomenon of intervention makes evident, the temporal structure of a life, an individual fate, is bound to the world order, which is to say, the meaning of an individual fate depends for its coherence on a communal destiny, on the public and shared world the individual inherited, produced and reproduced along with others,

What these reflections suggest is that death cannot be an absolute horizon of narrative reflection because the very being of a world is a necessary condition for death becoming the seal of an individual fate. If we revert to our consideration of Descartes the dependency of individual identity on the world becomes clear: Descartes' rejection of a narratable past as a condition for self-possession is precisely what made it impossible for him to produce an account of *his* identity; the rejection of the world implied by Cartesian doubt makes the self, its being through time, incapable of being narrated.[37] To lose or forget the world makes the life of an individual unnarratable; but a life incapable of being narrated becomes lost along with its world; if there is no world to be spoken, then there can be no saying of the self, saying who the self is. But what is the loss of the world except a community's loss of its ability to narrate its being through time? And conversely, is not a community's capacity to produce a narrative account of itself equivalent to a capacity to speak its historical identity, to speak the 'we' which gives all and every 'I' its sense? At the horizon of every individual narrative there exists, implicitly or explicitly, the narrative of a community, a history whose narration tells a people who they are.[38]

Now given what has been said thus far about individual narratives the very idea of a collective narrative raises what appears to be an immense problem, a problem which stands at the boundaries of the novel and at the very centre of Marxism's self-understanding. The problem can be stated simply thus: What is it in collective narratives which functions as a guarantor of closure and completeness in the same manner as death functions in individual narratives? What formal structure can replace death in collective narratives? To this question the tradition has provided an unequivocal answer, namely, God. H. Richard Niebuhr's statement of the thesis is clear and succinct: to be a self is to have a god; to have a god is to have history, that is, events connected in a meaningful pattern; to have one god is to have one history.'[39] All that is wrong with this statement is the ordering of its clauses, for it should say: to have a self is to have a history; to have a history is to have a god; to have one history is to have one god. A history, a narrative which employs a god as its source of closure is a contemplative history whose *telos* is a priori and transcendent with respect to the concrete social practices of particular worlds or social formations. When Marx and Engels claim that 'the history of all hitherto existing society is the history of class struggles' they are recognising the need for a narrative account of social identity; none the less, in stating the structure of that narrative as a contemplative truth they remain within the theological tradition of pre-capitalist narratives and the contemplative reduction of historical practice achieved by capital. When a Marixst theorist like Fredric Jameson follows Marx and Engels in asserting the narrative meaning of Marxism against the social scientific construal of Marxism he immediately sacrifices the political and practical significance of narrative reasoning by succumbing to a contemplative reading of the Marxist narrative.

Only Marxism can give us an adequate account of the essential *mystery* of the cultural past, which, like Tiresias drinking the blood, is momentarily returned to life and warmth and allowed once more to speak, and to deliver its long-forgotten message in surroundings utterly alien to it. This mystery can be reenacted only if the human adventure is one . . . . These matters [of cultural history] can recover their original urgency for us only if they are retold within the unity of a single great collective story; only if, in however disguised and symbolic a form, they are seen as sharing a single fundamental theme – for Marxism, the collective struggle to wrest a realm of Freedom from a realm of Necessity; only if they are grasped as vital episodes in a single vast unfinished plot.[40]

We can comprehend how speculative and contemplative Jameson's conception of collective history is by placing it into the situation of narrative which the history of modernism has bequeathed to us. Individual narratives, we have argued, can only be written against the background of a world. What happens, however, when the language and practices of a world systematically obscure and distort the worldliness of the world as such? What happens when the collective narrative supporting each individual narrative can no longer be spoken? To urge at this juncture that there *is* a collective history, an unfinished plot, breaks the fundamental connection between collective narratives and social identity; it makes the Marxist narrative transcendent to concrete social practices, and therefore transcendent to any particular world. Marxism thus becomes a collective narrative which is no one's narrative, a narrative searching for an agent, a hero to complete it.

It is inadequate simply to pose the Marxist historical narrative aginst the anti-narrative of modernism, employing the theoretical terms of the former to decode or decipher the historical meaning of the latter. To be sure the history of the novel points to the need for a different storytelling, a collective storytelling which the novel can not participate in for its story, its meaning is the absence of the collective subject which would give its many stories the meaning they desire, a meaning which would make their tellings redundant. Like Moses, they point to a land they are forever prohibited from entering. Yet, modernism tells us more than that there is no longer a collective narrative within which we can tell our individual stories; it tells us as well that the 'world' we find ourselves in is no world at all, that the dynamics of our social world occlude the conditions for narrative accounting. The reification of the social world is, in this setting, the becoming of anti-narrativity, the story of the undermining of the conditions for storytelling *uberhaupt*. Against this background, in this setting all universal histories stand exposed before the tribunal of history itself. As Adorno urges in his explication of the statement offered at the beginning of this section: 'After the catastrophes that have happened, and in view of the catastrophes to come, it would be cynical to say that a plan for a better world is manifested in history and unites it.'[41] *Pace* Jameson, no contemplation, no hermeneutical act of decipherment, can restore to history its missing narrative dimension.

The Theory of the Novel figures (in the mode of a ghostly absence) the need for a collective narrative to replace and displace the narratives of interiority provided by the novel. In *History and Class Consciousness* Lukács writes his account of the class praxis of the proletariat as a progressive narration, as the narrative production of a collective subject and its world. Even there, Lukács is careful to deny that Marxism is a universal history, that the meaning of history is trans-historical; he insists that the categories of Marxist analysis are themselves historical products of capital, and are not necessarily applicable to either pre- or post-capitalist social formations. He further insists that proletarian class consciousness is not given but forged through political struggle. None the less, the context of his writing was still a narrative context; he assumed the existence of the proletariat, the existence of a collective whose task it was to bring into being a consciousness and a world appropriate to their situation; he imaged the proletarian struggle as a narrative debate, as a conflict of on-going narrations. The 'time' of *History and Class Consciousness* was still a narrative time, a time figured in competing narratives and narrations; that time is now past. As continuing reification produced the anti-narrative of modernism, it produced as well the denial of the conditions for the narrative which was to replace the novel.

Lukács's programme of political narration is marred by an absence and an optimism. His theory of praxis is not overtly or consciously a theory of political narration; he describes the praxial process as an active and productive movement, but because he failed to identify that productivity as a *narration* he was unable to give an account of the *mechanisms* of that procedure. The continuation of Lukács's project would be the construction of a theory of praxis as a theory of political narration, a theory of the formation and re-formation of a collective identity through narratives whose telling would at once be a collecting and a making. But why should we believe that the theory of praxis might be adequate to the changed circumstances in which we find ourselves? It is here that Lukács's optimism, his living and writing in a narrative time, obscures the constructive components of his theory. The sign of his optimism in *History and Class Consciousness* is his assumption of the existence of a class whose narrative was yet to be written, his assumption that the minimal consciousness of alienation of proletarian individuals could be transformed into a class subjectivity. That optimism, we might say, is the direct cause of his failure to note the absence of a mechanism of narrative production, a mechanism wherby the 'I' of the individual proletarian and the 'we' of the collectivity could be intersubjectively mediated.[40] None the less, the theory of praxis not only does not preclude such an intersubjective mechanism, it positively instantiates the need for such a mechanism in its constructive characterisation.

In our earlier account of praxis and class consciousness we argued that proletaraian class consciousness was both a means to revolutionary action and the goal of that action; re-volutionary action would be impossible unless some class consciousness existed, but that class consciousness could not exist as a true 'we' within the existing social world. If Lukács takes more for granted than is permissible in his premise of there being some class consciousness, his account of the tran-sition, the movement from partial to full class consciousness through praxial interrogation and action does provide us with an image of how class consciousness can be formed without presupposing what the content of that consciousness is to be. Now what I want to suggest here is that this account of praxial production is narrative, that Lukács's description of praxis is a description of *narrative repetition* for a collective subject. In narrative repetition, we saw, the telling of the narrative is a necessary condition for the collecting of the potentialities latent in the past which make the narrative itself possible; thus the writing of the narrative, the activity of narration is the appropriation of the past which makes the narrative written possible. Our insistence of the dependency of identity on narrative makes the examples of Augustine and Proust emblematic rather than fortuitous in this context: the narrative collection of the potentialities of the past in narrative repetition produces the narrative which allows the narrator to say who he is. Finally, narrative repetition, we argued, *is* the existential experience of historicality, it is the mode of human activity in which the historicality of action is fully realised and thematised. Narrative repetition, then, is the image of a narrative praxis, narrative as a temporal movement that is productive rather than merely reproductive. Lukács's account of praxis explains how it is possible to begin a collective narrative without knowing the end, for only by beginning to try to make a narrative can the end of that narrative come into being. Analogously, only by attempting to collect the potentialities of the past can the collective for whom those remnants are potentialities come into being. Thus the premise of praxial action, of a collective narrating of experience, need not presuppose the actual existence of a collective consciousness. It does, of course, presuppose that there are spaces where such narratives can begin to be told; and further that there are potentialities for a telling, that the present contains grounds of shared interest and possibilities whose realisation depends on their being collectively recognised. These premises require defending and specifying; yet, short of a complete reification of the social world, a world in which even the imagining of an alternative to the present would be impossible, it is likely that the premises for the commencing of a collective narrative repetition will exist.

Collective narrative repetition is praxial because it replaces the teleological figures of death and the end of history (redemption or salvation in the theological tradition, a realm of freedom or communism in the Marxist tradition) by an ever-changing, always subject to revision collective intention. Arendt can ignore the praxial dimensions of narrative repetition because she presupposes the existence of what it is that the merely verbal and linguistic action of narrative is to transform into an identifiable 'who'. By presupposing a world and a finished life Arendt reduces the world-making of praxial narrative into the verbal art of identity making. We, however, cannot presuppose the world in which we attempt to narrate our lives; this is why the novel, the narrative form of our time, had to be a pseudo-*praxis* (and hence demonic (90)); and why, as well, our collective narrative, if it is ever to allow us to say who we are, must be a world-making as well as a naming. The narrative form of social praxis gives to praxis its rational form and shape, for to make a world is to produce a place and a way of life in which we can say who we are. Praxis is a world narration.

The historicality, the open-endedness of praxial narrative should not be regarded as a surrogate for a universal philosophy of history. On the contrary, the experience of the anti-narrativity of modernism reveals that universal philosophies of history were always contemplative reductions of the collective praxis of various peoples; universal philosophies of history figured the temporal synthesis of authentic human action in the mode of contemplation. The dependency of narrative totalisation on the synthesising movement of human action was long ago noted by Dilthey in his narrative hermeneutic.

We grasp the significance of a moment of the past. It is significant in so far as a linkage to the future was achieved in it, through action or through some external event.... The individual moment [has] significance through its connection with the whole, through the relation of past and future, of individual being and mankind. But what constitutes the peculiar nature of this relation of part to whole within life? It is a relation that is never entirely completed. One would have to await the end of one's life and could only in the hour of death survey the whole from which the relation of the parts could be determined. One would have to await the end of history to possess all the material needed for determining its significance. On the other hand, the whole is only there for us to the extent that it becomes comprehensible from the parts. Understanding moves constantly between these two modes of consideration. Our interpretation of the meaning of life changes constantly. Every plan of life is an expression of a comprehension of the significance of life. What we set as the goal of our future conditions the determination of the past's significance.[43]

Because narrative repetition realises the temporal synthesis of human action at the level of historicality it can provide the model for a collective praxis; and collective praxis, in its turn, can restore to narrative action its in-forming power by returning it to the worldly domain of political life where men and women gather, are gathered in the business of producing a world in which they might live.

The novel is, or was, the remembrance of significant, collective narrative under the dominion of the anti-narrative social relations of capital. By viewing the novel against the background of the epic we are able to recognise the dimensions of collective storytelling we have lost; the sign of that loss in the novel being the consignment of form to fictionality. As the worldless (because unnarratable) world of capital consigns form to fiction, it correlatively reduces political action to instrumentality, the calculating of appropriate means for given (by whom?) ends. Marxist political practice can succeed only by rejecting this image of the political; Marxist political practice can succeed only through the attempt to renarrativise experience, to construct a narrative whose narrating would be the production of a narratable world. In this light, we might say, *The Theory of the Novel* not only fulfils Lukács's prescriptions for a Marxist analysis of the novel, it equally forms a theoretical complement to his Marxist theory. In learning to see political action in terms of a collective narration we realise the truth of the pseudo-praxis of novel and simultaneously overcome the exclusion of form from non-literary domains. Praxis is a political narrating of experience; political narrative collects experience by collecting subjects into a collective subject; that collective subject becomes itself by producing a world in which it can say who it is.

The theory of Marxism is a theory of political narrative; the truth of Marxist theory is a political and narrative truth; its writing addresses us as possible members of a future collective subjectivity; our self-recognition in the story we hear, our grasping of our past and future in terms of the story told is an act of political identification by which we begin to become who we might be. Marxist theory offers us the terms in which we construct such political narratives, in which we can begin to give our lives a narrative comprehension, and thus begin to say who we are. Political narrative is always a construct in a situation; its truth is its capacity to collect subjects who can then continue the narrative making of their identity through the making of a world in which they can become who they are. How else, then, can we read *The Theory of the Novel* (or this telling of it) than as a political narration of the fate and meaning of narrative in our time? It addresses us by asking after the possibility of a collective subject who can continue the story of the novel in another domain, in another form of storytelling. And is not this address too a collecting and a narrating, offering to us a past and a story to come?

In answer to the question 'What is practice?' the philosopher Hans-Georg Gadamer responded in words I could not hope to better. 'Practice is conducting oneself and acting in solidarity. Solidarity, however, is the decisive condition and basis of all social reason. There is a saying of Heraclitus, the "weeping" philosopher: The *logos* is common to all, but people behave as if each had a private reason. Does this have to remain this way?'[44]

Notes

INTRODUCTION

1. (London: Pluto Press, 1979), p. 228.
2. 'Reconciliation Under Duress', translated by Rodney Livingstone, in *Aesthetics and Politics* (London: NLB, 1977), p. 151.
3. In *Illuminations*, translated by Harry Zohn (London: Fontana Books, 1973).
4. With respect to Benjamin, this thesis is implicitly argued for in Irving Wohlfarth's 'On the Messianic Structure of Walter Benjamin's Last Reflections' in *Glyph* 3 (London: Johns Hopkins Press, 1978). If the autonomous work of art is the key to Adorno's aesthetic, then this essay should underwrite this claim.
5. *Towards a Sociology of the Novel*, transalted by Alan Sheridan (London: Tavistock, 1975), ch. 1.
6. See Gillian Rose, *The Melancholy Science* (London: Macmillan, 1978), ch. 3; Susan Buck-Morss, *The Origin of Negative Dialectics* (Hassocks, Sussex: The Harvester Press, 1977), ch. 2; Lucien Goldmann, *Immanuel Kant*, translated by Robert Black (London: NLB, 1971), pp. 17–18.
7. See Gillian Rose, *Hegel Contra Sociology* (London: Athlone, 1981).
8. See e.g. David H. Miles, 'Portrait of the Artist, as a Young Hegelian: Lukács' *Theory of the Novel*', *PMLA* 94 (1979).
9. It could be argued at this juncture the *TN*'s status as a Hegelian reading of the novel is sufficient to explain its position in the writings of Hegelian Marxists, and that it is neither necessary nor possible to make any stronger claims for it. This suggestion is incoherent for it simply assumes that there exists a Hegelian methodology which can be applied to any contents whatsover; that is, it assumes that what is at issue in an authentically Hegelian reading of the novel is both non-problematic and straightforwardly distinguishable from what is at issue in a Marxist theory of the novel. But this thought makes nonsense of the premise of Hegelian Marxism, namely, that it is necessary in order to grasp

the validity of Marx's theory that it be read in terms of its Hegelian heritage, and that this requires us to apprehend the validity of Hegel's thought in Marxist terms. For a Hegelian Marxist the idea of a work being 'authentically' Hegelian but straightforwardly non-Marxist involves a contradiction in terms.

10. A. Arato and P. Breines, *The Young Lukács* (London: Pluto Press, 1979), p. 64, correctly note the premise – the productivity of spirit – but not its inadequacy. They equally fail to note the appearance in various places in *TN* of the Marxist-like premises or assumptions which Lukács had already used in his *Dramahistory*. See also Márkus, 'The Soul and Life', *Telos* 32 (1977).

11. 'Georg Lukács' *Theory of the Novel*; in his *Blindness and Insight* (New York: Oxford University Press, 1971), p. 53.

12. My conception of hermeneutics has been most influenced by Hans-Georg Gadamer, *Truth and Method* (London: Sheed & Ward, 1975), esp. pp. 258–325. That Gadamer's theory itself points in the direction which I have used it for has recently been argued by Richard J. Bernstein, 'From Hermeneutics to Praxis', *Review of Metaphysics* 35 (1982).

13. One of the reasons why *TN* has not been read as attempting to work through the Hegelian critique of Kant in a new setting is Lukács's affirmation at the end of *TN* of Fichte's statement that the novel is the 'form of the epoch of absolute sinfulness' (152). The concept of 'absolute sinfulness', however, signifies, roughly, Lukács's view of the *extent* of reification, the completeness of reification, and not the actual form of the novel itself.

14. Many writers on Kant would argue that the impositional construal of the categories fails to do justice to Kant's theory. I have defended this interpretation of Kant in my Ph.D. thesis, *Kant and Transcendental Realism* (University of Edinburgh, 1975); see also Paul Guyer's Kant of Apperception and A Priori Synthesis', *American Philosophical Quarterly* 17 (1980). More importantly, however, I am here merely using the impositional view as an expository device; a more traditional construal of Kant's formalism is all that is required for my argument.

15. See e.g. P.F. Strawson's *The Bounds of Sense* (London: Methuen, 1975); Dieter Henrich's *Idenität und Objektivität* (Heidelberg: Carl Winter Universitätsverlag, 1976); and Paul Guyer's useful review of Henrich, *Journal of Philosophy* 76 (1979).

16. Fredric Jameson, *Marxism and Form* (London: Princeton University Press, 1971), p. 179; Marthe Robert, *Origins of the Novel*, translated by Sacha Rabinovitch (Brighton, Sussex: The Harvester Press, 1980), ch. 1, passim.

CHAPTER 1

1. The best account in English of the tradition of metacritique can be found in Garbis Kortian's *Metacritique*, translated by John Raffan (Cambridge: Cambridge University Press, 1980).
2. That the critique of epistemology involves, essentially, the claim that 'the human nature's basis in the world as a whole, its relation to the world as such, is not that of knowing, anyway not what we think of as knowing', has been well brought out in Stanley Cavell, *The Claim of Reason* (Oxford: Clarendon Press, 1979); see especially pp. 37–48, 225–46. Cavell is right, I believe, in seeing this as what binds together the work of Heidegger and Wittgenstein.
3. Hubert Dreyfus uses this phrase in explicating Heidegger's conception of hermeneutics in his 'Holism and Hermeneutics', *Review of Metaphysics* 34 (September 1980), p. 14. Just how it is applicable to Lukács will be explicated below.
4. For a similar account, see Jurgen Habermas, *Theory and Practice*, translated by John Viertel (Boston: Beacon Press, 1973), pp. 1–3. Diagrammatically, the argument looks like this:

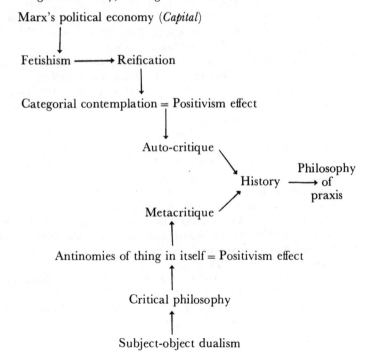

Marx's political economy (*Capital*)

Fetishism ⟶ Reification

Categorial contemplation = Positivism effect

Auto-critique

History ⟶ Philosophy of praxis

Metacritique

Antinomies of thing in itself = Positivism effect

Critical philosophy

Subject-object dualism

5. Karl Marx, *Capital*, vol. I, translated by Ben Fowkes (Harmondsworth: Penguin, 1976), p. 128.
6. Gillian Rose, *The Melancholy Science* (London: Macmillan, 1978), p. 47.
7. A commendable, if too sociological, account of Lukács's theory of reification can be found in Andrew Arato's 'Lukács' Theory of Reification', *Telos* 2 (1972).
8. It is, of course, only when contemplation becomes categorial that philosophy becomes epistemological. It is this capacity to identify the 'moment' of epistemology which gives Lukács's critique of epistemology its specificity and advance over rival accounts.
9. Since Heidegger's account of 'The Age of the World Picture' – in Martin Heidegger, *The Question Concerning Technology*, translated by William Lovitt (London: Harper Colophon Books, 1977) – restricts Descartes' interpretation of being and truth to 'modern metaphysics' it is not to be taken as contravening Lukács's analysis. What a Lukácsian would have to argue is that the meaning of 'modern metaphysics' cannot be detached from categorial contemplation in general, and hence from the 'connection' between metaphysics, social theory and social reality. Philosophy, for Lukács, while a relatively autonomous form of activity, is never absolutely autonomous from its social and historical context.
10. That Marx's essence – appearance doctrine should be interpreted in terms of scientific realism is assumed by, e.g. G.A. Cohen, *Karl Marx's Theory of Hostory* (Oxford: Clarendon Press, 1978), Appendix I; and Norman Geras, 'Marx and the Critique of Political Economy', in Robin Blackburn (ed.), *Ideology and Social Science* (London: Fontana, 1972). Their error, I believe, is to fail to recognise the Hegelian origins of Marx's terminology and usage here, hence e.g. their conflation of essence (*Wesen*) and reality (*Wirklichkeit*), or illusory being with appearance. One hint as to what has gone wrong in these analyses is to note the way in which the transparency of society achieved through scientific explanation is translated into the transparency of social relations themselves in a socialist society for Cohen. As I shall argue in more detail in my *Identity and Totality*, social scientific realism harbours the same desire for 'immediacy' and bias against historicality as that which structures Romantic utopian visions.
11. For a slightly different account, see *HCC*, p. 112.
12. Martin J. Scott-Taggart, 'The Ptolemic Counter-Revolution', in L.W. Beck (ed.), *Kant's Theory of Knowledge* (Dordrecht: D.Reidel, 1974), p. 12.
13. I shall say more about self-knowledge below in chapters V and

VI. For a good analysis of Kant's position on the self in this regard see Wilfrid Sellars, '"... this I or he or it (the thing) which thinks..."' in his *Essays in Philosophy and its History* (Dordrecht: D. Reidel, 1974).

14. On the ineliminability of the unconditioned in Kant see my *Kant and Transcendental Realism*. I mistakenly thought then that this must entail the validity of metaphysical realism, that realism was presupposed by transcendental idealism. I would now argue that these commitments are determined by the metaphysical structure of Kant's thought together with its fundamentally epistemological outlook. In fine, transcendental idealism is incoherent as an *epistemological* doctrine, i.e. it always ends affirming the realistic assumptions it seeks to displace, but succeeds as an anti-epistemological doctrine, as a doctrine which displaces knowing as our fundamental relation to reality.

15. John Silber, Introduction to I. Kant, *Religion Within the Limits of Reason Alone*, translated by T.M. Greene and H.H. Hudson (New York: Harper & Row, 1960), p. xcii.

16. *Science of Knowledge*, translated by Peter Heath and John Lachs (New York: Appleton-Century-Crofts, 1970), p. 254.

17. Kant does, of course, say more in the 'Third Antinomy'. See Chapter VI below.

18. Compare this with: 'man in capitalist society confronts a reality "made" by himself (as a class) which appears to him to be a natural phenomenon alien to himself; he is wholly at the mercy of its "laws"...' (p. 135).

19. *Critique of Practical Reason*, translated by L.W. Beck (New York: Bobbs-Merrill, 1958), p. 97.

20. In order to make his argument fully historical, Lukács follows the untying of the antinomies through the history of German Idealism: Fichte, Schelling, Hegel. With Hegel the problematic of history and historicality enter the scene so paving the way for Marx. Since that history is implicit in the conceptual untying of the antinomies, I have, for reasons of simplicity and space, compressed Lukács's analysis to these three steps.

21. On the Hegelian origins of the dialectic of immediacy and mediation in Lukács, see Arato, op. cit., pp. 52–61. For the hermeneutical version of this same dialectic, see Gadamer, op. cit., pp. 268–9.

22. For a more accurate appraisal of Hegel's 'spirit', see Merold Westphal, *History and Truth in Hegel Phenomenology* (New Jersey: Humanities Press, 1978), ch. 5.

23. Kenley Dove, 'Alienation and the Concept of Modernity', in A.

Tymieniecka (ed.), *Analecta Husserliana*, vol.V (Dordrecht: D. Reidel, 1976), p. 198.

24. *Adventures of the Dialectic*, translated by Joseph Bien (London: Heinemann, 1974), pp. 44–5. My argument generally in this chapter follows the line of interpretation originally suggested by Merleau-Ponty.

25. Andrew Feenberg, 'Lukács and the Critique of "Orthodox" Marxism', *The Philosophical Forum* 3 (1972), p. 456.

26. op. cit., p. 45.

27. Feenberg, op. cit., p. 438. As I hope to show at a later date, what is being theorised here is the 'collective' and therefore historical transformation of Aristotelian *phronēsis*.

28. Because he does not see how action is transformed by the overcoming of optical images of truth, Richard Rorty, *Philosophy and the Mirror of Nature* (Oxford: Basil Blackwell, 1980) fails in his critique of the epistemology to discover an adequate reformulation of the philosophical enterprise.

29. Merleau-Ponty, op. cit., p. 32.

30. See Andrew Feenberg, *Lukács, Marx and the Sources of Critical Theory* (Oxford: Martin Robertson, 1981), ch. 6; and Rose, *Hegel Contra Sociology*, op. cit., pp. 214–20.

31. Althusser appears to accept this contention in his thesis that there will never be an end to ideology.

32. See Feenberg, *Lukács, Marx and the Sources of Critical Theory*, op. cit., pp. 179–80.

33. ibid., p. 181.

34. The need to see agency and structure as two *moments* of the same process has recently been taken up again by social theorists (Giddens, Bhaskas, Sahlins, etc.); this view, however, has its origin in Hegel's concept of spirit. See Westphal, op. cit.

35. 'Linguistic and Poetics', in *Style in Language*, T. Sebeok (ed.) (Cambridge, Mass.: MIT Press, 1960), pp. 350–77.

36. ibid., p. 356.

37. ibid., p. 358.

38. For an excellent critique of Jakobson's critical practice along these lines, see Jonathan Culler, *Structuralist Poetics* (London: Routledge & Kegan Paul, 1975), pp. 55–74.

39. See e.g. Tony Bennett, *Formalism and Marxism* (London: Methuen, 1979), ch. 7; John M. Ellis, *The Theory of Literary Criticism* (London: University of California Press, 1974), ch. 2; Charles Altieri, *Act and Quality* (Brighton, Sussex: The Harvester Press, 1981), Part Two.

40. Ellis, ibid., p. 44.

41. Altieri, op. cit., p. 207.
42. See Peter Winch, 'Understanding a Primitive Society', in his *Ethics and Action* (London: Routledge & Kegan Paul, 1972), p. 41. I attempt to elaborate a theory of commensurability along these lines in my *Identity and Torality*.
43. Feenberg, *Lukacs, Marx,...*, op. cit., p. 134.

CHAPTER II

1. Translated by William Trask (Garden City, N.Y.: Anchor Books, (1957).
2. (New York: Oxford University Press, 1966).
3. op. cit., pp. 170–1.
4. In his *Structuralism in Literature* (London: Yale University Press, 1974), pp. 132–8, Scholes suggests a series of refinements to his earlier model. These refinements do not affect the present analysis.
5. op. cit., p. 12.
6. For the difficulties which an empirical approach to defining the specificity of the novel face compare Ian Watt's lucid conjectures in *The Rise of the Novel* (London: Chatto & Windus, 1957) with Diana Spearman's pointed refutations in *The Novel and Society* (London: Routledge & Kegan Paul, 1966). What are we to make of this debate? Neither writer directly faces the question: Why is the novel a problem for us? The so-called 'middle-class' theory of the novel, of which, after all, Lukács's theory is a version, is premised by this question, but then misconstrues its task as providing an empirical demonstration. For the necessity of making my divergence from this approach clear here I wish to thank Peter Hulme.
7. For a more detailed appraisal of these terms, see chapter III.
8. *Soul and Form*, translated by Anna Bostock (London: Merlin Press, 1974), p. 3.
9. G.W.F. Hegel, *Aesthetics*, translated by T.M. Knox (Oxford: Oxford University Press, 1975), vol. II, pp. 1048–9.
10. E. Said, *Beginnings* (New York: Basic Books, 1975), p. 13.
11. Jameson, op. cit, p. 159; de Man, op. cit., pp. 58–9.
12. op. cit., p. 3. The next four quotes from Auerbach are from pp. 14, 4, 5 and 11–12, respectively.
13. For this interpretation of early Greek tragedy, see e.g. J.-P. Vernant's 'Greak Tragedy', in R. Macksey and E. Donato (eds), *The Structuralist Controversy* (London: Johns Hopkins Press, 1972).

14. *Soul and Form*, op. cit., pp. 39–40.
15. See Auerbach, op. cit., p. 9.
16. For an account of this, as well as the next quote, see James M. Redfield, *Nature and Culture in the Iliad* (London: University of Chicago Press, 1975), p. 21.
17. op. cit., pp. 11–19; for the next quote, p. 15.
18. ibid., p. 109. For more on this see ch. III below.
19. Ference Fehér, 'Is the Novel Problematic?', *Telos* 15 (1973), p. 47.
20. Jameson, op. cit., pp. 179–80.
21. *Communication and the Evolution of Society*, translated by Thomas McCarthy (London: Heinemann, 1979), chapters 3–4.
22. Wohlfarth, op. cit., p. 176.
23. op. cit., pp. 54–55.
24. For an excellent account of how reading Aeschylus as a dramatist writing what we think of as 'literature' misconstrues his project, see Aspasia Velissariou, *Representations of Women in Aeschylus* (Ph.D., University of Essex, 1982); the title of this thesis is overly modest.
25. Wohlfarth, op. cit. p. 173. See Benjamin's 'The Task of the Translator', in *Illuminations*, op. cit.
26. The reference here is to Benjamin's 'The Storyteller', op. cit., pp. 93–7.
27. Wohlfarth, op. cit., p. 173.
28. I am here condensing a complex thesis into a few words. For an excellent philosophical account of this theory, see Laszlo Versényi's *Man's Measure* (Albany: State University of New York Press, 1974), chapters 1–2. The thesis is succinctly stated on p. 2: 'there is never any distance between living myth and its bearers; and since no distance, no reflection. The image a people gives itself in myth is an image in which it is reflected, and not one on which it reflects. *Mythos* and *logos*, imagination and thought, are not yet distinct.' See as well, of course, Eric Havelock's *Preface to Plato* (Oxford: Basil Blackwell, 1963). Neither Versenyi nor Havelock interprets the issues here hermeneutically.

CHAPTER III

1. Translated by Tom Bottomore and David Frisby (London: Routledge & Kegal Paul, 1978). Frisby has contributed a long and useful introduction to the translation. On Simmel generally I have benefited most from Andrew Arato's 'The Neo-Idealist Defense of Subjectivity', Telos 21 (1974); and Guy Oakes' monograph-length introduction to his translation of Georg

Simmel, *Essays on Interpretation in Social Science* (Manchester: Manchester University Press, 1980).

2. 'On the Concept and Tragedy of Culture', in Georg Simmel, *The Conflict in Modern Culture and Other Essays,* translated by K. Peter Etzkorn (New York: Teachers College Press, 1968), p. 42; *The Philosophy of Money,* pp. 56, 453–60. For the argument that Simmel's philosophy of culture does not depend on his *Lebensphilosophie,* see Arato, 'The Neo-Idealist Defense', p. 143 and n 134.

3. 'Subjective Culture', in *Georg Simmel on Individuality and Social Forms,* edited and translated by Donald N. Levine (London: University of Chicago Press, 1971), p. 230.

4. 'On the Concept and Tragedy of Culture', op. cit., p. 37.

5. *The philosophy of Money,* op. cit., pp. 453–60.

6. For a more substantial account of the tensions in Simmel's thought, see Arato, 'The Neo-Idealist Defence', op. cit., pp. 155–61.

7. Translated by Paul Breines, in Bart Grahl and Paul Piccone (eds), *Towards a New Marxism* (St Louis, Mo.: Telos Press, 1973). Also included in the volume is a helpful introductory essay by Breines.

8. ibid., p. 28.

9. 'Technology and Science as "Ideology"', in his *Towards a Rational Society,* translated by Jeremy J. Shapiro (London: Heinemann, 1971).

10. From Breines' Introduction, op. cit., p. 12.

11. ibid., p. 22.

12. ibid., p. 24.

13. ibid., p. 26.

14. 'Technology and Science as "Ideology"', op. cit., pp. 94–9.

15. op. cit., p. 25.

16. ibid., p. 26.

17. See e.g. Lucien Goldmann, 'The Early Writings of Georg Lukács', *Tri-Quarterly* 9 (1967).

18. *Soul and Form,* op. cit., pp. 152–3.

19. See 'Die Subjekt – Objekt Beziehung in der Äesthetik', *Logos* 2 (1917–18). For a good account of this essay see de Man, 'The Sublimation of the Self' in his *Blindness and Insight,* op. cit. This same argument is presented historically in *TN* as the 'Romanticism of Disillusionment'; see Chapter IV below.

20. op. cit., p. 35.

21. ibid., p. 40. I am condensing here a very subtle argument, for Lukács manages in the space of a few pages to encapsulate and criticise Kierkegaard's theory of stages and the argument of a work like, e.g. *Fear and Trembling.*

22. ibid.
23. ibid., p. 32; remarks in parentheses mine.
24. This is not to argue that tragedy could not change radically, or that the changes which have occurred *within* its forms are not radical. From within this hermeneutical frame, however, there are no grounds for imputing such a change *to* tragedy; even Beckett might to be seen as trying to produce an identification of the empirical and the intelligible, working against the dictates of his forms.
25. Although I would need a book to demonstrate the point, my claim for Lukács here parallels his analysis of Marx. *Capital* is not a representation of, say, the abstract object denominated 'the capitalist mode of production'; it is an interpretation of a set of practices, including the codification of these practices in the writings of the classical political economists.
26. *Grundrisse*, translated by Martin Nicolaus (Harmondsworth: Penguin, 1973), p. 472. For analogous conceptions of the differences between pre-capitalist societies and capitalist societies, see Jean Baudrillard, *The Mirror of Production*, translated by Marx Poster (St Louis, Mo.: Telos Press, 1975); and Claude Lefort, 'Marx: From One Vision of History to Another', *Social Research* 45 (1978).
27. Auerbach, op. cit., p. 165.
28. ibid., p. 171.
29. *S/Z*, translated by Richard Miller (London: Jonathan Cape, 1975), see references noted on p. 262.
30. Altieri, op. cit., p. 207.
31. See Culler, op. cit., pp. 192–202.
32. See Silber, op. cit., xcvii-ci; Lewis White Beck, *A Commentary on Kant's 'Critique of Practical Reason'* (London: University of Chicago Press, 1960), pp. 191–4. Both writers, who are profoundly sympathetic to Kant, suggest dropping causality as a constitutive category.
33. Silber, op.at., pp. xcvii-xcix.
34. My argument here is following part of John Rawls' unpublished lectures on Kant's ethics.
35. For a different account of the centrality of imagination in reason see John Sallis, *The Gathering of Reason*, (Athens, Ohio: Ohio University Press, 1980).
36. See Fehrer, op. cit., pp. 60–2.
37. Quoted in Culler, op. cit., p. 189.
38. See Fredric Jameson, 'The Ideology of the Text', *Salmagundi* 31–2 (1976), pp. 221–4.
39. That novels are so often long while causally conditioned by

changes in printing, forms of payment, forms of distribution (lending libraries and serial magazines), and changes in the reading public, it has its source in the novel's form.
40. op. cit. For the Koran, see pp. 81–2. For the next quote, see p. 84.
41. ibid., p. 142.

CHAPTER IV

1. For a clear statement of this dualism, see Johnathan Culler's 'Story and Discourse in Narrative', in his *The Pursuit of Signs* (London: Routledge & Kegan Paul, 1981). My point in calling this distinction a dualism is that because the distinction corresponds to the form–life distinction as it structures the novel there are grounds for scepticism about the ultimate status of the story – discourse distinction. I shall say something more about the issues here in Chapter VI.

2. See Louis Mink's illuminating essay, 'History and Fiction as Modes of Comprehension', in *New Directions in Literary History*, edited by Ralph Cohen (Baltimore: Johns Hopkins University Press, 1974). As will become evident later, while I am sympathetic to Mink's account of narrative activity and understanding, I think his explanation of narrative is too intellectualistic, too Kantian in its emphasis on the categorial character of narrative.

3. See Cynthia Chase, 'The Decomposition of Elephants: Double-Reading *Daniel Deronda*', *PMLA* 93 (1978).

4. See Fredric Jameson, 'Metacommentary', *PMLA* 86 (1971).

5. See Patricia Tobin, *Time and the Novel* (Guildford, Surrey: Princeton University Press, 1978). p. 218. Although I have said that the novel of plot presents an ideal fusion of time and meaning, it might be objected that the plots are so contrived in some eighteenth century novels that my thesis itself begins to look contrived. However, as Tobin rightly argues (pp. 30–4), it was precisely these novels' security about meaning, and corresponding lack of worry about time, which underwrites their narrative freedom.

6. For a clear exposition of Kant's schematism theory, see W.H. Walsh, 'Schematism', in *Kant*, edited by R.P. Wolff (London: Macmillan, 1968); or Lauchlan Chipman, 'Kant's Categories and Their Schematism', in *Kant on Pure Reason*, edited by Ralph Walker (Oxford: Oxford University Press, 1982). For an attempt to make the imagination and its schematising operations the metaphysical centre of the *Critique*, see Martin Heidegger, *Kant*

and the Problem of Metaphysics, translated by James S. Churchill (London: Indiana University Press, 1962).

6a.This, of course, is the strategy of Heidegger, ibid. For an elegant extension of Heidegger's conception of the transcendental imagination to practical reason, see John Llewelyn, 'Heidegger's Kant and the Middle Voice', in David Wood and Robert Bernasconi (eds), *Time and Metaphysics* (Coventry: Parousia Press , 1982).

7. All page references to *Sentimental Education*, marked with an asterisk (*), are to be Penguin edition (Harmondsworth, 1964), translated by Robert Baldick.

8. Said, op. cit., p. 146.

9. My rewriting of this section was informed by a reading of Paul Ricoeur's 'Narrative Time', *Critical Inquiry* 7 (1980). Originally I developed this argument from a hint given by Georg Henrik von Wright (see note 11 below), and some ideas about the nature of action provided by Lukács in his *The Ontology of Social Being*, Part Two, Chapter 1, *Labour*, translated by David Fernbach (London: Merlin Press, 1980).

10. Mink, op. cit., p. 121.

11. *Explanation and Understanding* (London: Routledge & Kegan Paul, 1971), p. 115. If the 'Is' of von Wright's statement is right, then we shall have to think again about what is involved in making intentionality the criterion for action as opposed to behaviour.

12. *Grundrisse*, op. cit., pp. 361–2. For an attempt to sketch a labour theory of time, see Carol Gould, *Marx's Social Ontology* (London: MIT Press, 1978), pp. 56–68.

13. Mink, op. cit., pp. 117–23.

14. op. cit., p. 180.

15. *The Human Condition* (Garden City, N.Y.: Doubleday Anchor Books, 1959), p. 166.

16. op. cit., p. 94; for the next quote, pp. 100–1.

17. In 'Theses on the Philosophy of History', in *Illuminations*, op. cit., pp. 263–4.

18. op. cit., p. 63.

19. 'The Eighteenth Brumaire of Louis Bonaparte', in Karl Marx, *Surveys From Exile* (Harmondsworth: Penguin, 1973), p. 170.

20. From the translator's introduction.

21. A splendid analysis of the relation between fiction and narration is provided by John Mepham, 'Figures of Desire: Narration and Fiction in *To The Lighthouse*', in *The Modern English Novel*, Gabriel Josipovici (ed.) (London: Open Books, 1976).

22. What I am trying to elucidate here is Flaubert's use of the imperfect tense, which does not fully parallel the English imper-

fect. For a shrewd account of this and what he calls the 'synthetic' mode of narration (as opposed to composite narration), see Richard Terdiman, *The Dialectics of Isolation* London: Yale University Press, 1976), ch. 8.

23. Said, op. cit., pp. 147–8, handles these last sections exactly right. Culler in his *Flaubert: The Uses of Uncertainty* (London: Elek, 1974), pp. 151–5, correctly notes Flaubert's attempt to create a 'purified' fiction in the final scenes which does not depend on previous development and thus remains disconnected from previous experience, but fails to draw a workable conclusion from this.

24. ibid., pp. 21, 23. Culler (p. 21) defends his enterprise against moral teleology with the claim that 'the process of interpretation forms a greater part of our experience than the making of fine moral judgements.' Is sheer quantity sufficient to legitimate a critical stance?

CHAPTER V

1. 'The Other Self: Thoughts about Character in the Novel', in *Sociology of Literature and Drama*, Elizabeth and Tom Burns (eds) (Harmondsworth: Penguin, 1973), p. 271.

2. Quoted in Paul de Man, *Allegories of Reading* (London: Yale University Press, 1979), p. 146.

3. Marthe Robert, *Origins of the Novel*, translated by Sacha Rabinovitch (Brighton: The Harvester Press, 1980), pp. 21–46, 81–148.

4. *Contexts of Criticism* (Cambridge, Mass.: Harvard University Press, 1958), p. 81.

5. Levin, ibid., p. 88, refers to Mann's *Doctor Faustus* in this regard.

6. See Pierre Vilar's instructive essay 'The Age of Don Quixote', *New Left Review* 68 (1977).

7. See Levin, op. cit., p. 94.

8. On Cervantes as a 'de-coder', see Fredric Jameson, *The Political Unconscious* (London: Methuen, 1981), p. 152.

9. E.S. Haldane and G.R.T. Ross (trans.), *The Philosophical Works of Descartes* (Cambridge: Cambridge University Press, 1969), vol. I, p. 152.

10. See Richard Kennington's 'The "Teaching of Nature" in Descartes' Soul Doctrine', *Review of Metaphysics* 26 (1972–3), p. 102.

11. op. cit., p. 145.

12. All further references in the text of this chapter marked with an astrisk (*) are to René Descartes, *Discourse on Method, Optics, Geometry and Meteorology* (New York: Bobbs-Merrill, 1965), translated by Paul J. Olscamp.
13. This line of interpretation is argued for by Hiram Caton, *The Origin of Subjectivity* (London: Yale University Press, 1973). pp. 66–73. There is little in English solely on the *Discourse;* the reason for this, I suspect, is that if it were taken seriously in its own right it would make the reading of the *Meditations* a good deal more problematical. My reading has been most influenced by Caton, chapter 2; Kennington, op. cit.; and Jean-Luc Nancy, '*Mundus est Fabula*', *MLN* 93 (1978), pp. 635–53. Nancy's article put the thesis that the *Discourse* is a novel (p. 647); but the Derridean setting into which he places his argument prohibits him from developing it adequately.
14. The full story is, of course, much more complex. See, for example, Gerd Buchdahl, *Metaphysics and the Philosophy of Science* (Oxford: Basil Blackwell, 1969), chapter III (2).
15. See Caton, op. cit., pp. 115–30.
16. As forcefully argued by Richard H. Popkin, *The History of Scepticism from Erasmus to Spinoza* (London: University of California Press, 1979), chapters II–IV, IX.
17. See Nancy, op. cit., p. 642.
18. From a late seventeenth-century paraphrase of Descartes' *Olympica*, translated by John F. Benton, *Philosophy and Literature* 4 (1980), p. 163. It might be argued that my reading the *Discourse* is premised by Descartes' dream; so it might be.
19. This thesis certainly requires a separate defence. My explicit identification of reason and identity here is a specification of a thesis Alisdair Macintyre forwards in his 'Epistemological Crises, Dramatic Narrative and the Philosophy of Science', *Monist* 50 (1977), pp. 444–5. See also Mike Marlies, 'Doubt, Reason, and Cartesian Therapy', in M. Hooker (ed.), *Descartes* (London: Johns Hopkins Press, 1978).
20. This paragraph till this point is a condensed version of the result of Kennington's analysis, op. cit. The connection between the new science of 'body', with its (non-Newtonian) conception of inertia, and infinite desiring is implicit or presupposed in Descartes; in Hobbes, of course, that same connection is made explicitly. See the *Leviathan* (any edition), chapters 6, 11. For a commentary on this issue, see Thomas A. Spragens, Jr, *The Politics of Motion* (London: Croom Helm, 1973), esp. pp. 176–85. There is a history to be written on this view of desire for it is not unique to Descartes and

Hobbes. Is not what Spinoza calls 'conatus' and Leibniz 'appetition' but a metaphysical rewriting of this new concept of (liberated, de-coded and thus infinite) desiring?

21. Haldane and Ross, op. cit., p. 401. Generosity is the will's own ethic, governing its relation to itself, and hence, by extension, each man's relation to himself generally. As a consequence it allows men to be 'masters of their passions' (p. 403), that is, masters over their 'natural' selves. Descartes' apparently innocuous divorce of esteem and contempt (disdain) from natural good and evil is hence the route by which the complete autonomy of the will from good and evil generally is established. (Generosity is the cause, and the only cause, of self-esteem for Descartes.) Our free will renders us 'in some way similar to God' (p. 401); and generosity, as the will's self-governance, is all that 'truly pertains' to us (ibid). Arguably, generosity is the ancester of and the link between Kant's 'Categorical Imperative' and Nietzsche's 'Will to Power'.

22. For this and the next quote, David Simpson, 'Putting One's House in Order: The Career of the Self in Descartes 'Method', *New Literary History* 9 (1977), p. 94.

23. op. cit., p. 645.

24. (Harmondsworth: Penguin, 1953), translated by J.M. Cohen.

25. I am agreeing with de Man, *Allegories of Reading*, op. cit., p. 262, that Rousseau's strategy is not governed by a *Morale de l' Intention*, and further that Rousseau's rhetoric of excuses is performative. What de Man does not explain is what explains or occasions this rhetoric. A Cartesian ethic of generosity is what lies behind the performative aspects of Rousseau's text, and creates the cognitive – performative paradox of modern autobiography generally.

26. For a more traditional account of this movement, see William C. Spengemann's *The Forms of Autobiography* (London: Yale University Press, 1980), pp. 62–72.

27. Haldane and Ross, op. cit., p. 6. Although this line of argument clearly supports Lukács's general view of the tradition, its inclusion here is to demonstrate how the form of self-consciousness which constitutes the novel, namely 'transcendental subjectivity', is formed through the negation of history and narrative as relevant to it. Hence the antinomic structure governing novel narratives. See also Dalia Judovitz's 'Autobiographical Discourse and Critical Praxis in Descartes', *Philosophy and Literature* 5 (1981), pp. 91–107.

28. Kant, of course, follows Descartes in this; *Critique of Pure Reason*, B xii, A 125: 'Thus the order and regularity in the appearances, which we entitle *nature*, we ourselves introduce. We could never

find them in appearances, had not we ourselves, or the nature of our mind, originally set them there'. Nancy, op.cit., p. 640, rightly claims in this regard that another world is 'true' because it is *invented*.

29. op. cit., p. 648.
30. This is a generally acknowledged feature of the *cogito*; see e,g, Bernard Williams, 'The Certainty of the *Cogito*', in Willis Doney (ed.), *Descartes* (Garden City, N.Y.: Anchor Books,1967), p. 108. Clearly, for Descartes this anonymity is intentional, for how else could the universality of mathematics, say, be grounded in subjectivity? Hence the irrelevance of criticisms of Descartes by writers from Gassendi to Geach on this point. Further, since science, the product and immediate object of anonymous subjectivity, is a means to private ends, Descartes could happily live with the thought that we are individuated by our bodies or by the mind/body composite (see Kennington, op. cit.). Problems, of course, do arise for this configuration when the context is practical and ethical rather than epistemic; but this is for the novel after Descartes to tell us about.
31. *Being and Time*, translated by John Macquarrie and Edward Robinson (New York: Harper & Row, 1962), p. 370.
32. Translated by A.V. Miller (Oxford: Clarendon Press, 1977), p. 125. Sceptical consciousness is a slave ideology.

CHAPTER VI

1. As stated this alternative is too radical. In Kant's ethics what the self provides is a 'form' (the Categorical Imperative) which all material statements of intention must accede to if they are to be permissible or obligatory. However, the Lukácsian problem arises later in Kant's analysis when he goes on to discuss the 'highest good' where, typically, the just get their proper deserts (happiness is matched to goodness). The highest good is almost nothing but a subjective desire, and certainly can not function as constitutive of moral experience itself. See Chapter III above, on reason and imagination in Kant's ethics.
2. This is, roughly, Hegel's point in the *Phenomenology*, op. cit., in the sections 'Reason as Lawgiver' and 'Reason as Testing Laws'.
3. Quoted in L.P. Wessell, Jr, 'The Antinomic Structure of Friedrich Schegel's "Romanticism"', *Studies in Romanticism* 12 (1973), p. 669. For a balanced appreciation of Schlegel on irony, see Anne K. Mellor, *English Romantic Irony* (London: Harvard University Press, 1980), ch. 1.

4. 'The Novel's Subjectivity: Georg Lukács's *Theory of the Novel'*, *Salmagundi* 28 (1975), p. 120. In her *Literature and Negation* (New York: Columbia University Press, 1979), p. 105, she makes a somewhat weaker claim for the achievement of irony.

5. ibid., pp. 122–3.

6. *The Concept of Irony*, translated by Lee M. Capel (London: Indiana University Press, 1965), p. 300. For an excellent account of Kierkegaard as ironist and theorist of irony, see Josiah Thompson's 'The Master of Irony' in his (ed.) *Kierkegaard* (Garden City, N.Y.: Anchor Books, 1972).

7. ibid., p. 336.

8. *Philosophical Fragements*, translated by H.V. Hong (Princeton: Princeton University Press, 1964), p. 55.

9. op. cit., p. 161.

10. We can state their derivations from Kant thus: In the same way as Schlegel mataphysically ratifies Kant's two-worlds thesis thus limiting human knowledge, so Kierkegaard radicalises the thesis that we must limit knowledge in order to make room for faith, and thus affirms the two-worlds thesis. For an interesting account of the relation between Kierkegaard and Kant, see G. Schrader's 'Kant and Kierkegaard on Duty and Inclination', in Thompson (ed.), op. cit.

11. For Schlegel this is something of an oversimplification for he adds to his theory the thesis that God 'is not [in] the world, but becomes *in* the world'. This cosmogonic touch changes nothing; since God becomes in the world 'infinitely', things are just as if we are set with the infinite task of reaching an unconditioned not in the world.

12. The theory of radical choice developed by Kierkegaard became the centre of Sartre's existentialist ethic. In a recent article – 'What is Human Agency', in T. Mischel (ed.), *The Self* (Oxford: Basil Blackwell, 1977) – Charles Taylor has argued that the idea of radical choice is internally incoherent. There would be no choice, Taylor argues (pp. 119–25), unless there were competing claims requiring judgement and evaluation. It is the incompatibility of certain claims, offering us different modes of self-understanding, that produces a situation in which it looks as if we must simply choose one of the alternatives. But no sense can be made of the notion of choice unless weighing and evaluating enter into our account; otherwise all we are left with is either (a) finding ourselves in one of the two alternatives; or (b) preferring one of the two alternatives. But neither of these two possibilities comes to anything like choice. The first either eliminates choice altogether or devolves into a situation of indifference; the second reduces to either indifference or utilitarian calculation. Taylor sums up his

view thus (p. 125): 'The notion of identity refers to certain evaluations which are essential because they are the fundamental horizon or foundation out of which we select and evaluate as persons.... A self decides and acts out of certain fundamental evaluations. This is what is impossible in a theory of radical choice. The agent of radical choice would at the moment of choice have *ex hypothesi* no horizon of evaluation.' Kierkegaard might admit that he thinks of the self in this way. Taylor's point, however, is that a self without a horizon of evaluation is unthinkable (does not conform to anything we might call a self). The self here is being conceived of practically rather than contemplatively; this of course is the fundamental assumption of the narrative construal of the self.

13. From *Uber Goethes Meister* (1978); quoted in Wessell, op. cit., p. 664.

14. This and the following criticism are hinted at by Hegel; see his *Aesthetics*, op. cit., pp. 64–9.

15. The passage from Baudelaire are from his essay 'On the Essence of Laughter', in *Selected Writings on Art and Artists*, translated by P.E. Charvet (Harmondsworth: Penguin, 1972), pp. 148, 160. for Culler, see his *Flaubert* (London: Elek, 1974), pp. 185–6. I have learned most about irony from de Man's superb and deeply mistaken essay 'The Rhetoric of Temporality' in Charles Singleton (ed.), *Interpretation: Theory and Practice* (Baltimore: Johns Hopkins Press, 1967).

16. *Problems in General Linguistics*, translated by R. Meek (Coral Gables, Fla.: University of Miami Press, 1971), pp. 224, 225, 226. For Kant, it is the I – It opposition which is central, but that, needless to say, is how his theory of the self goes wrong from the outset – or so argued Hegel in his account of the genesis of self-consciousness in the chapter of the *Phenomenology* on the Master – Slave dialectic. I defend Hegel's practical and inter-subjective construal of self and self-consciousness in my 'Act and Recognition', in Z. Pelczynski (ed.), *State and Civil Society* (Cambridge: Cambridge University Press, forthcoming).

17. *The Concept of Irony*, op. cit., p. 276.

18. Peter Szondi, 'Friedrich Schlegel und die Romantische Ironie', quoted in de Man, 'Rhetoric', op. cit., p. 201.

19. ibid., p. 203.

20. R. Barthes, *S/Z*, translated by Richard Miller (London: Jonathan Cape, 1975), p. 140.

21. (Harmondsworth: Penguin, 1968), translated by Lowe-Porter, p. 171; for the next quote, p. 245.

22. ibid., pp. 233–4.

23. Said, op. cit., p. 187. Said's few pages on Mann are the most pointed and accurate I have come across. For an elaborate but more traditional reading, see T.J. Reed, *Thomas Mann: The Uses of Tradition* (Oxford: Clarendon Press, 1974), pp. 360–402.
24. For more on Hegel's concept of spirit, see Westphal, op. cit. In his 'Hegel's Concept of "Geist"', in *Hegel*, A. Macintyre (ed.) (New York: Anchor Books, 1972), R.C. Solomon correctly notes how spirit is a rewriting of the Cartesian 'cogito' and Kant's 'I think', but fails to provide spirit with the concrete social historical grounding which Westphal and Hyppolite (see n. 25) have correclty claimed to be central to Hegel's concept.
25. Jean Hyppolite, *Genesis and Structure of Hegel's 'Phenomenology of Spirit'*, translated by Samuel Cherniak and John Heckman (Evanston: Northwestern University Press, 1974), p. 324, but see pp. 321–32 generally.
26. For a different account, see Martin Jay, 'The Concept of Totality in Lukács and Adorno', *Telos* 32 (1977).
27. 'Rhetoric', op. cit., p. 197; next quote, p. 203.
28. ibid., p. 207.

CHAPTER VII

1. See e.g. Tobin, op. cit., Conclusion.
2. R. Barthes, 'To Write: An Intransitive Verb', in R. Macksey and E. Donato (eds), *The Structuralist Controversy* (London: Johns Hopkins Press, 1972), p. 144. The presence of analyses of ideological forms in Barthes' S/Z (London: Jonathan Cape, 975) has led to the claim that neo-structuralist semiotics provides the appropriate apparatus for materialist critical practice. However, as the trajectory of Barthes *et al.*, has made clear, for them ideological forms arise *essentially* on the ground of the repression of textual productivity in the classical text. Thus the discovery of ideological forms in the classic (readerly) texts overlaps with the Marxist analysis because, as will be clearer in sequel, the masking of artifice, intertextuality and the submission to the interdictions of the practical ideology of the time are for both Marxits and structuralist constitutive of the classic text. But the Marxist will not a priori privilege the writerly (productive) text over the readerly text; rather, the writerly text will be submitted to the same kind of analysis as the readerly text, and analogous areas of progressive and regressive ideological forms will be found to be present. And this analysis will employ the properly materialist

categories of production, distribution and consumption. Without these categories the 'sociality' of texts is lost in the vague ether of intertextuality. In fine, because structuralists lack the appropriate categories for social analysis they tend to mislocate the locus of social relations, and consequently tend to over-valorise the simply anti-bourgeois.

3. For Heath (London: Elek, 1972), see ch. 1; for Josipovici (London: Macmillan, 1971), see e.g. chapter 5.

4. Heath, op. cit., p. 20. It is customary in this context to cite as well Gombrich's *Art and Illusion* (London: Phaidon, 1960).

5. For a useful account, see Barry Stroud, *Hume* (London: Routledge & Kegan Paul, 1977), chapter VI.

6. Said, op. cit., p. 6. This point has been generally recognised if not theoretically assimilated. See Heath, op. cit., p. 19; Josipovici, op. cit., pp. 260–1; on Said see J.H. Miller's review in *Diacritics* (Fall, 1976), pp. 5–7.

7. *The Meaning of Contemporary Realism*, translated by J.M. Mander (London: Merlin Press, 1963), p. 48.

8. In his *The Modes of Modern Writing* (London: Arnold, 1977), David Lodge offers a *neutral* definition of realism in literature: 'The representation of experience in a manner which approximates closely to descriptions of similar experience in nonliterary texts of the same culture' (p. 25). While allowing for historical and cultural variation, this account fails for two reasons:

(a) Either there may be no substantial nonliterary texts for the same culture (e.g. for primitive societies, for Homeric texts, and for early sections of the Bible – the last two central documents for the study of literature), or all the texts of that culture may obey rules of writing wholly at variance with oral practices such that calling any of the former 'realistic' is question begging internally to that culture.

(b) By treating realism as a synchronic category, Lodge begs the question against historical criteria, that is, against literary history as internal to literature as an institution.

While Lodge is perfectly correct in nothing that 'the realistic novel, from its beginnings in the eighteenth century, modelled its language on historical writings of various kinds . . . : biography, autobiography, travelogue, letters, diaries, journalism and historiography' (ibid.); he forgets both that there were pressures on these forms of discourse which also acted on the novel (especially biography, autobiography and historiography), and that the novel's assimilation of these forms was for reasons which are part of the novel's own dialectical development.

9. Georg Lukács, *Writer and Critic* (London: Merlin Press, 1970), p. 158.

10. 'Against a New Formalism', *The World in the Desert* (*Critical Quarterly* 10th Anniversary number, 1968), pp. 66–7.

11. Lukács, *The Meaning of Contemporary Realism*, op. cit., pp. 17–19 *et seq.*; and Irish Murdoch, 'Against Dryness'; in M. Bradbury (ed.), *The Novel Today* (London: Fontana, 1977).

12. See Lukács, *The Meaning of Contemporary Realism*, 'Franz Kafka or Thomas Mann?'

13. This is the central theme of Said's *Beginnings*. op. cit.; see especially pp. 83–4.

14. This term of art comes from Merleau-Ponty's *The Prose of the World*, translated by John O'Neill (London: Heinemann, 1974), p. 60.

15. 'Modern Fiction', *Collected Essays* (London: Hogarth Press, 1966), vol. II, p. 106.

16. A case similar to the one I am making here can be found in Fredric Jameson's 'Beyond the Cave: Demystifying the Ideology of Modernism', *Bulletin of the Midwest Modern Language Association* 8 (1975), pp. 1–20. However, I am in radical disagreement with Jameson's analytical apparatus. He employs the idea (from Deleuze and Guattari's *Anti-Oedipus*) of schizophernia as representing a pre-coded manifold of experiential flux which different forms of sociality (savage, barbaric, civilised) encode to different degrees and levels. The idea of such a pre-coded material is similar to Kristeva's distinction between the semiotic (pre-coded/uncoded) and the symbolic in her 'Signifying Practice and Mode of Production', *Edinburg 76 Magazine* 1 (1976). Both writers unconsciously employ an undialectical form – content distinction which reduces to a very undialectical mind – body dualism. There is no ever-present category of the raw and unmediated; body, content, nature are always determined with respect to some social formation; what social coding hides is the material *force* of both what it orders and what its ordering represses. Moreover, Jameson's theory fails to distinguish between schizophrenia as the breakdown of a signifying system and childhood autism which involves the failure ever to get hooked (interpellated) into one. Finally, even jazzed up, Jameson's Vichian Philosophy of history must look prematurely closed and therefore suspicious to us.

17. See Heath, op. cit., p. 27.

18. See Jameson, op. cit., p. 16.

19. As noted even by proponents of realism like Murdoch, op. cit., p. 27. Note also Henry James's comment that Balzac was fortunate enough to live amid 'social phenomena the most

rounded and registered, most organized and administered, and thereby most exposed to systematic observation and portrayal, that the world had been ... Balzac's France was both inspiring enough for an immense prose epic and reducible enough for a report or a chart.' *Notes on Novelists* (New York: Charles Scribner, 1914), pp. 112–13.

20. Jameson, op. cit., p. 15.
21. Kristeva, op. cit., pp. 65, 68–9.
22. Adorno, op. cit., p. 160. Another way of stating Adorno's point is this: This cognitive *appeal* of modernism attaches essentially, at least in the first instance, to the space it creates outside the assumptions governing the collusive writing of realism. Modernism, as a movement, *makes* realism, as a past, appear compromised and repressive and thereby denominates itself as radical and critical. It is because modernism refers to realism, because its own tacit self-understanding includes a critical understanding of realism, that there is a modernism – realism debate, and further, that modernism 'appears' (in the categorial sense of the term) as progressive. It is against this 'appearance' and its theoretical appropriation, that this chapter is directed. Moreover, a second approach to modernism reminds us that some modernists held (hold) ideologically reactionary beliefs, just as some realists held (hold) progressive social values. Naively, radical form may hide regressive values, and 'outmoded' forms may contain – as their content – progressive beliefs. Form – content is not just a bad, old dualism, but is as well a real discontinuity in literary practice. Modernism does not entail formalism, but rather forces us to confront the dislocation of form with respect to content.
23. The general thesis of James Naremore's excellent study, *The World Without a Self* (London: Yale University Press, 1973), passim.
24. A similar statement of this kind is offered by Jameson, op. cit., pp. 18–19.
25. Said, op. cit., p. 141.
26. This pattern of increasing isolation and frustration in the hero in the French novel is given an exemplary accounting in Teridman's, *Dialectics of Isolation*, op. cit.
27. e.g. M. Zeraffa, *Fictions* (Harmondsworth: Penguin, 1976), pp. 127–32; and F. Fehrer, 'Is the Novel Problematic?', *Telos* 15 (1973), p. 55.
28. See Naremore, op. cit., pp. 133–5; and John Mepham's 'Figures of Desire', in G. Josipovici (ed.), *The Modern English Novel* (London: Open Books, 1976).
29. ibid., p. 173.

30. On this and more, see Margot Norris. *The Decentered Universe of Finnegans Wake* (London: Johns Hopkins Press, 1976).
31. *Blindness*, op. cit., pp. 58–9.
32. *New Literary History* 8 (1976), p. 12 for this and the next quote.
33. ibid., p. 9.
34. ibid., p. 11.
35. op. cit., pp. 84–5. (This is probably the right place to answer a likely objection to my argument concerning the place of narrative in a cultural Marxism, namely, that Adorno and Benjamin would have been more appropriate sources than Arendt and Gadamer, and that as it stands the argument has a problematical 'existentialist' slant. The following three points should help to clarify my intentions here. (i) I have not followed Adorno and Benjamin because I believe that their different (and 'modernist') conceptions of ideological criticism lack precisely the narrative dimension, and hence conception of contingent rationality, that I am attempting to develop. (ii) None the less, I conceive of my version of narrative reason both to be a product of an ideological (and immanent) critique, and to function within the framework of ideological criticism as traditionally conceived of by cultural Marxism. (iii) I do not intend my use of the existentialist concept of 'world' to carry its *full* ontological meaning. On the contrary, my claim is that reification threatens the worldliness (or 'worldhood') of the world, and that only through ideological critique and narrative praxis can that worldliness be (re-)established.)
36. Gadamer, op. cit., pp. 401–5.
37. I take it that this is the way in which the incapacity of the *cogito* to name the self articulates with break between narrative and system, history and science.
38. Thus Macintyre, op. cit., p. 461, argues 'A tradition then not only embodies the narrative of an argument, but is only to be recovered by an argumentative retelling of that narrative ... ' All that needs to be added to Macintyre's progressive reformulation of the concept of tradition is the thought that what is provided by it is an historical identity for its tellers. To understand how narratives can be argumentative is to understand the relation between 'science' and narrative. Social scientific theories, for the most part, provide the parameters *for* narrative arguments, the terms and mechanisms for the construction of narrative accounts. Hence social theories 'confront' the world, not directly, but as components of a political dialogue, debate, argument or conflict. In my *Identity and Totality* I shall show how this conception of narrative, social theory and social identity can be used to conceptualise Gramsci's theory of hegeomony. (Since writing this I have had the opportunity to

read MacIntyre's *After Virtue* (London: Duckworth, 1981). There he both recognizes the anti-narrative pressures of modernity (p. 30) and explicitly forwards a theory which connects identity with narrativity; further, his theory takes the connection between identity and narrativity as a requiring the support of a 'world' or a 'community' (see in particular chapters 14–15). My general sympathy with his analysis and programme only serves to heighten my scepticism as to whether the programme can be coherently sustained outside the framework of Marxist theory and practice.)

39. *The Meaning of Revelation* (New York: Macmillan, 1967), p. 59.
40. *The Political Unconscious* (London: Methuen, 1981), p. 19.
41. *Negative Dialectics*, translated by E.B. Ashton (London: Routledge & Kegan Paul, 1973), p. 320.
42. See Arato and Breines, op. cit., pp. 136–9.
43. Quoted by Jurgen Habermas, 'A Review of Gadamer's *Truth and Method*', in F.R. Dallmayr and Th.A. McCarthy (eds), *Understanding and Social Inquiry* (London: University of Notre Dame Press, 1977), pp. 350–1.
44. *Reason in the Age of Science* (Cambridge, Mass.: MIT Press, 1982), p. 87.

Name Index

292

Subject Index

action 22, 129–31, 140
aesthetic form (as ethical) xvii, 76, 87, 100–5
amnesia 91, 229
antinomies: of bourgeois thought 15–22, 39; of literary modernism 230–9; of novel 42, 89, 229
author xxi, 51, 136, 151, 162, 183, 193
authority 51, 74, 76, 90, 94, 96, 104, 107–8, 110, 135–6, 160–2, 166, 240
autobiography 160, 163, 164, 167, 173–7, 178
auto-critique 1–2, 4, 5, 11
autonomy: of art 49, 69–71; of culture 12, 61; of economy 8, 10, 14, 26, 98, 124; of literature xxii–xxiii, 12–13, 39, 228, 231, 236, 240–6, 251–2; of reason 159, 163, 167; of self (man) 27, 40, 172, 177–8, 184, 234–5, 247; of truth 71

biography 149

Categorical Imperative 19, 21, 81, 100–1, 114, 283
categories 17, 49, 77–8, 111
class xi, xiii; consciousness 24–5, 28–34, 258
commensuration 41–2, 152–3
commodity fetishism 1–2, 6, 27, 77, 95
community 16, 51, 70–1, 161, 259, 260
contemplation (categorial) xv, 5, 8–16, 20–2, 25, 32–3, 35, 37, 39, 102, 108, 115, 186, 199, 219, 236, 257, 260, 271
Copernican Turn 16, 150, 152–3, 182
criticism (literary) 12–13, 14
culture 11, 14, 34–5, 45, 49, 73–4, 79–83, 223

death 126, 135–7, 140, 143, 144, 146, 148, 258–9
desire 166–7, 170–2, 179, 184, 281–2
dialectic 23, 26–7, 30, 73, 126–7, 138, 230

epic 51, 57, 59, 88, 94, 99. See also novel
epistemology 3, 11
ethic xxii, 70–1, 87–8, 100–3, 114–16, 193–4, 201. See also Moralität and Sittlichkeit

fiction xix, 40, 108, 116, 127, 144–5, 165–6, 179, 214–15, 217, 219, 231, 266
form: abstract 91, 98, 224; architectural 61, 95; autobiographical 92, 148–54, 173; biographical 92, 148–52; categories 77–8; and content 21, 39, 289; created 56, 66, 104; and culture 78–9; as ethical intent 91, 98, 104, 107; -giving xix, 91–2, 103, 104, 109, 152, 183, 199, 196, 215; and God 17, 61, 95–6, 261; inner 148, 149, 151; and life xx, 49–50, 84–5, 106, 107, 112–13, 139, 147; organic 61, 95, 138–9; outer 148; structural 23
freedom 19, 81–2, 168, 181, 185–6, 196, 208, 282; and necessity (causality) 20, 32–3, 203–5, 207; as subjective xix, 20, 113–16. See also generosity

generosity 171–2, 174–7, 178, 282
German Idealism 1, 15, 63, 162

hermeneutics xx, 64; of capitalism 27, 277; and epic 47–8, 54, 72–3; of novel xvi, 47, 89

294